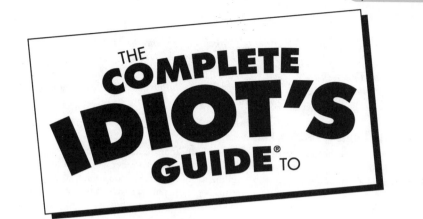

THE COMPLETE **IDIOT'S** GUIDE® TO

Grammar and Style

Second Edition

by Laurie E. Rozakis, Ph.D.

ALPHA

A member of Penguin Group (USA) Inc.

To my students, past, present, and future. Thank you for your hard work, determination, and support. You make teaching a privilege.

Special thanks to Tom Kennedy, Fred Church, and all the other students from years gone by who stay in touch. It's gratifying to know you're happy, successful, and masters of grammar and style!

Publisher: *Marie Butler-Knight*
Product Manager: *Phil Kitchel*
Senior Managing Editor: *Jennifer Chisholm*
Acquisitions Editor: *Gary Goldstein*
Development Editor: *Tom Stevens*
Senior Production Editor: *Christy Wagner*
Copy Editor: *Keith Cline*
Illustrator: *Chris Eliopoulos*
Cover/Book Designer: *Trina Wurst*
Indexer: *Brad Herriman*
Layout/Proofreading: *Becky Harmon, Mary Hunt, Ayanna Lacey*

Contents at a Glance

Contents

Foreword

According to most studies, people's number one fear is public speaking. Number two is death. Death is number two. Does that seem right? That means to the average person, if you have to go to a funeral, you're better off in the casket than doing the eulogy.

—Jerry Seinfeld, *SeinLanguage*

Picture this: You're standing in front of a large conference room full of business associates. You've put on your best new clothes for a special occasion: You're about to present the project you've been working on for six hard months. You know it's a good idea—you've considered it from every angle and you're sure it can't fail—but you're not sure you can sell everybody on it. In fact, you're scared to death of embarrassing yourself. Why?

If you're like most people, part of your fear comes from the worry that you might not use good grammar—wait, make that proper grammar—when you start speaking, or that somehow you've messed up the writing in the 60-page report you've just handed out. You don't have a run in your panty hose—you checked—but your infinitives might be split wide open. You can tell that your zipper's not down, but you've got this irrational fear that your participles are dangling. You're a smart dresser, for certain—but are you just plain smart?

In a word, yes. You are.

The most common myth about grammar is that people who don't use it correctly are somehow less intelligent than those who do. Wrong! Intelligence and grammar are unrelated. Consider Jerry Seinfeld, who is quoted at the start of this foreword. He's an incredibly clever comedian whose jokes are always built around insightful observations of the human condition. Now consider the quote itself. Frankly, if his grammar were a car, they'd be towing it away to the junkyard right about now. It's a lemon for sure—but that doesn't mean Jerry Seinfeld can't parallel park, if you know what I mean. His sentences have a style that's appropriate for his audience—and he's been so successful at it that people have been copying him for years.

Have you ever heard the joke about the boy named Cass who was absent for a few days in first grade, missed the lesson about the letter *C*, then for the next few days kept getting into trouble for signing a cuss word next to the date on his homework papers? This is how many people feel about grammar—that they were absent when their teachers taught the basic rules and have been paying for it ever since. The truth is, you were probably there when your teacher taught grammar. So why didn't you learn the proper rules? Well, honestly, it could be—at least partially—your teacher's fault.

If you were like almost every other unfortunate elementary school student, your teacher probably sat in front of the room carefully explaining—in a voice dull enough to make rocks start to fidget—how to parse sentences, how to conjugate irregular verbs, what past perfect tense means, what a gerund is, etc. Maybe you also got to read from a textbook—oh boy!—full of snappy, interesting sentences about Tom and Sue and Bob's plain brown dog. It was a recipe for failure. Somehow you passed the class, of course, but did you really take anything in? Did you master the English language? Of course not; nobody could—not in an environment like that. Your teachers were crazy to expect those lesson plans to work.

You did your best, under the circumstances—and now it feels impossible to go back and set things straight.

But it's not impossible, because the circumstances have just changed. Laurie Rozakis is your teacher now. Trust me, you're in good hands. I've been teaching with Dr. Rozakis for several years now, and what always amazes me is how she makes grammar fun. Her students laugh while they learn—and they definitely learn. She has a knack for making even the most complex concepts simple, understandable, and memorable. Her students love her.

They also respect her—she's not only an entertaining teacher, but a wise one. As far as I can tell, Laurie Rozakis knows everything there is to know about grammar and style.

This book is the next best thing to being in her classroom yourself. You'll remember what she teaches you and start using it in your daily life almost immediately. You'll look forward to reading this book just as much as you used to look forward to avoiding your homework. You'll be amazed at how easy it is. The conference room will never be quite as intimidating again, either—and, if you're lucky, you could pick up a joke for the lunchroom, too.

Read on and enjoy.

Gwydion Suilebhan

Gwydion Suilebhan is writing program coordinator and Curriculum Content Specialist for the Institute for the Academic Advancement of Youth at Johns Hopkins University. He also works as a freelance writer, teacher, and curriculum designer. A collection of his poems, *Inner Harbor*, was published in 1997 by Woods House Press.

Introduction

You know you have the intelligence, ambition, and resilience to succeed, but one problem holds you back. "I'm afraid of making embarrassing errors when I speak and write," you say to yourself. When it comes to expressing ideas or communicating your opinion, you're afraid your message is garbled or just plain incorrect.

Having washboard abs and a body-fat count lower than the inflation rate will get you only so far in life. You know you need to know the basics of good writing—grammar, usage, punctuation, capitalization, and spelling—to get where you want to go. That's why you bought this book.

Memorizing lists of grammar rules isn't the answer. Wading through dictionaries and grammar books is about as exciting as watching reruns of *Gilligan's Island* or *Green Acres*. Besides, you can never find what you need; there are so many words! Your online spell checker drives you mad; the grammar checker buzzes like a pinball machine.

You know you need to do the following:

- ◆ Understand how to use the different writing aids, including dictionaries, thesauruses, style guides, reference books, and computer programs.

- ◆ Identify the parts of speech and know when to use each kind.

- ◆ Make English grammar work for you.

- ◆ Write logical, complete, and graceful sentences.

- ◆ Use correct capitalization and punctuation.

- ◆ Write effective letters, memos, and electronic messages.

What You'll Learn in This Book

Success-conscious people are grammar-conscious people for many good reasons. You know that if you want to get ahead in almost any business or profession, you must speak and write reasonably correct English. That's what this book can help you achieve. You'll learn that business and personal writing is not a mysterious activity at which only a few people can succeed. Rather, writing is a craft, like barefoot aluminum foil dancing or cooking that can be learned by almost anyone willing to invest the required time and energy.

This book is divided into six sections that teach you the practical, hands-on grammar and usage rules you need. You'll understand why certain rules exist and what function they serve in writing and speech. Most of all, you'll finish this book convinced that writing is fun as well as useful and important.

Part 1, "No Uncertain Terms," first explores how many people feel about grammar, usage, and the mechanics of writing. This part provides the standards for effective communication, too. Next, you'll get the definitions of *grammar, usage, mechanics,* and *style,* so we're all starting this dance on the same foot. Then you'll assess your own writing strengths and shortcomings to find out how you can improve your writing—right now!

Part 2, "Under the Grammar Hammer," gets into the nitty-gritty of grammar: parts of speech, pronoun reference, pronoun case, verb usage, the difference between adjectives and adverbs, and subject-verb agreement. It's all the stuff you ignored in high school and English Comp 101 because you were too busy trying to get a date. This part concludes with a survey of the most common usage dilemmas. Along the way, there are lots of brand-new ways to make it easier for non-native English speakers to learn the basics of English.

Part 3, "Usage and Abusage," describes the building blocks of paragraphs: phrases, clauses, and sentences. You learn all about prepositional phrases, appositives and appositive phrases, verbal phrases, gerund phrases, and infinitive phrases. This part also covers sentence structure and function, fragments and run-ons, and sentence coordination and subordination. This sounds heavier than a sumo wrestler, but you know I'll make it fun.

Part 4, "Tools of the Trade," first explores the importance of using all the resources available to writers: dictionaries, computer spell-checkers, books of synonyms and antonyms, and reference books. Then I give you a complete refresher course in the signposts of our language: punctuation, capitalization, abbreviations, and spelling.

Part 5, "Style: All the Write Stuff," helps you give your writing grace, clarity, and that essential *je ne sais quoi* that separates your writing from everyone else's. This section also covers active and passive voice, conciseness, diction (word choice), and levels of language.

Part 6, "In Your Write Mind," helps you develop powerful writing strategies that enable you to write successful business and personal communications. This part covers such important writing situations as business and personal letters and e-mail. In the chapter on personal communication, you'll learn how to write effective letters to friends, companies, and people suffering losses.

Last, there's an appendix of model writing samples and a glossary of grammar and usage. The glossary of grammar and usage makes it easy for you to pinpoint specific writing issues and get the answers you need—*fast!*

More for Your Money!

In addition to all the explanation and teaching, this book contains other types of information to make it even easier for you to master writing and speaking skills. Here's how you can recognize these features:

Strictly Speaking

Want to dazzle your date? Stump your spouse? Have some witty chitchat for the next office party? Use these grammar teasers to astound and amaze your friends and enemies alike.

You Could Look It Up

Like every other skill worth knowing, grammar and usage have their own terminology. These definitions explain all those terms to prevent you from dangling your participles in public.

Take My Word for It

You could skip these tasty tidbits, but you won't want to because they're too much fun!

Danger, Will Robinson

These warnings help you stay on track—so you don't end up lost in space.

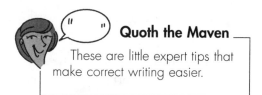

Quoth the Maven

These are little expert tips that make correct writing easier.

Acknowledgments

To my long-suffering husband, who endured bologna rather than turkey with his cranberries, stuffing, and gravy. (Okay, so I was a little preoccupied with this book to make the turkey. Bologna *is* a recognized food group.) He has always been my strongest supporter and staunchest friend.

And to my dear children Charles and Samantha, please stop referring to The Night Mom Forgot the Turkey. It is not a national holiday. I promise to remember the large dead bird at any and all appropriate future meals.

Also, a tip of the hat to Gary Goldstein, my editor for the second edition of this book. Tom Stevens, development editor, and Keith Cline, super copy editor, deserve credit for making me look much smarter and more careful than I am! And much gratitude to the amazing Christy Wagner, senior production editor, a fabulous colleague and production editor par excellence.

My deepest thanks to Marguerite Owens Kassinger, Amy Losi, Joanne Marrone, and Charles Rozakis for providing resumés. And a kiss for Pessha Snedeker, president of the southwest division of my fan club!

Special Thanks to the Technical Reviewer

The Complete Idiot's Guide to Grammar and Style, Second Edition, was reviewed by an expert who double-checked the accuracy of what you'll learn here, to help us ensure that this book gives you everything you need to know about grammar and style. Special thanks are extended to Doug Stein.

Doug Stein recently retired from the New York City School System, where he taught high school English and History for more than 35 years (and has lived to tell about it). He now does private tutoring in the New York City area in these subjects—when not rescuing dangling modifiers for Alpha Books and others fortunate publishers and writers. He now keeps busy freelance writing and editing for a number of local publications. When not working, he resides with his wife, Gail (the author of *The Complete Idiot's Guide to Learning Spanish on Your Own*) in New York City.

Trademarks

All terms mentioned in this book that are known to be or are suspected of being trademarks or service marks have been appropriately capitalized. Alpha Books and Penguin Group (USA) Inc. cannot attest to the accuracy of this information. Use of a term in this book should not be regarded as affecting the validity of any trademark or service mark.

Part 1

No Uncertain Terms

In 1983, a linguist named Geoffrey Nunberg published an essay called "The Decline of Grammar" in the *Atlantic Monthly* magazine. The article described the battle between different approaches to grammar and language usage. Truth be told, the article was about as dry as unbuttered melba toast. Nonetheless, the magazine was deluged with letters, many of them quite irate. When the smoke cleared, the editors realized that they had received one of the largest reader responses in years.

More than two decades later, most of the burning issues of the early 1980s have cooled, but interest in language usage remains as fierce as ever. And you thought your mother was the only one who cared if you said, "*Can* I go to the bathroom?" instead of "*May* I go to the bathroom?"

Now that you've finally gotten permission to go potty, it's time to see what grammar, usage, mechanics, and style are all about.

Are You Grammarphobic?

In This Chapter

- ◆ Learn how people feel about grammar
- ◆ Probe the influence of words on thought and speech
- ◆ Define grammar, usage, mechanics, and style

A favorite proverb of the arts-and-crafts set is "One picture is worth a thousand words." Nope. It really isn't so. Just try to use a picture to teach people. You'll quickly find out that you need a thousands words—or more!—to tell them exactly what to look at and why.

Whatever you might have heard about cultural illiteracy, the closing of the American mind, and TV rotting our brains, Americans are passionately in love with their language, perhaps more so now than ever before. And we greatly respect people who can use English correctly, with skill, grace, and flair. We know they tend to succeed in whatever they attempt, because they have the tools to communicate, persuade, and inform effectively, no matter what the message.

Take My Word for It

Most of us think the English we speak is the standard version. People who use other forms, we think, are speaking dialects. In fact, most of us speak a *dialect,* a language that reflects the speech of a particular region.

In this chapter, you learn that you're not alone in your desire to master the rules of standard written English—or in your fear of banging your head against a brick wall while trying to do so. Then you meet the movers and shakers of English: *grammar, usage, mechanics,* and *style.* Along the way, we explore your feelings about English.

How Can You Tell If You're Grammarphobic?

That said, we still have to contend with the fear factor. I'll bet you know what I mean. I whisper "grammar" and your eyes roll back in your head; I mutter "predicate nominative" and you pass out cold. How bad is it, bunky? Take this quiz to see if you're suffering from mild or acute "grammar-itis."

Put a check next to each answer that applies to you.

_____ 1. Knowing that I have to tell the difference between "lie" and "lay" makes me feel like General Pickett charging his doomed division up Cemetery Hill.

_____ 2. I think *euphemisms* are just another word for nothing left to lose.

_____ 3. Having to conjugate an irregular verb feels like a kick in the gut from Jackie Chan.

_____ 4. I'd rather shoot myself in the foot than be asked when and how to use the possessive case before a gerund.

_____ 5. Chewing ground glass is more appealing to me than having to write a resumé and a letter of application for a job (no matter how good the job sounds).

_____ 6. I'd rather dive into a pile of double-edge razor blades than have to distinguish between "who" and "whom."

_____ 7. I have to write a 20-page report on employee morale? Beam me up, Scotty.

_____ 8. Having my finger slammed in a car door is less painful than knowing if I should use an adjective or adverb after a linking verb.

_____ 9. I'd sit two inches from a speaker playing Whitney Houston when she hits that high C if it would get me out of writing a bad-news business letter.

_____ 10. Rip out my intestines with a fork? No problem. It's far preferable to having to send e-mail to my boss.

Bonus: I break into a cold sweat at the very thought of seeing my tenth-grade English teacher.

Answers

All checked	Your tenth-grade teacher really did a number on your head, didn't she?
7 to 9 checked	Everything will be okay, baby. Mama's here now.
4 to 6 checked	Help is just a few pages away.
1 to 3 checked	Liar, liar, pants on fire.
None checked	Want to write this book for me?

There's no denying that the rules of standard written English are scary, more frightening than a sail on the *Titanic* or a night with Michael Jackson. English rules are scary, yes—but difficult, no. Hey, you can program a VCR, ride on a New York City subway, and make withdrawals from an ATM. You can learn all you need to know to write a better report, memo, or letter. You know your efforts will be repaid manifold, like compound interest on a CD.

Word Power

"Give me a lever long enough and prop strong enough," Archimedes wrote, "and I can single-handed move the world." More than two thousand years later, the celebrated novelist Joseph Conrad responded: "Do not talk to me of Archimedes' lever. He was an absentminded person with a mathematical imagination. Give me the right word and the right accent, and I will move the world."

These comments are powerful confirmation of the marvel of language. For more than three thousand years, people have declared their love, made their demands, pledged their support, and taken on the IRS because of the flexibility and beauty of language. Millions of us, young and old alike, have turned words into communication thanks to our language. We've prayed at its altar, damned its rules, and stretched its limitations. We've molded it like so much Silly Putty to conform to our needs.

War of the Words

But not everyone worships language with the same enthusiasm. "Fine words butter no parsnips," observes an English proverb with noticeably less ebullience. Writer Franklin P. Adams cranked, "Words mean one thing on Monday and another on Tuesday." And an anonymous Romanian checks in with this saying: "With words alone, you don't make the soup."

That statements about the power of language can contradict each other only serves to prove the ability of language to express a wide variety of feelings and opinions.

The Force Be with You

Where do you stand on the power of English? Take this instant test to see. Put a check next to each statement you agree with.

_____ 1. Next to sex, language is the most exciting form of communication we have.

_____ 2. Words are as vital to life as food, drink, and sex, but on the whole we don't show as much interest in language as we do in the other pastimes.

_____ 3. If you write with confidence, you'll do better in nearly all aspects of your life.

_____ 4. Using correct English can help you get a better job.

_____ 5. The phrasing of a sentence has decided the fate of many a friendship, and for all we know, the fate of many a kingdom.

_____ 6. Knowing how to use English can improve your chances of getting a date on a Saturday night—a hot date, too.

_____ 7. People become great leaders through their command of words.

_____ 8. Much of the mischief in the world arises from words.

_____ 9. The whole purpose of writing and speech is to be understood.

_____ 10. You cannot get ahead if you can't write with confidence.

_____ 11. When words fail, wars begin. When the wars finally end, we settle our disputes with words.

_____ 12. Every word we know makes a difference, because every word is an idea.

_____ 13. Words are the only things that last forever; they are more durable than the hills.

_____ 14. Words are the most powerful drug we have.

_____ 15. Every time you write something, you say much more than you think you say.

Bonus: True or False: If the art of conversation stood a little bit higher, we would have a lower birthrate.

People who cherish language are not linguistic police who arrest the miscreants who split their infinitives or dangle their participles in public. Rather, they are people like you, people who recognize the need to speak and write with confidence.

Term Limits

This brings us to the matter of English itself. What exactly are the components of English? There are four standard conventions of written and spoken English:

- ◆ Grammar
- ◆ Usage
- ◆ Mechanics
- ◆ Style

Let's look at each standard convention of English in detail.

What Is Grammar?

"Grammar," Henry Fowler wrote in his soon-to-be famous 1926 *Dictionary of Modern English Usage*, is "a poor despised branch of learning." Henry was a bit cranky that day.

To the rest of us, *grammar* is a branch of linguistics that deals with the form and structure of words. It's an attempt to make explicit and conscious what the skilled writer and speaker of English does intuitively and unconsciously. When people are said to have "good" or "bad" grammar, the understanding is that they choose to obey or ignore the rules of accepted usage associated with their language.

You Could Look It Up

Grammar is a branch of linguistics that deals with the form and structure of words.

Grammar is one of the oldest fields of study, as well as one of the most durable. Even Plato can be labeled an early grammarian, because he was responsible for dividing the sentence into subject and verb (*onoma* and *rheme*), a division it has retained. Dazzle your friends; toss this out at the next cocktail party.

Take My Word for It

Grammarians are not necessarily writers, but writers must always be grammarians, whether they are aware of it or not.

What Is Usage?

Usage is the customary way we use language in speech and writing. Because we use language for different purposes, there are a various levels of usage. The following table lists the big three.

Level of Usage	Examples
1. Standard English: formal usage	They have done nothing.
2. Standard English: informal usage	They've done nothing.
3. Nonstandard usage	Dey ain't done nothin'.

You Could Look It Up

Usage is the customary way we use language in speech and writing.

The main difference between standard English and nonstandard English appears in the use of pronouns and certain verb forms. For example, where a speaker of standard English would use *brought*, a speaker of nonstandard English would use *brung*. There are also several words and expressions that are considered nonstandard, such as slang words.

" " Quoth the Maven

In most cases, substandard usage is associated with the uneducated. In a few rare cases, however, people have made substandard usage their trademark. Dizzy Dean, a pitcher for the St. Louis Cardinals who later became a radio and TV sports broadcaster, is a case in point. Typical of his utterance: "Didn't nobody come around after the game and ask whether we'd throwed or threw the ball in there to make a play. We won 'em, no questions asked."

The following table describes formal usage, informal usage, and nonstandard usage in more detail.

The Language Rank and File

Level of Usage	Uses	Characteristics
Formal	Business letters, resumés, cover letters, serious speeches, newspaper articles, scholarship	Standard verbs, adverbs with *-ly* endings, standard vocabulary, standard punctuation
Informal	Most books, magazines newspapers, business letters, many textbooks, political speeches	Standard verbs, adverbs with *-ly* endings, standard vocabulary, standard punctuation, contractions, some slang

Level of Usage	Uses	Characteristics
Nonstandard	Conversation, movies, television, radio, comic strips, regional expressions	Nonstandard verbs, adverbs without -ly, slang words, nonstandard punctuation, "creative" spelling

The correct level of usage is the one that is appropriate for the occasion. For example, you would use formal usage in a job application letter, resumé, and business letter. Informal usage is more fitting for a personal letter, greeting card message, and conversation. Even in these days when everything goes, nonstandard usage is as tacky as rhinestones on tweed.

Usage includes the following elements:

◆ Pronoun choice

◆ Verb conjugation

◆ Verb use

◆ Active and passive voice

◆ Correct word choice

◆ Subject/verb agreement

◆ Adjectives and adverbs

◆ Double negatives

◆ Parallel structure

◆ Misplaced modifiers

◆ Redundancy

◆ Parallel structure

◆ Coordination

◆ Subordination

There's more (isn't there *always?*), but that's enough to hit you with at once. I cover all these concerns (and more) in Parts 2 and 3.

What Is Mechanics?

As its name suggests, *mechanics* is the nuts and bolts of clear writing. The six members of the mechanics gang are as follows:

You Could Look It Up

Mechanics include abbreviations, capitalization, italics, numbers, punctuation, and quotation marks.

- ◆ Abbreviations
- ◆ Capitalization
- ◆ Italics
- ◆ Numbers
- ◆ Punctuation
- ◆ Quotation marks

Mechanics allow writers to show the grouping and relationship of words. They signal pace and intonation. Best of all, they help you say what you mean clearly and so avoid misunderstanding.

What Is Style?

In life, personal style is that essential *je ne sais quoi* that distinguishes Iman from Roseanne, Ethel Merman from Pee Wee Herman. People with style can wear white shoes after Labor Day and not get arrested by the Style Police; they never have lipstick on their teeth, toilet paper on their heels, or rings around their collars. Heck, they don't even have to *wear* collars to look sharp. Personal style is the way you dress, walk, and talk to make an impression on those you meet.

You Could Look It Up

A writer's **style** is his or her distinctive way of writing.

In writing, *style* is an author's distinctive way of writing. Style is made up of elements such as word choice, sentence length and structure, punctuation, figures of speech, and tone. Writers might change their style for different kinds of writing and to suit different audiences. In poetry, for example, writers might use more imagery than they would use in prose (nonpoetry).

Quoth the Maven

When it comes to writing style, the head weenie at the roast was *New Yorker* writer E. B. White. In the summer of 1957, White revised and reissued a slender writing guidebook he had used at Cornell, written by his professor, William Strunk. Fewer than 100 pages long, the book has never been out of print since—and with good cause; it's a honey.

A Civil Tongue: Standards for Effective Communication

Good writing and speaking meets five basic standards: It's clear, complete, correct, efficient, and effective. Here are some examples:

- **Clear.** The reader gets the meaning you, the writer, intended. There's no ambiguity or guesswork; everyone's on the same page. I cover issues of clarity in Chapter 19.

- **Complete.** Good writing is the bun and the beef; the reader gets the complete package. With effective communication, readers have everything they need to evaluate the message and act on it. See Part 5 for these issues.

- **Correct.** The writing is free from errors in grammar, usage, and mechanics. There are no bloopers in such areas as spelling, capitalization, word order, and sentence structure. All this is covered in Parts 2, 3, and 4.

- **Efficient.** The words are arranged on the page to save the reader time. The layout is clear and crisp, so the message is easy to track. Here are the Top Two of page arrangement:

    - Organization

    - Visual impact

  You'll learn all about these considerations in Part 6.

- **Effective.** Because all the ducks are in a row, effective writing conveys a positive image of the writer and his or her company, organization, or group. Because it treats the reader with consideration, good writing creates good feelings, too. See Part 6 for more on this.

Danger, Will Robinson

Cultural considerations are very important to effective writing and speech. Americans, for instance, value direct appeals. Check out any of our advertisements and you'll see what I mean. The Japanese, in contrast, prefer subtle messages where the point must be inferred.

The Least You Need to Know

- Grammar is a branch of linguistics that deals with the form and structure of words.

- Usage is the customary way we use language in speech and writing. The correct level of usage is the one that is appropriate for the occasion.

- Mechanics include punctuation, numbers, quotation marks, capitalization, abbreviations, and italics.

- A writer's style is his or her distinctive way of writing.

- Good communication is clear, complete, correct, efficient, and effective.

Chapter 2

Conan the Grammarian

In This Chapter

- ◆ Discover the most common grammar errors
- ◆ Assess your own writing strengths
- ◆ Find out how you can improve your writing—right now!

In this chapter, we'll explore how you can turn off your audience by making grammatical mistakes. They'll figure, "If you can't handle the language, how can you handle our business?" You'll be ready to handle anyone's business on my watch, captain.

We'll also examine the most common grammar and usage errors that people make. Then I'll guide you to take a look at your own writing to see where you should concentrate your efforts. Finally, I'll give you some concrete ways to improve your command of English skills now.

Sweet Dreams Aren't Made of These

Remember Miss Sour Puss, your eighth-grade English teacher? You know, the one with the bun, wire-rimmed glasses, and pursed lips. She probably taught you rules like these:

- ◆ A pronoun used as a predicate nominative takes the nominative case.
- ◆ A pronoun used in opposition with a noun is in the same case as that noun.

- After a helping verb, use the past participle (third principal part) rather than the past tense (second principal part).

- Make a pronoun agree with its antecedent.

Take My Word for It

English has far more lives than a cat. How do I know? People have been murdering English for years—and it refuses to die. If anything, it just keeps getting stronger.

I know, this is like showing someone *Jaws* before you take them swimming. But understanding the rules of our language is nowhere near as hard as assembling your child's new bicycle on Christmas Eve or drinking a screw-top chardonnay. So go ahead—amaze your doorman, dazzle your dentist, and shut up your prospective sister-in-law for good with your confident handling of mind-clouding grammar and usage rules. We may even have some fun along the way.

Puppy Love

Which of the following sentences is correct?

- Being an esteemed politician, the poodle lunged straight for Mr. Entwhistle's privates.

- The poodle, an esteemed politician, lunged straight for Mr. Entwhistle's privates.

- They both make a valid point.

Both the first two sentences state that the poodle is the politician. Now, this may be true, but it's unlikely (well, maybe not …). How can you rearrange this sentence to have it make sense? (*Hint:* Try making it into two separate sentences or giving the poodle to a deserving child.)

Misusing language is one thing; murdering it is another. I can help you correct errors in grammar and usage with surprising ease. After all, that's what this book is all about. Gross grammar abuse it another matter. There's no cure for *that*.

Has It Come to This?

Take this little quiz to separate the temporarily grammar-impaired from the hopeless dopes. Cross out every sentence that's just plain witless. Put a star next to the ones we can save with a little CPR (crisp pretty rewriting).

_____ 1. Many dead animals of the past changed to fossils while others preferred to be oil.

_____ 2. The plant was given to us by a friend that was supposed to flower in the spring.

_____ 3. Men are mammals and women are femammals.

_____ 4. Whom do you believe is the most capable?

_____ 5. The largest mammals are to be found in the sea because there's nowhere else to put them.

_____ 6. If you had been more patient, you might not have tore it.

_____ 7. Mushrooms always grow in damp places so they look like umbrellas.

_____ 8. The tomb of the Egyptian pharaoh commanded attention coming into the museum.

_____ 9. Water is composed of two gins, Oxygin and Hydrogin. Oxygin is pure gin. Hydrogin is gin and water.

_____ 10. Some people say we condescended from the apes.

Answers

Items 1, 3, 5, 7, and 9 are too idiotic to salvage. We *can* do something with items 2, 4, 6, 8, and 10, however. Here are the explanations.

Sentence	Correction	Chapter
2	*Misplaced modifier*	10
	The plant that was supposed to flower in the spring was given to us by a friend.	
4	Replace *whom* with *who*	6
6	Replace *tore* with *torn*	5
8	*Dangling modifier*	10
	The tomb of the Egyptian pharaoh commanded our attention as we came into the museum.	
10	Replace *condescended* with *descended*	24

Perversity Rules

So much to learn, so little time! Come on, let me make it easy for you, baby. We'll just stick one toe in the water. Here's an easy and fun way to remember key grammar and usage issues: Learn some perverse rules. Each perverse rule contains the error it describes.

Read the following 20 perverse rules. First identify each error. (*Hint:* It's mentioned in the rule.) Then rewrite each sentence so that it's correct. I did the first one for you. At the end of the list, I explain each rule and give you a cross-reference so you can get a more detailed explanation. (Aren't I just the nicest person?)

1. Remember to never split an infinitive.

   Error: <u>Split infinitive</u>

   Correction: <u>Remember never to split an infinitive.</u>

2. The passive voice should never be used.

   Error: _____

   Correction: _____

3. We never make misteaks.

   Error: _____

   Correction: _____

4. Avoid run-on sentences they are hard to read.

   Error: _____

   Correction: _____

5. Don't use no double negatives.

   Error: _____

   Correction: _____

6. Use the semicolon properly, always use it where it is appropriate; and never where it isn't.

   Error: _____

   Correction: _____

7. Reserve the apostrophe for it's proper use and omit it where its not needed.

   Error: _____

   Correction: _____

8. Verbs has to agree with their subjects.

   Error: _____

   Correction: _____

9. No sentence fragments.

   Error: _____

   Correction: _____

10. Proofread carefully to see if you any words out.

    Error: _____

    Correction: _____

11. Avoid commas, that are not necessary.

    Error: _____

    Correction: _____

12. If you reread your work, you will find on rereading that a great deal of repetition can be avoided by rereading and editing.

    Error: _____

    Correction: _____

13. Don't overuse exclamation marks!!!!

    Error: _____

    Correction: _____

14. Place pronouns as close as possible, especially in long sentences, as of 10 or more words, to their antecedents.

    Error: _____

    Correction: _____

15. Write all adverbs correct.

    Error: _____

    Correction: _____

16. Writing carefully, dangling participles must be avoided.

    Error: _____

    Correction: _____

17. Take the bull by the hand and avoid mixed metaphors.

    Error: _____

    Correction: _____

18. Everyone should be careful to use a singular pronoun in their writing.

    Error: _____

    Correction: _____

19. Always pick on the correct idiom.

    Error: _____

    Correction: _____

20. Last but least, avoid clichés like the plague; seek viable alternatives.

    Error: _____

    Correction: _____

Let Me 'Splain It to You, Lucy

1. *Error:* Split infinitive

    Correction: Don't put any word between "to" and the verb in an infinitive. There-fore, "to split" has to stay as one complete package. Only real sticklers get bent out of shape by this today. (Please don't call me if you're a stickler for this rule. And no, you cannot reach me by e-mail.) More on this in Chapter 10.

2. *Error:* Passive voice

    Correction: You should not use the passive voice. In addition to showing tense (time), verbs also show voice, the form of the verb that shows whether the sub-ject performs the action or received the action. English verbs have two voices: active and passive.

    A verb is active when the subject performs the action, as in this example:

    ◆ We made a mistake. (We are taking blame.)

    A verb is passive when its action is performed upon the subject, as in this example:

    ◆ A mistake has been made. (No one is taking credit for the mistake.)

    In general, use the active voice instead of the passive voice. The active voice was voted "Most Popular Voice" because it is less wordy. See Chapter 22.

3. *Error:* Spelling

    Correction: "Misteaks" do not refer to unmarried female rib roasts; the word is spelled "mistakes." See Chapter 18.

4. *Error:* Run-on sentence

   Correction: Avoid run-on sentences; they are hard to read. Or: Avoid run-on sentences because they are hard to read. A sentence is a group of words that express a complete thought. A sentence has two parts: a subject and a predicate. The subject includes the noun or pronoun that tells what the subject is about. The predicate includes the verb that describes what the subject is doing. A run-on sentence is two incorrectly joined sentences. See Chapter 13.

5. *Error:* Double negative

   Correction: Don't use any double negatives. See Chapter 8.

6. *Error:* Misused semicolon

   Correction: Use the semicolon properly; always use it where it is appropriate and never where it isn't. Use a semicolon between main clauses when the conjunction (and, but, for, or) has been left out. See Chapter 16.

7. *Error:* Apostrophe error

   Correction: Reserve the apostrophe for its proper use and omit it where it's not needed. Contractions are two words combined. When you contract words, add an apostrophe in the space where the letters have been taken out. See Chapter 16.

8. *Error:* Agreement of subject and verb

   Correction: Verbs have to agree with their subjects. See Chapter 9.

9. *Error:* Incomplete sentence

   Correction: Do not write any sentence fragments. See Chapter 13.

10. *Error:* Missing words

    Correction: Proofread carefully to see if you have left any words out. See Chapter 26.

11. *Error:* Unnecessary commas

    Correction: Avoid commas that are not necessary. See Chapter 16.

12. *Error:* Redundancy; unnecessary words

    Correction: If you reread your work, you will find that a great deal of repetition can be avoided. See Chapter 23.

13. *Error:* Unnecessary exclamation marks

    Correction: Don't overuse exclamation marks! See Chapter 16.

14. *Error:* Pronouns placed too far from their antecedents, the words to which they refer

    Correction: Place pronouns as close as possible to their antecedents, especially in long sentences, as of 10 or more words. See Chapter 7.

15. *Error:* Incorrect adverb use

    Correction: Write all adverbs correctly. See Chapter 8.

16. *Error:* Dangling participles

    Correction: When you write carefully, you must avoid dangling participles. See Chapter 10.

17. *Error:* Mixed metaphors

    Correction: Take the bull by the horns and avoid mixed metaphors. See Chapter 10.

18. *Error:* Pronoun agreement

    Correction: Everyone should be careful to use a singular pronoun in his or her writing. See Chapter 9.

Take My Word for It

What makes us human is our capacity to distinguish, compare, and evaluate—in words as well as life.

19. *Error:* Incorrect idiom

    Correction: Always pick the correct idiom. See Chapter 24.

20. *Error:* Clichés (shopworn phrases that have lost their punch)

    Correction: Write sentences that use fresh, new comparisons and expressions. See Chapter 25.

Personal Writing Inventory

How can you find the specific writing problems that afflict *you?* You can't rely on computerized grammar checkers because they usually cause more errors than they catch. In addition, computerized grammar checkers grind your style and reduce it to pap.

I suggest that you take the following writing inventory to zero in on your writing strengths and weaknesses.

Select several pieces of your writing, such as memos, letters, reports, or resumés. Follow these 10 steps as you complete the Writing Inventory:

1. Make at least five photocopies of the inventory.

2. Read the documents you selected for analysis several times.

3. Circle all the errors you find.

4. Ask a friend, colleague, or relative you know who is good in English to read the documents and find additional errors.

5. Enter all the errors on the following chart.

6. Count the number of errors in each category.

7. Enter these in each subtotal.

8. Take the inventory again after you finish each part of the book. This will tell you where you have made progress and what areas need additional review.

9. Read the whole book, but make a special effort to practice the skills covered in those chapters that match your biggest challenges.

10. Concentrate on these areas as you write.

>  **Quoth the Maven**
>
> To get the best results as you take the inventory, select writing samples that are at least a page long. That will give you sufficient text to analyze.

Writing Inventory

# of Errors	Type of Error
Grammar Errors	
_____	1. Misusing parts of speech
_____	2. Matching pronouns and antecedents
_____	3. Correct pronoun placement
_____	4. Using *who, which, that* correctly
_____	5. Using *who* and *whom* correctly
_____	6. Using the correct verb tense
_____	7. Using irregular verbs correctly
_____	8. Avoiding double negatives
_____	9. Using the correct comparative and superlative forms
_____	10. Using irregular adjectives and adverbs correctly
_____	11. Agreement of subject and verb

Writing Inventory   (continued)

# of Errors	Type of Error
_____	12. Pronouns and antecedent agreement
_____	13. Dangling construction and misplaced modifiers
_____	14. Ending with a preposition
_____	15. Split infinitives

Total Errors _____

Usage Errors

_____	1. Using phrases correctly
_____	2. Using clauses correctly
_____	3. Writing complete sentences
_____	4. Coordinating sentence elements
_____	5. Subordinating sentence elements

Total Errors _____

Mechanics Errors

_____	1. Using commas correctly
_____	2. Using semicolons correctly
_____	3. Using colons correctly
_____	4. Using apostrophes correctly
_____	5. Using other marks of punctuation correctly (including quotation marks, slashes, dashes, parentheses, brackets, and ellipsis)
_____	6. Using correct capitalization
_____	7. Using abbreviations correctly
_____	8. Spelling every word correctly

Total Errors _____

Style Errors

_____	1. Writing clear sentences
_____	2. Writing sentences that are logical and coherent
_____	3. Using active and passive voice correctly
_____	4. Avoiding unnecessary words
_____	5. Using the most appropriate words

Total Errors _____

Damage Control

Now that you know where you're most likely to need some added writing instruction and practice, try these three ideas to help you see where you should focus your efforts:

♦ Keep track of the writing errors you make by checking your own work or seeing what points your co-workers and supervisors mention repeatedly.

♦ For now, take it one chapter at a time. Concentrate on one element of your writing in turn. Don't try to master all of grammar and usage; you'll make yourself mad and very dull at parties.

♦ Remember that using standard grammar with confidence will help you build the credible image you want—and need—to succeed.

Danger, Will Robinson

Don't panic if you can't identify each type of error at this point. Just do the best you can. Remember: You're going to take the Writing Inventory again.

Danger, Will Robinson

When most managers complain that their employees "can't write," they are most often referring to errors their people make in grammar and usage.

Mission Possible

How can you succeed in improving your skills in grammar, usage, and mechanics? Try these 10 methods. I guarantee success!

1. First of all, recognize that you *can* succeed. Many, many people before you who weren't very good at grammar and punctuation have learned more than enough to get where they want to be.

2. Face the fact that it doesn't happen overnight. It will take you some time to get it all down.

3. Lose the fear of being criticized. You're no grammar wuss.

4. Decide that you *are* going to learn. Make a commitment to do it.

5. Practice, practice, practice. Look for opportunities to practice your writing and speaking skills.

6. Find someone who will read your writing and give you an honest critique.

7. Take courses in basic English and reading. Check out adult education in your local school district or community college.

Quoth the Maven

Don't have time to sit in class? You don't need to! Some community colleges offer basic writing courses for adults on trains and buses rather than in traditional classrooms; many companies now give "mini-courses" and writing seminars in their conference rooms. What could be more convenient?

8. Try a computer tutorial program. It has the advantage of being private; just you and your 'puter.

9. Keep a journal of your work habits, strengths, and accomplishments. Not only is it good writing practice, but it's also handy to have at review time. When you talk to your superior about promotions and raises, you can refer to this journal for specific examples of your accomplishments.

10. Just do it! Don't put off writing that proposal for six months because you think your writing isn't good enough yet.

The Least You Need to Know

◆ Most writers make the same grammar, usage, mechanical, and spelling errors over and over.

◆ Assess your writing strengths and weaknesses to help you concentrate on the areas that need specific improvement.

◆ You can improve your writing now by following the methods outlined in this chapter.

Part 2

Under the Grammar Hammer

Believe it or not, *grammar* comes from the same word that *glamour* comes from. In the 1700s, *grammar* meant "enchantment, magic" (among other things). A sloppy speaker here, a sloppy speaker there, the *r* became an *l*. Voilà! A new word is born: *glamour*. To most of us, however, Tom Cruise has glamour, Liz Taylor has glamour, even Rin Tin Tin had some glamour (even though it's a little furry). Grammar does not have glamour. Neither does grammar have much magic, unless it's the witches' caldron variety.

But you've been misled. I'm here to tell you that grammar can have glamour. It can even be sexy. In this part of the book, you learn the nitty-gritty of using English properly, including parts of speech, pronoun reference, case, verb tense, agreement, and solutions to a host of other common usage dilemmas.

Parts of Speech: Coming to Terms

In This Chapter

◆ Learn four of the eight parts of speech: nouns, verbs, conjunctions, and prepositions

◆ Understand the concept of subject and object

◆ See how words are put together to create meaning

English words are divided into eight different parts of speech according to their function in a sentence. The parts of speech are (the envelope, please): *adjectives, adverbs, conjunctions, interjections, nouns, pronouns, prepositions,* and *verbs.* In this chapter, you learn all about nouns, verbs, conjunctions, and prepositions. I explain the other four parts of speech in Chapter 4. You learn how to recognize parts of speech so you have a standard way to describe how words work together to create meaning.

Nouns: Prime-Time Players

A *noun* is a word that names a person, place, or thing. Nouns, like house guests, come in different varieties. House guests include those you want, those you hate, and those you're stuck with regardless. Nouns come in these varieties: *common nouns, proper nouns, compound nouns,* and *collective nouns.*

You Could Look It Up

A **noun** is a word that names a person, place, or thing.

Take My Word for It

The word *noun* comes from the Latin word *nomen*, which means "name." Now, wouldn't that make a great pick-up line?

1. *Common nouns* name any one of a class of person, place, or thing.

   ◆ boy

   ◆ city

   ◆ food

2. *Proper nouns* name a specific person, place, or thing.

   ◆ Bob

   ◆ New York City

   ◆ Rice-a-Roni

3. *Compound nouns* are two or more nouns that function as a single unit. A compound noun can be two individual words, words joined by a hyphen, or two words combined.

   ◆ individual words: time capsule

   ◆ hyphenated words: great-uncle

   ◆ combined words: basketball

4. *Collective nouns* name groups of people or things.

   ◆ audience

   ◆ family

   ◆ herd

   ◆ crowd

Take a few seconds to catch your breath. Then underline the nouns in each of the following sentences.

1. A hungry lion was roaming through the jungle looking for something to eat.

2. He came across two men.

3. One man was sitting under a tree and reading a book; the other man was typing away on his typewriter.

4. The lion quickly pounced on the man reading the book and devoured him.

5. Even the king of the jungle knows that readers digest and writers cramp.

Answers

1. lion, jungle, something

2. men

3. man, tree, book, man, typewriter

4. lion, man, book

5. king, jungle, readers, writers

Possessive Nouns: $^9/_{10}$ of the Law

In life, possession shows success; in grammar, *possession* shows ownership. Follow these rules to create possessive nouns.

1. With singular nouns, add an apostrophe and *s*.

   ◆ girl: girl's manuscript

   ◆ student: student's ideas

2. With plural nouns ending in *s*, add an apostrophe after the *s*.

   ◆ girls: girls' manuscript

   ◆ students: students' ideas

3. With plural nouns not ending in *s*, add an apostrophe and *s*.

   ◆ women: women's books

   ◆ mice: mice's tails

Possess It!

Reduce each of the following sentences to fewer words by using the possessive form. Doing so will improve your writing style. Here's an example:

Original: The comedy routines of the Three Stooges aren't funny to me.

Revised: The Three Stooges' comedy routines aren't funny to me.

1. The original name of Mel Brooks was Melvin Kaminsky.

   _____

2. The quack of a duck doesn't echo, and no one knows why.

   _____

3. The placement of the eyes of a donkey in its head enables it to see all four feet at all times.

   _____

4. The original name of Mickey Mouse was Mortimer Mouse.

   _____

5. The real name of Hulk Hogan is Terry Bollea.

   _____

6. The milk of a camel does not curdle.

   _____

7. In *Fantasia* by Disney, the name of the Sorcerer is Yensid, which is Disney backward.

   _____

8. The urine of a cat glows under a black light.

   _____

9. The favorite hobby of my mother-in-law is playing cards with her computer.

   _____

10. Keep the boss of your boss off the back of your boss.

    _____

Answers

1. Mel Brooks' original name was Melvin Kaminsky.

2. A duck's quack doesn't echo, and no one knows why.

3. The placement of a donkey's eyes in its head enables it to see all four feet at all times.

4. Mickey Mouse's original name was Mortimer Mouse.

5. Hulk Hogan's real name is Terry Bollea.

6. Camel's milk does not curdle.

7. In Disney's *Fantasia*, the Sorcerer's name is Yensid, which is Disney backward.

8. A cat's urine glows under a black light.

9. My mother-in-law's favorite hobby is playing cards with her computer.

10. Keep your boss's boss off your boss's back.

Plural Nouns: Two's Company, Three's a Crowd

Here are the guidelines for creating plural nouns.

1. Add *s* to form the plural of most nouns.

   ◆ boy: boys

   ◆ girl: girls

   ◆ computer: computers

2. Add *es* if the noun ends in *s*, *sh*, *ch*, or *x*.

   ◆ class: classes

   ◆ wish: wishes

   ◆ inch: inches

   ◆ box: boxes

3. If a noun ends in consonant *-y*, change the *y* to *i* and add *es*.

   ◆ city: cities

   ◆ lady: ladies

4. If a noun ends in vowel *-y*, add *s*. Words ending in *-quy* don't follow this rule (as in *soliloquies*).

   ◆ essay: essays

   ◆ monkey: monkeys

Too Much of a Good Thing?

Before I overwhelm you with the rules, take a break and make each of the following singular words plural. Write your answer in the space provided.

Singular	**Plural**
1. roach	_____
2. alto	_____
3. cameo	_____
4. lily	_____
5. sex	_____

6. cry _____

7. potato _____

8. kitten _____

9. silo _____

10. fez _____

Answers

1. roaches   6. cries

2. altos   7. potatoes

3. cameos   8. kittens

4. lilies   9. silos

5. sexes   10. fezzes

5. Add *s* to most nouns ending in *f.* However, the *f* endings are so irregular as to be nearly random. If you have any doubts at all, consult a dictionary.

Singular	Plural
◆ brief	briefs
◆ chief	chiefs
◆ proof	proofs

Exceptions: In some cases, change the *f* to *fe* or *v* and add *es:*

Singular	Plural
◆ self	selves
◆ wolf	wolves
◆ leaf	leaves

Exception: This rule doesn't hold for names. When you're dealing with names, just add *s.* Thus, Mr. and Mrs. *Wolf* becomes the *Wolfs.*

6. In compound words, make the main word plural.

Singular	Plural
◆ mother-in-law	mothers-in-law
◆ passerby	passersby
◆ sister-in-law	sisters-in-law

There are two exceptions. Here's the first: If there is no noun in the compound word, add *s* to the end of the word, as in these examples:

Singular	**Plural**
◆ mix-up	mix-ups
◆ takeoff	takeoffs

Here's the second: If the compound word ends in *-ful*, add *s* to the end of the word.

Singular	**Plural**
◆ cupful	cupfuls

7. Some nouns change their spelling when they become plural.

Singular	**Plural**
◆ child	children
◆ foot	feet
◆ goose	geese
◆ louse	lice
◆ man	men
◆ mouse	mice
◆ ox	oxen
◆ tooth	teeth
◆ woman	women

8. Some nouns have the same form whether they are singular or plural.

Singular	**Plural**
◆ deer	deer
◆ moose	moose
◆ Portuguese	Portuguese
◆ series	series
◆ sheep	sheep
◆ species	species
◆ swine	swine

Like the word "Portuguese," the names of other nationalities ending in *-ese* have the same singular and plural form.

9. The only plurals formed with apostrophes are the plurals of numbers, letters, and words highlighted as words. Here are some examples:

   ◆ How many 3's make 9?

   ◆ Be sure to mind your p's and q's.

10. Some words from other languages form plurals in other ways, often determined by the laws of the language of their origin. Here are some examples:

Singular	**Plural**
◆ analysis	analyses
◆ axis	axes
◆ bacterium	bacteria
◆ index	indices
◆ parenthesis	parentheses

Combo Platter

Make each of the following words plural.

Singular	**Plural**
1. spoonful	_____
2. sheriff	_____
3. Vietnamese	_____
4. chief	_____
5. moose	_____
6. axis	_____
7. wolf	_____
8. criterion	_____
9. stimulus	_____
10. basis	_____

Answers

1. spoonfuls
2. sheriffs
3. Vietnamese
4. chiefs
5. moose

6. axes
7. wolves
8. criteria
9. stimuli
10. bases

A Note on Nouns for Non-Native Speakers

Nouns sometimes take the definite article *the*. Follow these rules:

1. Use *the* with specific singular and plural nouns.

   ◆ I need *the hammer* and *the nails*.

   ◆ I need *the tools*.

2. Use *the* with one-of-a-kind objects.

   ◆ Look at *the sun!*

   ◆ This is *the last* cupcake.

3. Use *the* with the names of oceans, seas, rivers, deserts.

   ◆ *the Atlantic Ocean*

   ◆ *the Sahara Desert*

4. Use *the* with the names of colleges and universities containing the word *of*.

   ◆ She studied at *the University* of New Mexico.

At other times, nouns do not take the definite article *the*.

Do not use *the* with the names of people, general positions, continents, states, cities, streets, religious place names, titles of officials, fields of study, names of diseases, and names of magazines and newspapers (unless it is part of the title).

◆ George Bush, *not* the George Bush

◆ Europe, *not* the Europe

◆ New Jersey, *not* the New Jersey

◆ Main Street, *not* the Main Street

◆ heaven, *not* the heaven

- Queen Mary, *not* the Queen Mary
- chemistry, *not* the chemistry
- cancer, *not* the cancer
- *Newsweek*, not the *Newsweek*
- *The New Yorker* (part of title)

Verbs: All the Right Moves

Verbs are words that name an action or describe a state of being. Verbs are seriously important, because there's no way to have a sentence without them.

While we're on the topic, every sentence must have two parts: a *subject* and a *predicate*.

- A *subject* tells who or what the sentence is about. The subject is a noun or a pronoun.
- A *predicate* tells what the subject is or does. The *verb* is found in the predicate.

You Could Look It Up

Verbs are words that name an action or describe a state of being.

Strictly Speaking

The action of an action verb can be a *visible action* (such as gamble, walk, kvetch) or a *mental action* (such as think, learn, cogitate).

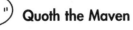

Quoth the Maven

To determine if a verb is transitive, ask yourself, "Who?" or "What?" after the verb. If you can find an answer in the sentence, the verb is transitive.

There are four basic types of verbs: *action verbs, linking verbs, helping verbs, verb phrases.*

Action Verbs: Jumping Jack Flash

Action verbs tell what the subject does. For example: jump, kiss, laugh.

- The mobsters *broke* Irving's kneecaps.
- Some people *worry* about the smallest things.

An action verb can be *transitive* or *intransitive*. *Transitive verbs* need a direct object.

- The boss *dropped* the ball.
- The workers *picked* it up.

Intransitive verbs do not need a direct object.

- Who *called?*
- Icicles *dripped* from his voice.

Chain Gang: Linking Verbs

Linking verbs join the subject and the predicate. *Linking verbs* do not show action. Instead, they help the words at the end of the sentence name and describe the subject. Here are the most common linking verbs: *be, feel, grow, seem, smell, remain, appear, sound, stay, look, taste, turn, become.*

Although small in size as well as number, linking verbs are used a great deal. Here are two typical examples:

- The manager *was* happy about the job change.

- He *is* a fool.

Many linking verbs can also be used as action verbs. For example:

- *Linking:* The kids *looked* sad.

- *Action:* I *looked* for the dog in the pouring rain.

 **Quoth the Maven**

To determine whether a verb is being used as a linking verb or an action verb, use *am, are,* or *is* for the verb. If the sentence makes sense with the substitution, the original verb is a linking verb.

Mother's Little Helper: Helping Verbs

Helping verbs are added to another verb to make the meaning clearer. Helping verbs include any form of *to be*. Here are some examples: *do, does, did, have, has, had, shall, should, will, would, can, could, may, might, must.*

Verb phrases are made of one main verb and one or more helping verbs.

- They *will run* before dawn.

- They *do have* a serious problem.

Verb-O-Rama

Identify each of the verbs in the following sentences. Remember to look for action verbs, linking verbs, and helping verbs.

1. A group of chess enthusiasts had checked into a hotel.

2. They were standing in the lobby discussing their recent tournament victories.

3. After about an hour, the manager came out of the office and asked them to disperse.

4. "But why?" they asked as they moved off.

5. "Because," he said, "I can't stand chess nuts boasting in an open foyer."

Answers

1. had checked

2. were standing, discussing

3. came, asked, disperse

4. asked, moved

5. said, can't stand, boasting

One more time, with gusto! Underline the verbs in each of these sentences.

1. I can please only one person per day. Today is not your day.

2. I love deadlines. I especially like the whooshing sound they make as they fly by.

3. Tell me what you need, and I'll tell you how to get along without it.

4. Accept that some days you are the pigeon and some days the statue.

5. Everybody is somebody else's weirdo.

6. I don't have an attitude problem; you have a perception problem.

7. Last night I lay in bed looking up at the stars in the sky, and I thought to myself, where the heck is the ceiling?

8. My reality check bounced.

9. On the keyboard of life, always keep one finger on the escape key.

10. Never argue with an idiot. They drag you down to their level, then beat you with experience.

Answers

1. can please, is

2. love, like, make, fly

3. tell, tell, get

4. accept, are

5. is

6. don't have, have

7. lay, looking, thought, is

8. bounced

9. keep

10. argue, drag, beat

Conjunctions: The Ties That Bind

Conjunctions connect words or groups of words and show how they are related. There are three kinds of conjunctions: *coordinating conjunctions, correlative conjunctions,* and *subordinating conjunctions.* Let's look at each one.

1. *Coordinating conjunctions* link words or word groups. Here are the seven coordinating conjunctions:

   ◆ for

   ◆ and

   ◆ but

   ◆ or

   ◆ yet

   ◆ so

   And now for some examples:

   ◆ Eat one live toad the first thing in the morning *and* nothing worse will happen to you the rest of the day.

   ◆ Meddle not in the affairs of dragons, *for* thou art crunchy and taste good with ketchup.

You Could Look It Up

Conjunctions connect words or groups of words and show how they are related.

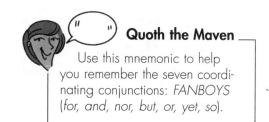

Quoth the Maven

Use this mnemonic to help you remember the seven coordinating conjunctions: *FANBOYS* (for, and, nor, but, or, yet, so).

All Tied Up

Underline the coordinating conjunctions in each sentence.

1. There are two kinds of air travel in the United States: first class and with children.

2. Almost certainly not Oscar Wilde's last words: "Either this wallpaper goes or I do."

3. Winston Churchill said, "History will be kind to me, for I intend to write it."

4. The only reason I intend to take up jogging is so that I can hear heavy breathing again.

5. It's lonely at the top, but you eat better there.

Answers

1. and

2. or

3. for

4. so

5. but

2. *Correlative conjunctions* also link similar words or word groups, but they are always used in pairs. Here are the correlative conjunctions:

   - both … and
   - either … or
   - neither … nor
   - not only … but also
   - whether … or

   Some examples:

   - He lost *both* his shirt *and* his pants.
   - *Either* you come with us now, *or* you will miss the boat.

3. *Subordinate conjunctions* link an independent clause (a complete sentence) to a dependent clause (a fragment). There are only seven coordinating conjunctions and five correlative conjunctions, but you have more subordinating conjunctions than Custer had Native Americans. Here are the most often used subordinating conjunctions:

   - after
   - although
   - as
   - as if
   - as long as
   - as soon as
   - as though
   - because

- before
- even though
- if
- in order that
- since
- so, so that
- though

- till
- unless
- until
- when
- whenever
- where
- wherever

And a few examples culled from actual insurance forms:

- The guy was all over the road *so* I had to swerve a couple of times before I finally hit him.

- I had been driving for 40 years *when* I fell asleep at the wheel and had an accident.

Fit to Be Tied

Underline the conjunctions in each sentence.

1. Never argue with an idiot. They drag you down to their level, then beat you with experience.

2. Don't be irreplaceable—if you can't be replaced, you can't be promoted.

3. After any salary raise, you will have less money at the end of the month than you did before.

4. When you don't know what to do, walk fast and look worried.

5. You can go anywhere you want if you look serious and carry a clipboard.

6. As I told you, work with me, baby.

7. Since my car is costlier, newer, and flashier than yours, I have the right-of-way.

8. No sense being pessimistic because it probably wouldn't work anyway

9. Unless you have a doctor's note, it is illegal to buy ice cream after 6 P.M. in Newark, New Jersey.

10. When confronted by a difficult problem, you can solve it more easily by reducing it to the question, "How would the Lone Ranger handle this?"

Answers

1. then
2. if
3. after
4. when
5. if

6. as
7. since
8. because
9. unless
10. when

Prepositions: Good Things Come in Small Packages

Prepositions are the mighty mites of grammar and writing, small but powerful little puppies. Prepositions are words that link a noun or a pronoun to another word in the sentence.

Use this list to help you recognize some of the most common prepositions:

- about
- above
- across
- after
- against
- along
- amid
- around
- as
- at
- before
- behind
- below
- beneath
- beside

- between
- beyond
- but
- by
- despite
- down
- during
- except
- for
- from
- in
- inside
- into
- like
- near

- of
- off
- on
- onto
- opposite
- out
- outside
- over
- past

- since
- through
- toward
- under
- underneath
- until
- upon
- with
- within

You Could Look It Up

Prepositions are words that link a noun or a pronoun to another word in the sentence.

A noun always follows a preposition. A *prepositional phrase* is a preposition and its object. A prepositional phrase can be two or three words long, as these examples show:

- on the wing
- in the door

However, prepositional phrases can be much longer, depending on the length of the preposition and number of words that describe the object of the preposition. Here are two super-size prepositional phrases:

- *near* the violently swaying oak trees
- *on* account of his nearly depleted bank account

Joined at the Hip

Circle the preposition or prepositions in each sentence. Then write the noun or noun phrase that follows it. (*Hint:* Look for the noun markers *a*, *an*, and *the*.)

1. You are slower than a herd of turtles stampeding through peanut butter.

2. A pat on the back is only a few centimeters from a kick in the butt.

3. He wants the magic fingers vibrating bed regardless of the cost.

4. Of course he will help himself to the biggest portion; he's a piggy.

5. If it wasn't for the last minute, nothing would get done.

Answers

Preposition(s)	Noun(s)
1. of, through	peanut butter, turtles
2. on, from, in	the back, a kick, the butt
3. of	cost
4. to	the biggest portion
5. for	the last minute

A Note on Prepositions for Non-Native Speakers

Using prepositions correctly presents special problems for people whose first language is not English. That's because so many prepositional phrases are *idiomatic:* They have evolved through use and do not necessarily make logical sense. Here are some guidelines:

1. Use *in* before seasons of the year. Also use *in* with months and years not followed by specific dates.

   ◆ *in* the summer

   ◆ *in* January

   ◆ *in* 2003

2. Use *on* before days of the week, holidays, and months, if the date follows.

   ◆ *on* Wednesday

   ◆ *on* Thanksgiving

   ◆ *on* July 20

3. *Like* is a preposition that means "similar to." Therefore, it is followed by an object (usually a noun or pronoun).

   ◆ *like* T'Aysha

   ◆ *like* you

4. Use the preposition *of* to show possession.

   The preposition of is often used to show possession instead of the possessive form of a pronoun.

I hear a puppy's bark.

Or:

I hear the bark of a puppy.

Never use the preposition *of* with proper nouns.

Incorrect: I wore the dress of Nina.

Correct: I wore Nina's dress.

5. Following is a list of idiomatic prepositional phrases and examples. *Always* use these prepositional phrases as units; don't substitute other prepositions.

Prepositional Phrases	Examples
acquainted with	Nico is acquainted with my cousin Raul.
addicted to	I am addicted to coffee.
agree on (a plan)	They finally agreed on a plan.
agree to (someone else's proposal)	Did Betty agree to their demands?
angry at or about (a thing)	The commuters are angry about the fare hike.
angry with (a person)	They are angry with the mayor.
apply for (a job)	Apply for a job.
approve of	Did she approve of the vacation plan?
consist of	The casserole consists of squirrel and noodles.
contrast with	The red shirt contrasts with the pink pants.
convenient for	Is Monday convenient for you?
deal with	How do you deal with that awful child?
depend on	Everything depends on the bus schedule.
differ from (something)	The airplane differs from the train.
differ with (a person)	I differ with your argument.
displeased with	Nina is displeased with the plan.
fond of	We are all fond of Mrs. Marco.
grateful for (something)	The child was grateful for a snow day.

grateful to (someone)	We are grateful to the doctor.
identical with	This cake is identical with hers.
interested in	Chris is interested in martial arts.
interfere with	Homework can interfere with you social life.
object to	We object to the income tax hike.
protect against	An umbrella protects against rain.
reason with	You can't reason with a two-year-old.
responsible for	I am responsible for bringing the salad.
shocked at	We are shocked at your hair color!
similar to	It is similar to a rainbow.
specialize in	The hairdresser must specialize in humor.
take advantage of	They surely take advantage of kids!
worry about	I worry about you.

The Least You Need to Know

- ◆ Nouns name a person, place, or thing.

- ◆ Verbs express action, condition, or state of being.

- ◆ Conjunctions connect words or groups of words.

- ◆ Prepositions link a noun or pronoun to another word.

Chapter 4

Terms of Endearment: More Parts of Speech

In This Chapter

- ◆ Learn the other four parts of speech: adjectives, adverbs, pronouns, and interjections

- ◆ See how words are put together to create meaning

As you learned in Chapter 3, English words are divided into eight different parts of speech according to their function in a sentence. In this chapter, you explore the remaining four parts of speech: *adjectives, adverbs, pronouns,* and *interjections.* (Hey, would I cheat you? You get all eight for your money!)

Adjectives: Happy Little Clouds

Adjectives are words that describe nouns and pronouns. They're the color commentators of language, the words that give your writing and speech flavor. Adjectives answer the questions "What kind?" "How much?" "Which one?" and "How many?" For example:

- ◆ What kind? red nose, gold ring

- ◆ How much? more sugar, little effort

- ◆ Which one? second wife, those nuts
- ◆ How many? several wives, six husbands

Spice Up Your Sentences with Adjectives

There are five kinds of adjectives: *common adjectives*, *proper adjectives*, *compound adjectives*, *articles*, and *indefinite adjectives*.

You Could Look It Up

Adjectives are words that modify—describe or limit—nouns and pronouns.

1. *Common adjectives* describe nouns or pronouns.

   - ◆ *strong* man
   - ◆ *green* plant
   - ◆ *pretty* child

2. *Proper adjectives* are formed from proper nouns.

   - ◆ *California* vegetables
   - ◆ *Mexican* food

3. *Compound adjectives* are made up of more than one word, like these two examples:

   - ◆ *far-off* country
   - ◆ *teenage* person

4. *Articles* are a special type of adjective. There are three articles: *a*, *an*, and *the*.

   - ◆ *The* is called a "definite article" because it refers to a specific thing.

   - ◆ *A* and *an* are called "indefinite articles" because they refer to general things. Use *a* when the word that follows begins with a consonant sound; use *an* before words that begin with vowel sounds.

5. *Indefinite adjectives* don't specify the amount of something. Instead, they describe general quantities. Most of the indefinite adjectives were pronouns in their first lives. For example:

   - ◆ all
   - ◆ another
   - ◆ any
   - ◆ both
   - ◆ each
   - ◆ either
   - ◆ few
   - ◆ many
   - ◆ more
   - ◆ most

- neither
- other
- several
- some

A Note on Adjectives for Non-Native Speakers

The indefinite articles *a* and *an* are grammatically the same. They both mean "one of many." They are used only with singular nouns. As you learned earlier, use *a* when the word that follows begins with a consonant sound; use *an* before words that begin with vowel sounds. Here are some additional guidelines:

1. *A* is sometimes used with the words "little" and "few." The meaning is slightly different, depending on whether you use the article *a* before the words "little" and "few." Study these examples:

   > *a little*, *a few* = a small amount of something
   > *little*, *few* = less than expected

   - a few carrots, few carrots

   - a little sugar, little sugar

2. *A* and *an* are rarely used with proper nouns.

Have Fun with Adjectives

Now that you know what adjectives are, it's time to learn how to use them. Follow these easy-as-pie guidelines:

1. Use an adjective to describe a noun or a pronoun.

2. Use vivid adjectives to make your writing more specific and descriptive.

3. Use an adjective after a *linking verb*. A linking verb connects a subject with a descriptive word. Here are the most common linking verbs: *be* (*is, am, are, was, were,* and so on), *seem, appear, look, feel, smell, sound, taste, become, grow, remain, stay,* and *turn*.

   - Chicken made this way <u>tastes</u> more *delicious* (not *deliciously*).

And in This Corner ...

Identify the adjective or adjectives in each of the following sentences. (They are all winners in a contest in which contestants were asked to take a well-known expression in a foreign language, change a single letter, and provide a definition for the new expression. So ignore the foreign expressions.)

1. ¿HARLEZ-VOUS FRANCAIS?—Can you drive a French motorcycle?

2. ¡IDIOS AMIGOS!—We're wild and crazy guys!

3. PRO BOZO PUBLICO—Support your local clown.

4. MONAGE A TROIS—I am three years old.

5. QUIP PRO QUO—A fast retort

6. PORTE-KOCHERE—Sacramental wine

Answers

1. French

2. wild, crazy

3. local

4. three

5. fast

6. Sacramental

Adverbs: Who Ya Gonna Call?

Adverbs are words that describe verbs, adjectives, or other adverbs. Adverbs answer the questions "When?" "Where?" "How?" or "To what extent?" For example:

♦ When? left yesterday, begin now

♦ Where? fell below, move up

♦ How? happily sang, danced badly

♦ To what extent? partly finished, eat completely

Fortunately for us, most adverbs are formed by adding *-ly* to an adjective. This makes recognizing an adverb fairly easy. Of course, we don't want things to be *too* easy, so there are a bunch of adverbs that don't end in *-ly*. Here are some of the most common non-*ly* adverbs:

♦ afterward   ♦ already

♦ almost   ♦ back

- even
- far
- fast
- hard
- here
- how
- late
- long
- low
- more
- near
- never
- next
- now
- often
- quick
- rather
- slow
- so
- soon
- still
- then
- today
- tomorrow
- too
- when
- where
- yesterday

Have Fun with Adverbs

Now, what can you do with an adverb? Try this: Use an adverb to describe a verb, an adjective, or another adverb.

1. Use an adverb to describe a verb.

   - Experiments using dynamite must be done *carefully*.

2. Use an adverb to describe an adjective.

   - Charles had an *unbelievably* huge appetite for chips.

3. Use an adverb to describe another adverb.

   - They sang *so clearly*.

Conjunctive Adverbs: An Adverb Disguised as a Conjunction

Conjunctive adverbs are used to connect other words. Therefore, conjunctive adverbs act like conjunctions, these wily devils—even though they are not technically considered to be conjunctions. Despite their tendency to be mislabeled, conjunctive adverbs are very useful when you want to link ideas and paragraphs. Here are the fan favorites:

- ◆ accordingly
- ◆ again
- ◆ also
- ◆ besides
- ◆ consequently
- ◆ finally
- ◆ for example
- ◆ furthermore
- ◆ however
- ◆ indeed
- ◆ moreover
- ◆ nevertheless
- ◆ on the other hand
- ◆ otherwise
- ◆ then
- ◆ therefore

Hunt and Peck

Underline the adverb or adverbs in each sentence.

1. America is a large, friendly dog in a small room. Every time it wags its tail, it knocks over a chair.

2. Bigamy: One wife too many. Monogamy: Same idea.

3. There is never enough time—unless you're serving it.

4. Fashion is a form of ugliness so intolerable that we have to alter it every six months.

5. Upon hearing that Ronald Reagan had been elected governor of California, movie studio head Jack Warner said, "It's our fault. We should have given him much better parts."

Strictly Speaking
Conjunctive adverbs are also called *transitions* because they link ideas.

Answers

1. large

2. too

3. never

4. so, every

5. much

Pronouns: Pinch Hitters

Say you wrote this sentence:

> Mr. Hufnagle gave Mr. Hufnagle's pen
> to Mr. Hufnagle's wife, Mrs. Hufnagle;
> Mrs. Hufnagle was grateful for the pen.

You Could Look It Up

Pronouns are words used in place of a noun or another pronoun. An **antecedent** is the noun that the pronoun stands for.

You would be reduced to this sorry state were it not for the delightful and ever useful little *pronoun*. Thanks to Mr. Pronoun, you can write this graceful sentence instead:

> Mr. Hufnagle gave *his* pen to *his* wife,
> Mrs. Hufnagle; *she* was grateful for *it*.

Now, I know you have to agree that the pronoun is a thing of beauty indeed.

A pronoun is a word used in place of a noun or another pronoun. Pronouns help you avoid unnecessary repetition in your writing and speech.

A pronoun gets its meaning from the noun it stands for. The noun is called the *antecedent*. Here's an example:

Take My Word for It

The word *antecedent* comes from a Latin word meaning "to go before." However, as in the example here, the noun doesn't have to appear before the pronoun in a sentence. The things you learn in this book!

 ◆ Although *Seattle* is damp, *it* is my favorite city.

              antecedent   pronoun

Of course, there are different kinds of pronouns. Most of them have antecedents, but a few do not. Meet the pronoun family.

1. *Personal pronouns* refer to a specific person, place, object, or thing. Here are the major players:

	Singular	**Plural**
First person	I, me, mine, my	we, us, our, ours
Second person	you, your, yours	you, your, yours
Third person	he, him, his, she,	they, them, their,
her, hers, it	theirs, its	

2. *Possessive pronouns* show ownership. The possessive pronouns are yours, his, hers, its, ours, theirs, whose.

    ◆ Is this nice dead cat *yours?*

    ◆ Yes, it's *ours.*

3. *Reflexive pronouns* add information to a sentence by pointing back to a noun or pronoun near the beginning of the sentence. Reflexive pronouns end in *-self* or *-selves.*

    ◆ Herman bought *himself* a life-size inflatable woman.

    ◆ They all enjoyed *themselves* at Herman's expense.

4. *Intensive pronouns* also end in *-self* or *-selves,* but they just add emphasis to the noun or pronoun.

    ◆ Herman *himself* blew up the doll.

    ◆ Herman said that he would be able to deflate the doll *himself.*

5. *Demonstrative pronouns* direct attention to a specific person, place, or thing. Not to panic—there are only four demonstrative pronouns: *this, that, these,* and *those.*

    ◆ *This* is the invisible car that came out of nowhere, struck my car, and vanished.

    ◆ *That* was the slow-moving, sad-faced old gentleman who bounced off the roof of my car.

6. *Relative pronouns* begin a subordinate clause. Only five, folks: *that, which, who, whom,* and *those.*

    ◆ Mr. Peepers claimed *that* the other car collided with his without giving warning of its intention.

    ◆ Louise was the driver *who* had to swerve a number of times before she hit the other car.

7. *Interrogative pronouns* ask a question. High fives: *what, which, who, whom,* and *whose.*

    ◆ *Who* claimed he was coming home when he drove into the wrong house and collided with a tree he doesn't have?

    ◆ *Which* insurance adjuster had these headaches?

8. *Indefinite pronouns* refer to people, places, objects, or things without pointing to a specific one.

Here are the most common indefinite pronouns:

Singular	Plural	Singular or Plural
another	both	all
anyone	few	any
each	many	more
everyone	others	most
everybody	several	none
everything		some
much		
nobody		
nothing		
other		
someone		
anybody		
anything		
either		
little		
neither		
no one		
one		
somebody		
something		

Face the Music

Circle the pronouns in the following jokes. The number of pronouns in each joke is indicated in parentheses at the end of each one. The same pronoun may be used more than once in each sentence.

1. Observation attributed to Professor Robert Wilensky of the University of California at Berkeley: "We have all heard that a million monkeys banging on a million typewriters will eventually reproduce the works of Shakespeare. Now, thanks to the Internet, we know this is not true." (5)

2. There was a man who entered a local paper's pun contest. He sent in 10 different puns, in the hope that at least 1 of the puns would win. Unfortunately, no pun in 10 did. (5)

3. A man told his psychiatrist, "Doc, I keep having these alternating recurring dreams. First I am a teepee; then I am a wigwam; then I am a teepee; then I am a wigwam. It is driving me crazy. What's wrong with me?"

   The doctor replied, "It is very simple. You are two tents." (12)

Answers

1. We, all, that, this, we

2. There, who, He, that, one

3. his, I, these, I, I, I, I, It, me, me, It, you

Interjections: Zap! Pow! Wow!

Unlike movie stars Steven Seagal and Morris the Cat (okay, so he's dead), *interjections* show strong emotion. Because interjections are not linked grammatically to other words in the sentence, they are set off from the rest of the sentence with a comma or an exclamation mark.

You Could Look It Up

Interjections show strong emotion. Often, interjections will be set off with an exclamation mark. Although any word that shows strong feelings can be an interjection, look for the usual suspects: *Wow!, Zap!, Pop!,* and the rest of the family.

◆ *Oh!* What a shock you gave me with that gorilla suit.

◆ *Wow!* That's *not* a gorilla suit?

With interjections, a little goes a long way. Use these marks of punctuation as you would hot pepper or hysterics, because they are strong and edgy.

Just When You Thought It Was Safe to Take a Shower ...

How long did it take you to get over *Psycho?* Still have nightmares about checking into the Bates Motel? Well, grammar has its own scary points. Let me give it to you straight because I know you can take it: Some words can function as more than one part of speech. Yes, you heard me right. This means you can't memorize a word like *fish* as a noun—because the slimy sucker can also be a verb. Here's an example of one that didn't get away:

◆ Noun: I ate a *fish* for dinner.

◆ Verb: We *fish* in the lake every Tuesday.

Adverbs disguise themselves as prepositions in certain sentences; in other sentences, a word you thought was a died-in-the-wool adjective turns out to be a card-carrying noun. What's a writer to do?

Just as no man or woman is an island (except perhaps for Michael Jackson), so no part of speech exists in a vacuum. To correctly identify a word's part of speech, you have to see how the word functions in a specific sentence. Try this pleasant little exercise to see what you've learned so far.

Seventh-Inning Stretch

Identify the part of speech of each underlined word. Write your answer in the space provided.

1. The <u>outside</u> of the boat needs scraping.

2. You should scrape the boat without <u>outside</u> help.

3. Let's sit <u>outside</u> and laugh at you as you work in the blazing sun.

4. The ambulance is parked right <u>outside</u> the yard, next to the beehive and poison ivy.

5. The Reverend repented of his <u>past</u> mistakes.

6. Turn right <u>past</u> the store with the "Deli/Guns" sign in the window.

7. Did you hear that song <u>before</u>?

8. Always follow <u>through</u> what you start.

9. The remark went right <u>through</u> one ear and out the other.

10. The gardener mowed the lawn <u>after</u> he reread *Lady Chatterly's Lover.*

Answers

1. noun

2. adjective

3. adverb

4. preposition

5. adjective

6. preposition

7. adverb

8. adverb

9. preposition

10. conjunction

The Least You Need to Know

◆ Adjectives describe nouns and pronouns.

◆ Adverbs are words that describe verbs, adjectives, or other adverbs.

◆ Pronouns are words used in place of a noun or another pronoun.

◆ Interjections express strong emotions.

◆ This all sounds a lot harder than it really is.

Chapter 5

Altered States: Verbs

In This Chapter

- Find out why verbs are tense
- Learn about a verb's person, number, and mood
- Get the scoop on the active and passive voice

In writing and speaking, you often have to show when something happens. Is it taking place now? Later? Did it happen earlier in the day, a week ago, a year ago, or when dinosaurs roamed the earth? In English, *tense* is used to show when something happens.

In this chapter, you learn how to use verbs to indicate when an action occurred. First, I explain the different tenses and how they are used. The focus here is on regular verbs (the nice cooperative ones) and irregular verbs (the ones that need bran cereal). There's even a special section on *lie/lay*, the verb duo that reduces even linebackers and mothers-in-law to quivering masses of jelly. The rest of the chapter covers verbs and their person, number, mood, and voice. Not to worry if you don't know these terms now; I promise that by the end of the chapter you'll be slinging them around like a short-order cook hauls hash 'n' eggs.

Shape Shifters

You learned in Chapter 3 that *verbs* are words that name an action or describe a state of being. There are four basic types of verbs: *action verbs, linking verbs, helping verbs,* and *verb phrases.* Verbs tell what's happening, what has happened, and what will happen. They're just happenin' kinds of words.

Verbs are all this and more! Verbs also convey information through changes in their form. Here are the five different things you can find out from a verb:

◆ Tense (when the action takes place: past, present, or future)

◆ Person (who or what experiences the action)

◆ Number (how many subjects act or receive the action)

◆ Mood (the attitude expressed toward the action)

◆ Voice (whether the subject acts or is acted upon: the active or passive voice)

Still with me? Of course you are. Now it's time to take a look at each of these verb functions in detail.

Verb Tense: Nothing a Little Prozac Wouldn't Cure

Like people, verbs show the passage of time by changing form. Over the years, some of us get a little thick around the middle while the rest of us get a bit more blond. The *tense* of a verb shows its time. Verbs add a final *-ed* or *-d* to the simple form, use an auxiliary verb, or change their form completely to show that time flies.

You Could Look It Up

The **tense** of a verb shows its time.

There are six verb tenses in English. Each of the six tenses has two forms: *basic* and *progressive* (also known as "perfect"). The following table shows the six forms for the verb *to talk.*

I'm All Shook Up: Examples of the Six Verb Tenses

Tense	Basic Form	Progressive Form
Present	talk	am talking
Past	talked	was talking
Future	will talk	will be talking

Tense	Basic Form	Progressive Form
Present perfect	have talked	have been talking
Past perfect	had talked	had been talking
Future perfect	will have talked	will have been talking

I Feel Your Pain: Principal Parts of Verbs

As the preceding table indicates, you form verb tense from principal parts and helping verbs. Every English verb has four main parts, as the following table shows.

Principal Verb Parts

Present	Present Participle	Past	Past Participle
talk	talking	talked	talked
play	playing	played	played

♦ The *present* is used to form the present tense (*I talk*) and the future (*I will talk*). Notice that you have to use the helping verb *will* to show the future tense.

♦ The *present participle* forms all six of the progressive forms (*I am talking*, *I was talking*, and so on).

♦ The *past* forms only one tense—you guessed it, the past (*I talked*).

♦ The *past participle* forms the last three tenses: the *present perfect* (*I have talked*), the *past perfect* (*I had talked*), and the *future perfect* (*I will have talked*). To form the past participle, start with a helping verb such as *is*, *are*, *was*, or *has been*. Then add the principal part of the verb.

> **Strictly Speaking**
>
> The *simple form* of the verb is also called the *base form*. The simple form shows action, occurrence, or state of being that is taking place right here and now (*I pout*). The simple form is also the base for the future form (that is, *I will pout, they will pout*).

A Class Act: Forming Past Tenses

English verbs are traditionally divided into two classes, according to the ways they form their past tense and past participles.

You Could Look It Up

Regular verbs form the past tense and past participle by adding *-d, -ed,* or *-t* to the present form. They don't change their vowel. **Irregular verbs** don't form the past by adding *-ed* or *-d*. They form the past tense in many other ways.

Take My Word for It

Over time, we have come to accept regular verbs as the "normal" ones, so now we usually just add *-ed* or *-d* to new verbs, as in *televise, televised.*

1. Some verbs are *regular.* This means they form the past tense and past participle by adding *-d, -ed,* or *-t* to the present form but don't change their vowel, as in *walk, walked, walked.*

2. *Irregular verbs* don't form the past by adding *-ed* or *-d.* The principal parts of irregular verbs are formed in many different ways. This could be why they need bran.

   ◆ Sometimes, irregular verbs change tense without changing their endings. Instead, they usually travel in time by changing a vowel and adding *-n* or *-en,* as in *begin, began, begun.*

   ◆ Other times, they change their vowel and add *-d* or *-t,* as in *lose, lost, lost.*

   ◆ Or they may not change at all, such as *set, set, set,* and *put, put, put.*

The following chart shows the most common irregular verbs.

Present Tense	Past Tense	Past Participle
arise	arose	arisen
bear	bore	born or borne
beat	beat	beaten
become	became	become
begin	began	begun
bend	bent	bent
bite	bit	bitten
blow	blew	blown
break	broke	broken
bring	brought	brought
burst	burst	burst
catch	caught	caught
choose	chose	chosen
come	came	come
creep	crept	crept
dig	dug	dug

Present Tense	Past Tense	Past Participle
dive	dived or dove	dived
do	did	done
draw	drew	drawn
drink	drank	drunk
drive	drove	driven
eat	ate	eaten
fall	fell	fallen
fight	fought	fought
fly	flew	flown
forget	forgot	forgotten
forgive	forgave	forgiven
freeze	froze	frozen
get	got	gotten or got
give	gave	given
go	went	gone
grow	grew	grown
hang	hung	hung
hang (execute)	hanged	hanged
hide	hid	hidden
hold	held	held
hurt	hurt	hurt
kneel	knelt	knelt
know	knew	known
lay	laid	laid
lead	led	led
lie (horizontal)	lay	lain
lie (falsehood)	lied	lied
lose	lost	lost
prove	proved	proved or proven
ride	rode	ridden
ring	rang	rung
rise	rose	risen
run	ran	run
say	said	said

continues

continued

Present Tense	Past Tense	Past Participle
see	saw	seen
shake	shook	shaken
show	showed	showed or shown
shrink	shrank	shrunk
sing	sang	sung
sink	sank	sunk
speak	spoke	spoken
spring	sprang	sprung
steal	stole	stolen
strive	strove	striven
swear	swore	sworn
swim	swam	swum
take	took	taken
teach	taught	taught
tear	tore	torn
throw	threw	thrown
wake	woke or waked	woken or waked
wear	wore	worn
write	wrote	written

Now I ~~Lay Lie~~ Lay Me Down to Sleep

You can argue whether men are from Mars and women are from Venus, but everyone agrees that *lie* and *lay* are definitely from another planet. These two verbs may be the most commonly confused pair of words in English. Here's the problem: They're just plain evil.

Danger, Will Robinson

The verb *to be* is the most irregular verb in English. Beware of this quick-change artist. Its principal parts are: *be, being, was, were, been, am, are, is.*

Seriously, *lie* is an irregular verb that conjugates *lie, lay, lain. Lay*, in contrast, is a regular verb that conjugates *lay, laid, laid*. Because *lay* is both the present tense of *to lay* and the past tense of *lie*, many speakers and writers use *lay* when they mean *lie*.

To add to the confusion, *lie* and *lay* have different meanings. *Lie* means "to repose"; *lay* means "to put." It's enough to make you learn Esperanto.

Try these hints to sort out *lie/lay:*

♦ *Lie* means "to repose"; *lay* means "to put."

♦ *Lie* is an intransitive verb. That means that it never takes a direct object. For example: "If you are tired, you should *lie* down."

♦ *Lay* is a transitive verb. That means that *lay* always takes a direct object. For example: "*Lay* the book on the table, please."

Study the following table to further clarify *lie* and *lay.* Or have it tattooed in your palm for ready reference.

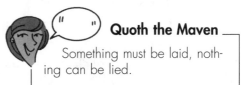

You Could Look It Up

When you **conjugate** a verb, you list the singular and plural forms of the verb in a specific tense.

Quoth the Maven

Something must be laid, nothing can be lied.

The Various Forms of Lie and Lay

Verb	Meaning	Examples
lie	to repose flat	Present tense: Fido lies down.
		Past tense: Fido lay down.
		Future tense: Fido will lie down.
		Perfect tense: Fido has lain down.
lay	to put down	Present tense: Lay your cards down.
		Past tense: He laid the cards down.
		Future tense: He will lay his cards down.
		Perfect tense: He has laid his cards down.

Party Pooper: Test Time

I know you need this quiz like Sinatra needs singing lessons, but humor me. Circle the correct form of each verb in parentheses. Then identify the verb as regular or irregular.

1. Martin Buser (took/taking/taked) his third Iditarod title in the grueling Alaskan dogsled race. However, the team from Beverly Hills has yet to finish. Apparently, French poodles weren't the way to go.

The verb is (regular/irregular).

2. President Clinton has (proposed/proposing) free TV time for candidates. "Not good," said one commentator. "This could mean Sonny Bono will be back on television."

   The verb is (regular/irregular).

3. NBA's Dennis Rodman's announcement that he would (choose/chose) professional wrestling has caused a stir. "I hope that sport doesn't turn him into some weird spectacle," said one viewer.

   The verb is (regular/irregular).

4. When he heard that Tonya Harding described herself as "the Charles Barkley of figure skating," Barkley was (going/went/gone) to sue Tonya Harding for defamation of character. "But then I realized that I had no character," he said.

   The verb is (regular/irregular).

5. The feud between East Coast and West Coast rappers continues. It all (started/starting) over the usual: Who controls what, who insulted whom, whether the theories of Kierkegaard still have relevance …

   The verb is (regular/irregular).

6. My karma just (run/ran) over your dogma.

   The verb is (regular/irregular).

Answers

1. took; irregular

2. proposed; regular

3. choose; irregular

4. going; irregular

5. started; regular

6. ran; irregular

All Tensed Up: Using Verb Tense Correctly

Okay, so now you know that verbs form different tenses to show different times. Now you have to learn how to use the tenses correctly to show the timing of one event in relation to another. And we all know that in life, timing is *everything*.

Get your bearings with the following table. It shows how the tenses are related.

Verb Tense and Time

Past	Present	Future
Simple past	Simple present	Simple future
Present perfect		Future perfect
Past perfect		
Past progressive	Present progressive	Future progressive
Present perfect progressive		Future perfect
Progressive		
Past perfect progressive		

◆ Use the two present forms (*simple present* and *present progressive*) to show events that take place now.

◆ Use the six past forms (*simple past, present perfect, past perfect, past progressive, present perfect progressive*, and *past perfect progressive*) to show events that took place before the present.

◆ Use the four future forms (*simple future, future perfect, future progressive*, and *future perfect progressive*) to show events that take place in the future.

Get the inside skinny in the following sections.

Past Tense

What's past may be past, but only if you get your past tenses straight. Use the following table to leave the past in the past.

Past Tenses

Tense	Use	Example
Simple past	Completed action	We finished the tofu.
	Completed condition	We were sad; no more tofu.
Present perfect	Completed action	We have finished the tofu.
	Completed condition	We have been sad.
	Continuing action	We have burped for hours.
	Continuing condition	I have been here for days.

continues

Past Tenses (continued)

Tense	Use	Example
Past perfect	Action completed before another	I had eaten all the tofu before you returned.
	Condition completed before another	I had been sad before the new tofu arrived.
Past progressive	Continuous completed action	I was snoring that week.
Present perfect progressive	Action going into present	I have been snoring all week.
Past perfect progressive	Continuing action interrupted by another	I had been snoring when the house collapsed.

Back to the Future

This table explains the future tenses.

Future Tenses

Tense	Use	Example
Simple future	Future action	The sponge will dry.
	Future condition	I will be happy when it does.
Future perfect	Future action done before another	By the time you read this, the sponge will be dry.
	Future condition done before another	The sponge will have been on the window for a week.
Future progressive	Continuing future action	They will be buying sponges this week.
Future perfect progressive	Continuing future action done before another	When we lunch next week, I will have been pumping iron for at least a week.

A Note on Verbs for Non-Native Speakers

Verbs present special problems for people whose first language is not English. Here are some guidelines to make your life easier (at least as it relates to verbs).

1. Use the correct form of verbs.

   The following chart can help you remember how to use verbs correctly.

   ## Nonstandard and Standard English

Nonstandard English Present Tense	Standard English
I	I
you	you
we walks	we walk
they	they
he, she, it walk	he, she, it walks
Past Tense	
I	I
you	you
we walk	we walk**ed**
they	they
he, she, it walk	he, she, it walk**ed**

2. When used as a helping verb, *be, do,* and *have* change form to agree with a third-person singular subject. The main verb does not add *-s.*

   Incorrect: Does the store opens at 10?

   Correct: Does the store open at 10?

3. *Can* and *could*

   ◆ *Can* means *am/is/are able.* It may be used to show the *present tense.*

   Today, I can sleep late.

   I can clean the house—but I won't.

   ◆ *Could* means *was/were able* when used to show the *past tense* of *can. Could* also means "might be able, a possibility or wish."

   In the past, I could touch my toes.

   I wish I could touch my toes now.

   Can and *could* (along with *might, must, shall, should, will, would*) never change form.

4. Idiomatic expressions with *can, could, might, must, shall, should, will, would*

   These words are called "modals." Here's a list of the most common expressions.

Idiomatic Expressions with Modals

Example	Meaning
I *would rather* walk than ride.	I prefer to walk.
I *would sleep* during foreign films.	I always sleep in foreign movies.
Shall we meet again?	I'm inviting you to meet again.
Would you mind turning off the radio?	Would you be against doing this?
Do you mind turning it off?	Please turn it off.

5. Invert the subject and all or part of the verb to form questions.

   The subject and verb change places to form questions. The following examples show this.

Question Forms

Statements	Questions
He is absent today.	*Is he* absent today?
Mara can help us.	*Can Mara* help us?
They are working here.	*Are they* working here?
It has made this noise before.	*Has it* made this sound before?

It's All in the Timing

Here's the rule: Pick a tense and stick with it. Avoid shifting tenses in the middle of a sentence or paragraph. This confuses readers and makes them battier than they are already. Study this example:

Wrong: I *was walking* to lunch when a huge dog *jumps up* and *attacks* me.

Right: I *was walking* to lunch when a huge dog *jumped up* and *attacked* me.

The following recipe for chocolate cake (1040 version) contains many errors in tense. Rewrite the paragraph to correct the tenses. Don't make the cake.

Chocolate Cake 1040

Line 1: Butter, a minimum of half a pound, but not to be exceeding 1 cup (see Line 4).

Line 2: Sugar, light brown or white, unless you or your spouse will be having a financial account in a foreign account in 2004, in which case do not substitute molasses or honey.

Line 3: Eggs, six or a half-dozen, whichever was greater.

Line 4: Semisweet chocolate. Nonfarm families may chosen the optional method of using cocoa powder. Multiplying by .9897 per ounce of substitution. For additional details on cocoa conversion, seen Form 234a.

Line 5: Salt, ⅓ teaspoon (optional). If you was a head of household with dependents and be born during a leap year, you must add salt. Now cream the mixture.

Line 6: Incorporate eggs, one at a time, into creamed mixture. If the eggs will be from a farm of which you are the sole owner, you may have been eligible for a Fowl Credit. See Form 9871m, "For the Birds."

Note: If you weighed 20 percent more (or higher) than your ideal weight (see chart on page 56), ignore this recipe and complete Schedule F, "Fresh Fruit Desserts."

Answers

Line 1: to exceed

Line 2: had

Line 3: is

Line 4: choose, multiply, add, see

Line 5: were, were

Line 6: are from a farm, be eligible

Note: weigh

Person, Number, and Mood

Verbs do it all. Well, not *everything*. They can't do the laundry, sing on key, or draw a straight line. I lied; so sue me. Actually, verbs *can* do a whole lot. Here are three things they show:

◆ They show person.

◆ They show number.

◆ They show mood.

In detail, maestro …

Person

Remember that, concerning verbs, *person* is who or what experiences the action. Here's the crowd:

◆ First person: the person speaking (I, me)

◆ Second person: the one being spoken to (you)

◆ Third person: the person being spoken about (he, she, they)

Number

Number shows how many subjects act or receive the action.

◆ One subject: singular verb

◆ More than one subject: plural verb

Mood

Mood shows the attitude expressed toward the action. It refers to the ability of verbs to convey a writer's attitude toward a subject. English has three moods: *indicative*, *imperative*, and *subjunctive*.

You Could Look It Up

Mood shows the attitude expressed toward the action. It refers to the ability of verbs to convey a writer's attitude toward a subject.

1. *Indicative:* used for statements and questions of fact. For example:

   ◆ Ohio rejected this license plate motto: Don't judge us by Cleveland.

   ◆ Kentucky did not like this motto: Tobacco is a vegetable.

2. *Imperative:* expresses commands and direct requests. The imperative mood always uses the simple form of the verb. The subject may be omitted. In these cases, the subject is always assumed to be *you* or one of the indefinite pronouns, such as *anybody* and *somebody*. Here are some examples:

   ♦ Please shut your mouth.

   ♦ Watch out! (The subject, *you*, is omitted.)

3. *Subjunctive:* expresses conditions, recommendations, speculations, and indirect requests. For instance:

   ♦ Whether it be now or later, we must eventually face the truth.

   ♦ If she were going to stay, I would crack open a fresh box of Twinkies.

The subjunctive is used in certain standard expressions. Here are a few of the most popular ones:

   ♦ Please let me be …

   ♦ If only I were there …

   ♦ If I were you …

   ♦ Come what may …

   ♦ Be that as it may …

   ♦ Far be it from me …

And there's more … These verbs are real party animals.

Active and Passive Voice: A Mistake Has Been Made

Verbs also show *voice*, the form of the verb that shows whether the subject performs the action or received the action. English verbs have two voices: *active* and *passive*.

1. A verb is *active* when the subject performs the action, as in these examples:

   ♦ We made a mistake. (*We* are taking blame.)

   ♦ I played a blank tape on full volume. The mime next door complained. (*I* am doing the action in the first sentence; the *mime* is doing the action in the second sentence.)

2. A verb is *passive* when its action is performed upon the subject, as in these examples:

- ◆ A mistake has been made. (No one is taking credit for the mistake.)

- ◆ A tape was played by me at full volume. A complaint was made by the mime next door. (The action is performed upon the subjects.)

In general, use the active voice instead of the passive voice. The active voice was voted "Most Popular Voice" because it is less wordy. As a result, sentences written in the active voice tend to be crisp and direct. This is a very good thing in writing and speech—unless you work for the Department of Motor Vehicles, the Post Office, or any other branch of the government. In these cases, it's better to make all speech and writing as wordy and difficult to understand as possible.

There are two instances where the passive voice is preferable over the active voice. Here they are:

1. Use the passive voice when you don't want to assign blame to or emphasize who or what performed the action. This is especially important in business if you ever want to get promoted. Here's an example:

- ◆ The office doors were left unlocked over the weekend.

2. Use the passive voice when you don't know who did the action. For instance:

- ◆ The phone call was made at 6 A.M.

Not So Fast ...

Can't have you being passive, now can I? To keep you active, rewrite the following passive sentences to make them active. (*Hint:* Not all the sentences are passive …)

1. In the men's room at work, a sign had been placed by the boss directly above the sink.

2. It had a single word on it—"Think!"

3. The next day, the men's room was entered by Harvey.

4. The sign was looked at by him.

5. Right below the sign, immediately above the soap dispenser, another sign had been written by someone.

6. The sign read—"Thoap!"

Answers

1. In the men's room at work, the boss had placed a sign directly above the sink.

2. It had a single word on it—"Think!"

3. The next day, Harvey went to the men's room.

4. He looked at the sign.

5. Right below the sign, immediately above the soap dispenser, someone had written another sign.

6. The sign read—"Thoap!"

 **Take My Word for It** _____

The most suspect grammatical construct from the past wigglings of pinned-down public figures is "mistakes were made." Some wag dubbed this last-ditch concession of error the "exonerative passive."

The Least You Need to Know

◆ A verb's tense shows when the action takes place. Use the right order of tenses to show the correct order of events.

◆ Verbs show person, who or what experiences the action.

◆ A verb's number shows how many subjects act or receive the action. A verb can be singular (one subject) or plural (more than one subject).

◆ Verbs show mood, the attitude expressed toward the action.

◆ Voice shows whether the subject acts (active voice) or is acted upon (passive voice). In general, use the active voice instead of the passive voice.

Chapter 6

Woe Is I: Pronouns and Case

In This Chapter

- ◆ Learn pronoun case
- ◆ Untangle who and whom

When Quentin Crisp told the people of Northern Ireland that he was an atheist, a woman in the audience stood up and said, "Yes, but is it the God of the Catholics or the God of the Protestants *in whom* you don't believe?" Hey, we don't need religious strife—we have *who* and *whom* to contend with. And that's not to mention all the rest of the pronouns. You've got to figure out how to use them correctly, too.

In this chapter, you learn about the grammatical role a pronoun plays in a sentence. Armed with this knowledge, you can use *all* pronouns—even the dreaded *who* and *whom*—correctly, with skill and confidence.

Why Can't a Pronoun Be More Like a Noun?

Can't live with 'em, can't live without 'em. Between you and I, pronouns drive myself crazy, and I bet they do yourself, too. A quick look at the disastrous last sentence and a brief survey of English explains why pronouns are more maddening than a hormone-crazed teenager.

Old English, like Latin, depended on word endings to express grammatical relationships. These endings are called *inflections*. For example, consider the Old English word for *stone*, "stan." Study this chart.

Case	Word
Nominative and accusative singular	*stan*
Genitive singular	*stane*
Dative singular	*stane*
Nominative and accusative plural	*stanas*
Genitive plural	*stana*
Dative plural	*stanum*

Fortunately, contemporary English is greatly simplified from Old English. (Would I lie/lay to you?) Today, nouns remain the same in the nominative and accusative *cases* and inflect only for the possessive and the plural. Here's how our version of "stan" (*stone*) looks today: *stone, stone's, stones,* and *stones'.* Huh? Sounds like Greek? Not to worry. It will all be clear by the end of this chapter.

Pronouns, on the other hand, have retained more of their inflections, and more's the pity. The first-person pronoun, for example, can exist as *I, me, mine, my, myself, we, us, our, ours, ourself,* and *ourselves*—11 written forms! Because pronouns assume so many more forms than nouns, these otherwise adorable words can be a real pain in the butt.

Head Case: The Three Cases

Case is the form of a noun or pronoun that shows how it is used in a sentence. English has three cases: *nominative*, *objective*, and *possessive*. The following chart shows the three cases.

Nominative (Pronoun as Subject)	Objective (Pronoun Showing Object)	Possessive (Pronoun as Ownership)
I	me	my, mine
you	you	your, yours
he	him	his
she	her	her, hers
it	it	its
we	us	our, ours
they	them	their, theirs
who	whom	whose
whoever	whomever	whoever

The Rules

Let's review the rules for using pronouns so these little words won't make you crazy as you write and speak.

1. Use the nominative case to show the subject of a verb. Remember that the subject is the noun or pronoun that performs the action of the verb.

   > *Question:* I know of no other person in the company who is as smarmy as (*he, him.*)

   > *Answer: He* is the subject of the understood verb *is.* Therefore, the sentence would read: "I know of no other person in the company who is as smarmy as *he.*"

   > *Question:* (*Who, Whom*) do you believe is the best writer?

   > *Answer: Who* is the subject of the verb *is.* Therefore, the sentence would read, "*Who* do you believe is the best writer?"

You Could Look It Up

In the **nominative case,** the pronoun is used as a subject; in the **objective case,** the pronoun is used as an object; in the **possessive case,** the pronoun is used to show ownership.

Quoth the Maven

To help you choose the correct pronoun, mentally supply the missing verb. For example, "Herbert knows the material better than (he/him)." Supplying the missing verb "does" tells you that the correct pronoun is he.

Of course, anything associated with grammar can't be *that* easy. Here's the exception to the rule you just learned: *A pronoun used as the subject of an infinitive is in the objective case.* For example: "Billy Bob expects Frankie Bob and (I, me) to make squirrel stew." The correct pronoun here is *me*, because it is the subject of the infinitive *to make*.

2. A pronoun used as a predicate nominative is in the nominative case. A *predicate nominative* is a noun or pronoun after some form of *to be* (is, was, might have been, and so on).

You Could Look It Up

A predicate nominative is a noun or pronoun after some form of to be (is, was, might have been, and so on).

Quoth the Maven

Ignore interrupting expressions such as *do you believe, do you think, do you suppose* (and so on). They do not affect pronoun case.

Predicate nominatives are the bad boys in the back row of homeroom because they equal trouble. Here's what I mean:

The verb *to be*, in all of its forms, is the same as an equal sign. Whatever comes before it (almost always a pronoun in the nominative case) must also follow it.

It	was	we.
nominative	=	nominative

Question: It was (*they, them*) who first suggested getting the 90-pound puppy.

Answer: It was *they* who first suggested getting the 90-pound puppy.

3. Use the objective case to show that the noun or pronoun receives the action.

   Question: (*Who, Whom*) can you send to help us?

   Answer: Whom is the direct object of the verb *can send*. Therefore, the sentence should read: "*Whom* can you send to help us?"

Quoth the Maven

With a who/whom question, change the word order: "You can send whom to help us?" This shows that *you* is the subject and *whom* is the object of *can send*.

Question: The taxidermist promised to notify Herman and (*I, me*) of his plans for the moose.

Answer: Me (together with Herman) is the object of the infinitive *to notify*. Therefore, the sentence should read: "The taxidermist promised to notify Herman and *me* of his plans for the moose."

Question: It is always a pleasure for (*we, us*) employees to have a day-long meeting.

Answer: Here, *us* is the object of the preposition *for.* Therefore, the sentence should read: "It is always a pleasure for *us* employees to have a day-long meeting."

Question: The Internet gave my sister and (*I, me*) some interesting ideas.

Answer: Me (together with *my sister*) is the *indirect object* of the verb *gave.* Therefore, the sentence should read: "The Internet gave my sister and *me* some interesting ideas."

Danger, Will Robinson

Direct objects appear in more guises than a quick-change artist. A pronoun can be the direct object of a verb, the object of an infinitive, the object of a preposition, or an indirect object.

You Could Look It Up

An **indirect object** tells to or for whom something is done.

  Quoth the Maven _____

When you have a pronoun combined with a noun (such as *we employees, us employees*), try the sentence without the noun. You can usually "hear" which pronoun sounds right.

It is always a pleasure for we to have a day-long meeting.

It is always a pleasure for us to have a day-long meeting.

Doesn't that second choice just sound better? (Don't answer that!)

You can tell a word is an indirect object if you can insert *to* or *for* before it without changing the meaning. For example: The Internet gave (to) my sister and (to) me some interesting ideas.

4. A pronoun used in apposition with a noun is in the same case as the noun. An *appositive* is a noun or pronoun placed after another noun or pronoun to identify, explain, or rename it.

Question: Two bond traders, Alice and (*she, her*) were given bonuses large enough to buy their own banana republic.

Answer: The pronoun must be in the nominative case (*she*) because it is in apposition with the noun *bond traders,* which is in the nominative case. Therefore, the sentence should read: "Two bond traders, Alice and *she,* were given bonuses large enough to buy their own banana republic."

5. Use the possessive case to show ownership.

> *Question:* The manager refused to acknowledge that the memo was (*her's, hers*).

> *Answer: Hers* is the correct spelling of the possessive case, which is needed her to express ownership (belonging to her). Therefore, the sentence should read: "The manager refused to acknowledge that the memo was *hers.*"

Be careful not to confuse possessive pronouns and contractions. To help you remember the difference, carve this chart into your desk at work.

Possessive Pronouns	**Contractions**
its (belonging to *it*)	*it's* (it is)
your (belonging to *you*)	*you're* (you are)
their (belonging to *them*)	*they're* (they are)
whose (belonging to *whom*)	*who's* (who is)

> *Question:* The boss disapproves of (*me, my*) leaving the office early.

> *Answer:* The meaning of the sentence requires the possessive case: *my.* Therefore, the sentence should read: "The boss disapproves of *my* leaving the office early."

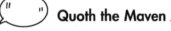

Quoth the Maven

Ask yourself what the sentence is saying. Here, ask yourself what does the boss disapprove of? Certainly not me! Rather, he disapproves of *my leaving the office early.*

You Could Look It Up

Linking verbs indicate a state of being (*am, is, are,* and so on), relate to the senses (*look, smell, taste,* and so on), or indicate a condition (*appear, seem, become,* and so on).

6. Use the subjective case after *linking verbs.* Remember that a linking verb connects a subject to a word that renames it. This one actually makes perfect sense: Because a pronoun coming after a linking verb renames the subject, the pronoun must be in the subjective (nominative) case.

> *Question:* The flasher of the month was (*I, me*).

> *Answer:* Use *I,* because the pronoun renames the subject, the flasher of the month.

> *Question:* The one who will benefit from this honor is they and (*me, I*).

> *Answer:* Again, go with I, because the pronoun renames the subject.

7. Use *-self* forms correctly with reflexive and intensive situations.

As you learned in Chapters 5 and 6, *reflexive pronouns* reflect back to the subject or object. Check out these examples:

- The superhero embarrassed *himself.*

- Unfortunately, he had to rely on *himself* to save the day.

Don't use reflexive pronouns in place of subjects and objects:

> *Question:* The diner and (*myself, I*) had a chat.

> *Answer:* The diner and *I* had a chat. (Use the pronoun subject *I*, not the reflexive form.)

Remember that *intensive pronouns* provide emphasis; they make another word stronger. They're like the vitamin B_{12} of pronouns. Here's an example:

- The superhero felt that his reputation *itself* was at stake.

> **Strictly Speaking**
>
> Pronouns that express ownership never get an apostrophe. Watch for these possessive pronouns: *yours, his, hers, its, ours, theirs.*

> **Danger, Will Robinson**
>
> Avoid nonstandard reflexive and intensive pronouns as you would no-class kinfolk, the ones with federal box office addresses. Here are the words to shun: *theirself, theirselves, themself, themselfes,* and any other variations the human brain can hatch. Nonstandard expressions such as these are not accepted as correct written or spoken English in business settings.

Sorry, Wrong Number

What should you say on the phone: "It is me?" or "It is I?" Maybe you should just hang up the phone and send a fax.

The rivalry between "It is me" and "It is I" is right up there with Pepsi and Coke battling for market shares.

The "It is I" camp argues that forms of the verb *to be,* such as *is* and *was,* should be followed by pronouns in the nominative case. Therefore, here the pronoun would be *I.*

On the other hand, the "It is me" camp counters with the argument that noun case in English has disappeared. Further, they contend that the pronoun case has become so weakened that the force of word order now overrides the force of case.

Strictly Speaking

Should the childhood mecca be "Toys R We"? Should Sammy Davis Jr. have sung "I Gotta Be I"? (According to grammar frumps, yes!)

The placement of the pronoun in the object part of the sentence "It is me" and "It is us" has become increasingly acceptable as standard usage even in boardrooms. But if you're speaking with a language purist who is likely to become offended by today's more relaxed standards of speech and writing, use the time-honored "It is I" instead of "It is me."

Seventh-Inning Stretch

Stand up, wave your arms around wildly, then sit a spell and take this brief quiz. Score yourself, party hearty to celebrate your victory, then look back over the sentences that gave you a headache.

1. Gary and (I/me) have decided to become Pat Boone imitators.

2. The victims are (they/them).

3. (We/Us) actuaries are going to run away and join the World Wrestling Federation.

4. The cause is unquestionably (she/her).

5. Madness takes (it's/its) toll. Please have exact change.

6. Her kisses left something to be desired—the rest of (her/she).

7. Human beings, (who/whom) are almost unique in having the ability to learn from the experience of others, are also remarkable for their apparent disinclination to do so.

8. Sam and (me/I) heard that the Internal Revenue Service wants to improve its image; they will no longer answer the phone with "Next victim," and a new mascot, Timmy the Tax Collector, will replace the Grim Reaper.

9. The only difference between (I/me) and a madman is that I am not mad.

10. Those (whom/who) make peaceful revolution impossible will make violent revolution inevitable.

Answers

1. I	5. its	8. I
2. they	6. her	9. me
3. We	7. who	10. who
4. she		

Who Versus *Whom* (or Should I Just Shoot Myself Now?)

Contemporary writer and humorist Calvin Trillin once claimed, "*Whom* is a word invented to make everyone sound like a butler. Nobody who is not a butler has ever said it out loud without feeling just a little bit weird."

Trillin isn't alone in his frustration with who/whom. More than half a century ago, a professor named Arthur H. Weston voiced his feelings over who/whom this way:

> It's hard to devise an appropriate doom
> For those who say *who* when they ought to say *whom*.
> But it's even more hard to decide what to do
> With those who say *whom* when they ought to say *who*.

No one will argue that *who* and *whom* are the most troublesome pronouns in English. Anyone who has ever grappled with *who* and *whom* might use stronger language than that, but this is a family-type book. Here are some reasons why *who/whom* are so perplexing:

- *Who* is used as an interrogative pronoun in questions.

- *Who* is also used as a relative pronoun in complex sentences (see Chapter 13 for more on this).

- *Whoever* is usually found only in complex sentences (again, see Chapter 13).

- Who knows how to use these suckers?

We can't do much about the national debt, frown lines, or those Mets, but we *can* straighten out *who/whom* use. Even though I discussed *who/whom* earlier in this chapter, these little words cause such distress that they deserve their own subsection. Let's start by looking back at our pronoun-use chart for a moment.

Quoth the Maven

Remember, the main purpose of language is communication. Good grammar is "that language which creates the least discomfort among the largest number of participants." (Robert Pooley)

Strictly Speaking

Don't get scared by who/whom in questions. At the beginning of a question, use *who* if the question is about the subject or *whom* if the question is about the object.

	Nominative (Subject Case)	Objective (Object Case)	Possessive (Ownership)
Singular	who	whom	whose
	whoever	whomever	whosoever
Plural	who	whom	whose
	whoever	whomever	whosoever

This Hurts You More Than It Hurts Me

Only three itty-bitty rules to know for who/whom:

1. Use *who* or *whoever* when the pronoun is the subject of a verb.

   ◆ *Who* said, "I am not a vegetarian because I love animals; I am a vegetarian because I hate plants?"

   ◆ *Who* won the prize for employee of the month—the guy from accounting who was just fired?

   ◆ I wonder *who* thought up that bright idea.

2. Use *who* or *whoever* when the pronoun is the predicate nominative.

   ◆ The winner was *who?*

   ◆ No one knew *who* the loser was.

3. Use *whom* or *whomever* when the pronoun is the direct object of a verb or the object of a preposition.

   ◆ *Whom* did he marry this time?

   ◆ Of course, he can marry *whomever* he wants (as long as it's not me).

   ◆ With *whom* were you dancing at his wedding?

I Dare You

The proof is in the pudding, or something like that. Take your best shot with these questions. Circle who or whom in each sentence.

1. From (who/whom) did you buy that wooden nickel?

2. (Who/Whom) is your parole officer?

3. The boss selected (who/whom)?

4. (Who/Whom) in the office knows how to operate the phone system?

5. With (who/whom) have you agreed to carpool?

6. No one knew (whom/who) the bean counter was.

Answers

1. whom (object of the preposition *from*)

2. who (subject of the verb)

3. whom (direct object of the verb)

4. who (subject of the verb)

5. whom (object of the preposition *with*)

6. who (predicate nominative)

Seventh-Inning Stretch

Let's have some fun, bunny. Choose the correct pronoun to complete each sentence.

On a transatlantic flight, a plane passed through a severe storm. "Oh Lord," a passenger screamed. (1 Who/Whom) can You send to help us?" a passenger yelled. Things went from bad to worse when one wing was struck by lightning. Two women in particular, Hermione and (2 she/her) lost it. The second woman jumped up screaming, "I'm too young to die!" she wailed. "Well, if I'm going to die, I want my last minutes on Earth to be memorable! Is there anyone on this plane (3 who/whom) can make me feel like a real woman?"

For a moment there was total silence. Everyone had forgotten (4 they/their) own peril as (5 they/them) stared, riveted, at the desperate woman in the front of the plane. "(6 You're/Your) in a bad way, lady," one man muttered.

Then a man stood up in the rear of the plane. "(7 Me/I) can make you feel like a woman," he said. Tall, dark, and handsome, he started walking slowly up the aisle, unbuttoning (8 his/him) shirt one button at a time. "(9 We/Us) are in for a treat," a few passengers whispered. The woman was breathing heavily in anticipation as the stranger approached. (10 Him/He) removed his shirt. Muscles rippled across his chest as he reached (11 she/her) and extended the arm holding his shirt to the trembling woman. (12 Him/He) whispered:

"Iron this."

Answers

1. Whom
2. She
3. Who
4. their
5. they
6. You're
7. I
8. his
9. We
10. He
11. her
12. He

The Least You Need to Know

◆ Case is the form of a noun or pronoun that shows how it is used in a sentence.

◆ English has three cases: nominative, objective, and possessive.

◆ Use the nominative case to show the subject of a verb; use the objective case to show the object of a verb; use the possessive case to show ownership.

Multiple-Vehicle Wrecks: Pronoun Reference

In This Chapter

◆ Define pronoun reference

◆ Find out how unclear pronoun reference occurs

◆ Learn how to keep pronoun reference clear

So what the dickens is *pronoun reference?* A new low-fat, high-fiber break-fast cereal? A nonslip floor wax? A painless hair removal system? Stop! You're all correct—pronoun reference is all this and more!

Just kidding, folks. Actually, the term "pronoun reference" refers to the fact that the meaning of a pronoun comes from its *antecedent,* the noun or pronoun to which it refers. In this chapter, you first learn all about clear pronoun reference—and ways in which unclear pronoun reference can occur in your writing and speech. Then I teach you how to fix all your unclear pronouns. By the end of this section, your pronouns will be as clear as a politician's agenda (if not clearer).

How's That Again?

Read the following passage and summarize what it says. *Warning:* No fair scratching your head as you try to figure the passage out.

> 1945: Churchill, Roosevelt, and Stalin take another meeting, this time at Yalta, an old czarist summer resort on the Black Sea. Victory over Germany and Japan is in sight, but how are the Allied Powers to deal with it? Likewise, with them? Roosevelt miscalculates, choosing to trust him too much, listen to him—a past master of keep-your-distance diplomacy—too little. Russia not only gets most of Eastern Europe, but also walks away with parts of it, too.

What's wrong with this passage? The pronoun references are unclear. As a result, you don't know who's doing what to whom and where … much less *why*. Here are the places where you were likely confused:

> 1945: Churchill, Roosevelt, and Stalin take another meeting, this time at Yalta, an old czarist summer resort on the Black Sea. Victory over Germany and Japan is in sight, but how are the Allied Powers to deal with *it? (What's the "it"—victory or the defeated?)* Likewise, with *them? (Who's the "them"—the victors, the defeated, or each other?)* Roosevelt miscalculates, choosing to trust *him (Whom?—Churchill or Stalin?)* too much, listen to *him (Whom?—Churchill or Stalin?)*—a past master of keep-your-distance diplomacy—too little. Russia not only gets most of Eastern Europe, but also walks away with parts of *it (What's the it?—another country?)*, too.

Carelessly placed pronouns can create unintentionally funny sentences as well as confusing ones. Consider the difference between what the writer *thinks* he or she said and what is *really* being said in each of these sentences:

- Antinuclear protesters released live cockroaches inside the White House Tuesday, and *these* were arrested when they left and blocked the security gate. (That's what happens when you nuke a roach.)

- My mother wants to have the dog's tail operated on again, and if it doesn't heal this time, *she'll* have to be put away. (Are we sending Mom or the pooch to the happy hunting ground?)

- About a year ago, a wart appeared on my right foot, and I want *it* removed. (Is that before or after you take "it" out of your mouth?)

- Guilt, bitterness, and cruelty can be emotionally destructive to you and your family. You must get rid of *them*. (Who? Guilt and bitterness, or the family?)

There are three ways to prevent this kind of confusion with pronouns:

♦ Make a pronoun clearly refer to a single antecedent.

♦ Place pronouns close to their antecedents.

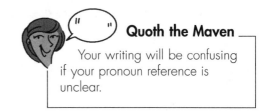

Quoth the Maven

Your writing will be confusing if your pronoun reference is unclear.

♦ Make a pronoun refer to a definite antecedent.

Let's look at each guideline in detail.

It Just Proves There's Someone for Everyone

To prevent unclear pronoun reference, make a pronoun clearly refer to a single antecedent. A common writing problem occurs when the same pronoun refers to more than one antecedent. For example, in the last example in the preceding section, "them" can refer to *guilt, bitterness, and cruelty* as well as *your family.*

Can you hear the logic in that sentence circling the drain? Can you hear your reader screaming for mercy? Thank goodness, help is on the way. Clarify the sentence by replacing the unclear pronouns with nouns. That way, all the remaining pronouns will clearly refer to a single antecedent. Here are two ways you could rewrite this sentence:

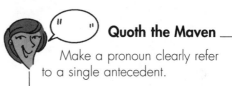

Quoth the Maven

Make a pronoun clearly refer to a single antecedent.

♦ Guilt, bitterness, and cruelty can be emotionally destructive to you and your family. You must get rid of *these emotions.*

Or:

♦ Guilt, bitterness, and cruelty can be emotionally destructive to you and your family. You must get rid of *these destructive feelings.*

Strictly Speaking
Remember that a pronoun replaces a noun. To make sure that your writing is clear, always use the noun *before* you use the pronoun.

The Numbers Game

There's no rule that limits the number of pronouns you can use—as long as each pronoun clearly refers to a single antecedent. For example:

◆ The office manager bought cheap, knock-off *keyboards* for *his* steno pool, but *they* fell apart quickly because *they* were not suited to heavy use.

The pronoun "his" refers to the office manager; the pronoun "they" refers to the "keyboards."

Tag, You're It

How about giving it a shot? Rewrite each of the following sentences to make the pronouns clearly refer to their antecedents. Not to panic: Remember that there's more than one way to skin a cat, make decent coffee, and fix unclear pronoun references.

1. When Fred and Louie return home, he will call.

   _____

2. When Dennis spoke to Keith that morning, he did not realize that he might win the lottery by the end of the day.

   _____

3. When the rain started, we pulled out an umbrella and opened it. It dampened our spirits for a while, but we decided to stick it out.

   _____

4. If you asked Doug to describe Nick, he would say that he was sly, boring, and cheap—and then he would chuckle.

   _____

5. Ask Nick about Doug, and he would say that, while he couldn't be a gossip, he was sure that he had links with the Young Republicans.

   _____

6. He didn't consider him a safe driver, either.

   _____

Answers

Possible responses:

1. When Fred and Louie return home, Fred will call. (Or Louie could be doing the calling just as easily.)

2. When Dennis spoke to Keith that morning, Dennis did not realize that he might win the lottery by the end of the day. (Again, Keith might just as easily have been the winner.)

3. When the rain started, we pulled out an umbrella and opened it. The rain dampened our spirits for a while, but we decided to stick it out.

4. If you asked Doug to describe Nick, Doug would say that Nick was sly, boring, and cheap and—then Doug would chuckle.

5. Ask Nick about Doug, and Nick would say that, while he couldn't be a gossip, he was sure that Doug had links with the Young Republicans.

6. Nick didn't consider Doug a safe driver, either.

Location, Location, Location: Placement of Pronouns

Another way to avoid confusing pronoun reference is to go for the squeeze play: Place pronouns as close to their antecedents as logically possible. If too many phrases come between a pronoun and its antecedent, the pronouns may get muddied. This can happen even if the intervening material is logically related to the rest of the sentence. Here are some examples:

Confusing: The statement that the dog catcher made and that she issued it as a formal policy inflamed the city council, who knew it would result in widespread anger.

Clear: The dog catcher made a statement and the Mayor issued a formal policy. This inflamed the City Council, which knew this policy would result in widespread anger.

Confusing: Prehistoric people used many inorganic substances difficult to find at archaeological sites, which included clay and rock.

Clear: Prehistoric people used many inorganic substances, including clay and rock, which are difficult to find at archaeological sites.

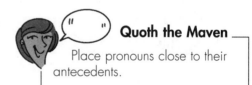

Quoth the Maven

Place pronouns close to their antecedents.

Take My Word for It

When you start a new paragraph, repeat the noun from the previous paragraph rather than using a pronoun in its place. Repeating the noun (usually a name) can help your reader more easily follow your logic.

A Match Made in Writer's Heaven

Just as there's a pot for every lid, so there's an antecedent for every pronoun. The pronoun's antecedent must be clearer than the Mississippi River, or your writing will be as murky as the Big Muddy's depths. How to achieve pronoun clarity? *Make a pronoun refer to one specific antecedent.* As simple as that.

Here are some guidelines to follow as you filter your writing to sift out pronoun errors.

Take My Word for It

Pronouns are among the most frequently used words in English. Among the top 100 words: *he, it, his, I, they, you, she, we, him.*

Quoth the Maven

When the possessive quality is added to a noun, that noun becomes an adjective and is no longer suitable to be an antecedent.

Strictly Speaking

Not in the mood to put the pronoun in the possessive case? Instead, you can revise the sentence so the noun provides the reference for the pronoun.

Possession and Pronouns

Don't use a pronoun to refer to a noun's possessive form (the form that shows ownership). You can't use a noun's possessive form as the antecedent to a pronoun, unless the pronoun is also in the possessive case. This sounds a lot trickier than it is, trust me ... and read these examples:

Confusing: The proctologist's discovery brought him fame.

(Because the pronoun *him* is not possessive, it cannot be used to refer to the possessive *proctologist's*.)

Clear: The proctologist became famous because of his discovery.

Confusing: Leroy's report was superb. Does he know that?

Clear: Leroy wrote a great report. Does he know that?

It's a Lock

Be sure the pronouns *it, this, that,* and *which* refer to only one antecedent. These four sweet little pronouns are especially prone to unclear pronoun reference. Here are some examples:

Confusing: Karate is a form of martial arts in which people who have had years and years of training can, using only their hands and feet, make some of the worst movies in the history of the world. *This* is interesting.

(*What* is interesting? Karate? Bad movies? The relationship between karate and bad movies?)

Clear: Karate is a form of martial arts in which people who have had years and years of training can, using only their hands and feet, make some of the worst movies in the history of the world. *This phenomenon* is interesting.

Confusing: If a woman has to choose between catching a fly ball and saving a baby's life, she will choose to save *that* without even considering if there are men on base. (What will she choose to save?)

Clear: If a woman has to choose between catching a fly ball and saving a baby's life, she will choose to save the baby's life without even considering if there are men on base.

Confusing: According to some sources, a rain of comets lasting hundreds of centuries hits the earth every few million years or so. Maybe *that is* how the dinosaurs perished in a mass extinction 65 million years ago.

Clear: According to some sources, a rain of comets lasting hundreds of centuries hits the earth every few million years or so. Maybe such a rain of comets killed the dinosaurs 65 million years ago.

Confusing: I told my friends that I was going to be a circus rouster which annoyed my boss.

Clear: My boss was annoyed because I told my friends that I was going to be a circus rouster.

> **Strictly Speaking**
>
> Avoid using a pronoun to refer to the title of a document in the document's first sentence. For example, if the title is "Big Bank's Role in Mutual Funds," the first sentence cannot be "It is important and we must stress it." What's the *it?*

It and They

Ever heard, "It said on television that ..." or "In the office they say ..."? Such expressions are sloppy, imprecise, and confusing. Who are these mysterious "it"s and "they"s? Eliminate this error by using the pronouns *it* and *they* carefully.

Give it a shot. Repair the following sloppy statements by straightening out the sloppy use of "it"s and "they"s.

1. It said on the radio that it's going to rain tomorrow.

   _____

2. In a book they say that animal testing is a bad idea; the animals all get nervous and give the wrong answers.

   _____

3. It said that a Freudian slip is when you say one thing but mean a mother.

   _____

4. In a company they say that a committee is a group of the unwilling, picked from the unfit, to do the unnecessary.

   _____

5. The book says that applying computer technology is simply finding the right wrench to pound in the correct screw.

   _____

Answers

1. The radio announcer said that it's going to rain tomorrow.

2. The author said that animal testing is a bad idea; the animals all get nervous and give the wrong answers. (Better yet, give the author's name.)

3. A Freudian slip is when you say one thing but mean a mother.

4. Employees say that a committee is a group of the unwilling, picked from the unfit, to do the unnecessary.

5. The author says that applying computer technology is simply finding the right wrench to pound in the correct screw. (Better yet, give the author's name.)

It Mania

It has become a fast-food word, more commonplace than burgers, fries, and a shake. Advice for life: Don't eat too much junk food, wear your galoshes when it rains, and don't overuse *it*.

The word *it* has three uses:

   ◆ **As a personal pronoun.** Chris wants to see how long he can stay in the clothes dryer, but *it* is broken.

   ◆ **As an expletive.** *It* is fun to eat raw cookie dough and feel sorry for yourself when you're home alone on Saturday night.

   ◆ **As an idiomatic expression for weather, time, or distance.** It is cloudy today. It is noon. It is quite a distance to the home.

The unclear "it" problem arises when these uses are combined in one sentence, like this one:

Confusing: Because our electric knife was overheating, it came as no surprise that it broke just as it was time to carve the bird.

Clear: It came as no surprise that the electric knife broke just as it was time to carve the bird.

Confusing: It will be a successful project if the computer doesn't overload its memory.

Clear: The project will succeed if the computer doesn't overload its memory.

Confusing: It is clear that it is not fulfilling its duties.

Clear: Clearly, the board of directors is not fulfilling its duties.

> **CAUTION**
>
> **Danger, Will Robinson**
>
> Avoid using an unnecessary pronoun to repeat the subject. Here's a no-no: "The shorter woman, who nodded at me, she knew me." The sentence should be written: "The shorter woman, who nodded at me, knew me."

Who's on First?

Another confusing issue concerns the pronouns *who*, *which*, and *that*. Here, the rule is a snap:

1. *Who* refers to people or animals (only animals with names or special talents, like Socks the First Cat or Rex the Wonder Pooch). Here's an example or three:

   ◆ The student, who was a dope, said, "Professor Zigler, I don't believe I deserve this F you've given me."

   ◆ The professor, who was a sensible man, said, "I agree, but unfortunately it is the lowest grade the university will allow me to give."

   ◆ Lassie, who was known for his intelligence and courage, was actually played by a series of collies.

2. *That* and *which* refer to things, groups, and unnamed animals. The choice between *which* and *that* depends on whether the clause introduced by the pronoun is *restrictive* or *nonrestrictive*. Use *that* or *which* for restrictive clauses and *which* with nonrestrictive clauses. Here are some examples:

> **You Could Look It Up**
>
> A **restrictive clause** is essential to a sentence; a **nonrestrictive clause** adds extra meaning, is set off by commas, and can be removed from the sentence. See Chapter 12 for a more detailed description of clauses.

Strictly Speaking

Like my thighs, the distinction between *that* and *which* is becoming less firm. Some writers still reserve *that* for restrictive clauses and *which* for nonrestrictive clauses. Others don't.

- Once, at a social gathering, Gladstone said to Disraeli, "I predict, sir, *that* you will die either by hanging or by some vile disease." (restrictive clause)

- Disraeli replied, "*That* all depends, sir, upon whether I embrace your principles or your mistress." (restrictive clause)

- Sacred cows, *which* are holy, make the best hamburger. (nonrestrictive clause)

Give it a shot. Fill in the blanks with *who*, *which*, or *that*.

1. The car _____ hit me rolled into a ditch … and so did I.

2. My car, _____ came from Rent-a-Wreck, had relatively little damage.

3. The concept _____ intrigued the Securities and Exchange Commission involved insider trading.

4. The report _____ I wrote recommended the concept.

5. The woman _____ came to visit me in jail was my former boss.

Answers

1. The car *that* hit me rolled into a ditch … and so did I.

2. My car, *which* came from Rent-a-Wreck, had relatively little damage.

3. The concept *that* intrigued the Securities and Exchange Commission involved insider trading.

4. The report *that* I wrote recommended the concept.

5. The woman *who* came to visit me in jail was my former boss.

Quoth the Maven

A clause introduced by *that* will almost inevitably be restrictive. Do not use a comma around restrictive clauses, as in this example: "The menu that the waiter handed me made my mouth water."

The Least You Need to Know

- Make a pronoun clearly refer to a single antecedent.

- Place pronouns close to their antecedents.

- Make a pronoun refer to a definite antecedent.

Chapter 8

How to Write and Speak Good: Adjectives Versus Adverbs

In This Chapter

- ◆ Explore the positive, comparative, and superlative degrees
- ◆ Learn about irregular adjectives and adverbs
- ◆ Cope with adjectives and linking verbs
- ◆ Deal with double negatives

You know it's going to be a bad day when …

- ◆ Your twin forgets your birthday.
- ◆ You open the newspaper and find your picture under a caption that reads: "WANTED: DEAD OR ALIVE."
- ◆ You have to figure out whether to use *bad* or *well* in a sentence.

That last scenario is the *real* killer.

You learned in Chapter 4 that *adjectives* and *adverbs* are describing words; the former describes a noun or pronoun; the latter, a verb, adjective, or other adverb. Here, you learn how to use these words with skill and confidence so you'll never again face the dreaded *bad/well* dilemma.

They Walk Alike, They Talk Alike: You Could Lose Your Mind

Both adjectives and adverbs are *modifiers*—words that describe other words. For example:

> *Adjective:* The *quick* fox jumped.

> *Adverb:* The fox jumped quickly.

Ah ha! you say. Adverbs end in *-ly;* adjectives don't, so that's how I can tell these suckers apart. Not so fast, kemosabe. *Some* adverbs end in *-ly,* but not all. Further, some adjectives also end in *-ly,* such as *lovely* and *friendly.* As a result, the *-ly* test doesn't cut the mustard. Instead, the key to telling the difference between adjectives and adverbs is understanding how they work:

- *Adjectives* describe a noun or pronoun.
- *Adverbs* describe a verb, adjective, or other adverb.

As you learned in Chapter 4, the only dependable way to tell whether you should use an adjective or an adverb is to see how the word functions in the sentence. If a noun or pronoun is being described, use an adjective. If a verb, adjective, or other adverb is being described, use an adverb. Here's an example to refresh your memory:

> He is a *skillful* driver.

> (The adjective *skillful* describes the noun *driver.*)

> The cabby drove *skillfully.*

> (The adverb *skillfully* describes the verb *drove.*)

Graphic Proof

Use the following table to keep adjectives and adverbs straight. That way, we'll all be reading from the same sheet music as we play together in the rest of this chapter.

In the Know: Adjective or Adverb?

Modifier	Function	Example
Adjectives	Describe nouns	The busy bee never rests. (The noun is *bee*.)
Adjectives	Describe pronouns	She felt disappointed. (The pronoun is *she*.)
Adverbs	Describe verbs	The child cried bitterly. (The verb is *cried*.)
Adverbs	Describe adverbs	The child cried very bitterly. (The adverb is *bitterly*.)
Adverbs	Describe adjectives	The child was truly annoyed. (The adjective is *annoyed*.)

I'm Ready for My Close-Up Now, Mr. DeMille

Reality check: Are you still with me? Find out by taking this little quiz. Identify the underlined word or words in each of the following sentences. Hint: The answer will be either "adjective" or "adverb." Those are better odds than you get in Vegas.

_____ 1. My <u>school</u> colors were "clear."

_____ 2. Question: How many surrealists does it take to screw in a light bulb? Answer: Two. One to hold the giraffe <u>firmly</u> and the other to fill the bathtub with <u>brightly</u> <u>colored</u> machine tools.

_____ 3. If the cops arrest a mime, do they tell her that she has the right to remain <u>silent</u>?

_____ 4. Maybe you're right. Maybe I should have been insulted when the mind reader charged me <u>half</u> price.

_____ 5. For three days after death, hair and fingernails continue to grow <u>slowly</u>, but phone calls taper off.

_____ 6. Diplomacy is the art of saying "nice doggy" until you can find a <u>big</u> rock.

_____ 7. Is it true that cannibals don't eat clowns because they taste <u>funny</u>?

_____ 8. Murphy's Oil Soap is the chemical <u>most</u> commonly used to clean elephants.

_____ 9. Giraffes have no <u>vocal</u> cords.

_____ 10. A man ordered a taco. He asked the server for "<u>minimal</u> lettuce." The server said he was sorry, but they only had iceberg.

Answers

1. Adjective
2. Adverb, adjective
3. Adverb
4. Adjective
5. Adverb

6. Adjective
7. Adverb
8. Adverb
9. Adjective
10. Adjective

Three Degrees of Separation

Often, you'll want to compare things rather than just describe them. Not to worry; English has this covered. Adjectives and adverbs have different forms to show degrees of comparison. We even have a name for each of these forms of degree: *positive, comparative*, and *superlative*. Let's meet the whole gang.

Strictly Speaking
What do these three words have in common: *childish, yellowish,* and *flowery?* They are all adjectives created from nouns. Creating adjectives from nouns: another hobby you might want to consider.

◆ *Positive degree:* the base form of the adjective or adverb. It does not show comparison.

◆ *Comparative degree:* the form an adjective or adverb takes to compare *two* things.

◆ *Superlative degree:* the form an adjective or adverb takes to compare *three* or more things.

The following table shows the three degrees of comparison with some sample adjectives and adverbs.

Comparative Levels of Adjectives and Adverbs

Part of Speech	Positive	Comparative	Superlative
Adjective	low	lower	lowest
Adjective	big	bigger	biggest
Adjective	fat	fatter	fattest
Adverb	highly	more highly	most highly
Adverb	widely	more widely	most widely
Adverb	easily	more easily	most easily

As you can see from this table, the comparative and superlative degrees of adjectives and adverbs are formed differently. Here's how:

1. All adverbs that end in *-ly* form their comparative and superlative degree with *more* and *most*.

> quickly, more quickly, most quickly
>
> slowly, more slowly, most slowly

2. Avoid using *more* or *most* when they sound awkward, as in "more soon than I expected." In general, use *-er/-est* with one- and two-syllable modifiers.

> fast, faster, fastest
>
> high, higher, highest

3. When a word has three or more syllables, use *more* and *most* to form the comparative and superlative degree.

> beloved, more beloved, most beloved
>
> detested, more detested, most detested

You Could Look It Up

The **positive degree** is the base form of the adjective or adverb. It does not show comparison. The **comparative degree** compares two things; the **superlative degree** compares three or more things.

Strictly Speaking

Less and *least* can also be used to form the comparative and superlative degrees of most adjectives and adverbs, as in *less attractive* and *least attractive*.

Less and *fewer* cannot be interchanged. *Less* refers to amounts that form a whole or can't be counted (*less money, less filling*), while *fewer* refers to items that can be counted (*fewer coins, fewer calories*).

Size *Does* Matter

Now that you know how to form comparisons with adjectives and adverbs, follow these guidelines to make these comparisons correct.

1. Use the comparative degree (*-er* or *more* form) to compare two things.

> Your memory is *better* than mine.
>
> Donald Trump is *more* successful than Donald Duck, Don Ameche, or Don Ho.

2. Use the superlative form (*-est* or *most*) to compare three or more things.

> This is the *largest* room in the house.

> This is the *most* awful meeting.

3. Never use *-er* and *more* or *-est* and *most* together. One or the other will do the trick nicely.

> *No:* This is the *more heavier* brother.

> *Yes:* This is the heavier brother.

> *No:* He is the *most heaviest* brother.

> *Yes:* He is the heaviest brother.

Good, Gooder, Goodest: Irregular Adjectives and Adverbs

Of course, life can't be that easy in the land of adjectives and adverbs. And so it isn't. A few adjectives and adverbs don't follow these rules. They sneer at them, going their own separate ways. Like errant congressmen, there's just no predicting what these adjectives and adverbs will do next.

The following table shows the most common irregular adjectives and adverbs. Tap the noggin and memorize these forms.

Inconsiderate Adjectives and Adverbs

Positive	Comparative	Superlative
good	better	best
well	better	best
bad	worse	worst
badly	worse	worst
far	farther	farthest
far	further	furthest
late	later	later or latest
little (amount)	less	least
many	more	most
much	more	most
some	more	most

Take My Word for It _____

Irregular adjective/adverb use, like much of life, is the result of accidents. In this case, it arose from the way the language formed. *Good*, for instance, has Indo-European roots; *worse* and *worst*, in contrast, originated in Old English. So here's one reason English isn't consistent, Mouseketeers.

Keep Your Balance

In most cases, the comparative and superlative degree shouldn't present any more difficulty than doing pick-up brain surgery with a screw driver or dealing with your two-year-old. Upon occasion, however, the way the sentence is phrased may make your comparison unclear. You balance your tires and your checkbook, so balance your sentences. Here's how:

♦ Compare similar items.

♦ Finish the comparison.

No: Nick's feet are bigger than Charles's. (Charles's *what?*)

Yes: Nick's feet are bigger than Charles's feet.

No: My wife's CD collection is larger than my son's.

Yes: My wife's CD collection is larger than my son's CD collection.

Other and Else

Another common error is illogical comparisons. Why bother creating new illogical situations, when the world is filled with existing ones that fit the bill so nicely?

Because the thing you're comparing is part of a group, you have to differentiate it from the group by using the word *other* or *else* before you can set it apart in a comparison. Therefore, to avoid adding to the world's existing stock of stupidity, when you compare one item in a group with the rest of the group, be sure to include the word *other* or *else*. Then, your comparison will make sense.

Dopey: The Godfather was greater than any modern American movie.

Sensible: The Godfather was greater than any <u>other</u> modern American movie.

Dopey: Francis Ford Coppola won more awards than anyone at the ceremony.

Sensible: Francis Ford Coppola won more awards than anyone <u>else</u> at the ceremony.

Tough Sledding: Using Adjectives After Linking Verbs

Remember that *linking verbs* describe a state of being or a condition. They include all forms of *to be* (such as *am, is, are, were, was*) and verbs related to the senses (*look, smell, sound, feel*). Linking verbs connect the subject of a sentence to a word that renames or describes it.

Sticky situations arise with verbs that sometimes function as linking verbs but other times function as action verbs. Life just isn't fair sometimes. As linking verbs, these verbs use adjectives as complements. As action verbs, these verbs use adverbs. For example:

> Charlie looks cheerful.
>
> (*looks* is a linking verb; *cheerful* is an adjective)
>
> Charlie looks cheerfully at the buffet table.
>
> (*looks* is an action verb; *cheerfully* is an adverb)

The Badlands

The adjective *bad* and the adverb *badly* are especially prone to such abuse. For instance:

> *No-No:* The guest felt badly.
>
> *Yes-Yes:* The guest felt bad.
>
> *No-No:* The food tasted badly.
>
> *Yes-Yes:* The food tasted bad.

Good News; Well News

Good and *well* are as dicey as *bad* and *badly*. That's because *well* functions both as an adverb and as an adjective:

1. *Good* is always an adjective.

   > You did a *good* job.
   >
   > You're a *good* egg.

2. *Well* is an adjective used to describe good health.

   > You look *well*.
   >
   > You sound *well* after your recent bout with pneumonia.

3. *Well* is an adverb when it's used for anything else.

    You cook *well*.

    They eat *well*.

Once More into the Breach, Dear Friends

Complete each sentence by adding the correct form of the adjective or adverb in parenthesis or by selecting the correct word in parenthesis.

1. KTHI-TV in Fargo, North Dakota, owns the _____ (tall) television tower in America.

2. *People Magazine* has a (high) _____ circulation than *TV Guide*, but *AARP Magazine* has the (high) _____ circulation of all.

3. January and February are the (cold) _____ months of the year; not coincidentally, they are also the (heavy) _____ months for watching television in the United States.

4. The Navahos form the (more, most) _____ populous Indian tribe in the United States and Canada.

5. ABC's "Turn-On" became the (short) _____ running series in TV history: It lasted only one day.

6. Of all the fruits sold, bananas are the (more, most) profitable item in American supermarkets.

7. Silas is a (good, well) _____ cook; he cooks (good, well) _____ .

8. This year, *Castaway* was the (bad) _____ movie of all, much (bad) _____ than *Plan Nine from Outer Space*.

9. According to the U.S. Census, (more, most) _____ Americans trace their ancestry to Germany than to any other country.

10. Rocco asked (good, well) _____ questions at the meeting and the boss answered them (good, well).

Answers

1. tallest	5. shortest	9. more
2. higher, highest	6. most	10. good, well
3. coldest, heaviest	7. good, well	
4. most	8. worst, worse	

A Note on Adjectives and Adverbs for Non-Native Speakers

When you make comparisons using adjectives and adverbs, pay attention to elements that can be counted and those that cannot. As you read earlier, remember that *less* and *fewer* cannot be interchanged. *Less* refers to amounts that form a whole or can't be counted (*less money, less filling*), while *fewer* refers to items that can be counted (*fewer coins, fewer calories*).

1. For nouns that can be counted, use *few, fewer,* or *fewest* rather than *little, less,* or *least* to count down.

    Incorrect: Carrot sticks have *less* calories than chocolate.

    Correct: Carrot sticks have *fewer* calories than chocolate.

    Because *calories* can be counted, use the adjective *fewer* rather than the adjective *less.*

2. For mass nouns (which cannot be counted) use *little, less,* or *least* rather than *few, fewer,* or *fewest* to count down.

    Incorrect: There's *fewer* water in this bucket than I expected.

    Correct: There's *less* water in this bucket than I expected.

    Because *water* is a mass noun that cannot be counted, use the adjective *less* rather than the adjective *fewer.*

3. For nouns that can be counted, use the adjective *many,* not *much.*

    Incorrect: Foi gras has *much* calories.

    Correct: Foi gras has *many* calories.

    Because *calories* can be counted, use the adjective *many* rather than the adjective *much.*

Don't Use No Double Negatives

A *double negative* is a statement that contains two negative describing words. For instance:

Double negative: The shopper did *not* have *no* money left over after the binge.

Correct: The shopper did *not* have *any* money left over after the binge.

Or:

The shopper had *no* money left over after the binge.

To avoid this grammatical faux pas, use only one negative word to express a negative idea. Here are the most frequently used negative words:

You Could Look It Up

A **double negative** is a statement that contains two negative describing words.

- ◆ no
- ◆ never
- ◆ not
- ◆ none
- ◆ nothing
- ◆ hardly
- ◆ scarcely
- ◆ barely

Quoth the Maven

Many negative words begin with *n*, just like *no: not, nothing, never, none, nothing*. Use this trick to help you remember negative words.

Double negatives are sneaky little critters. They are especially likely to cause problems with contractions. When the word *not* is used in a contraction—such as *isn't, doesn't, wouldn't, couldn't, don't*—the negative tends to slip by. As a result, writers and speakers may add another negative.

Double negative: He didn't say nothing.

Correct: He didn't say anything.

Or:

He said nothing.

Take My Word for It

From the 1400s to the 1700s, it was customary to crowd as many negative words as possible into a sentence. See, you were just born too late.

Don't Be Making No Mistakes

To make sure that you keep those double negatives straight, rewrite each of the following sentences to eliminate the double negative.

1. Sadly, I didn't have no cash.

   _____

2. Louie won't talk to nobody until his lawyer arrives.

   _____

3. Now, I can't eat nothing.

_____

4. They couldn't hardly finish their meal on time.

_____

5. Ms. Packasandra hasn't never been to HoHoKus before.

_____

Answers

Possible responses:

1. Sadly, I didn't have any cash.

   Or:

   Sadly, I had no cash.

2. Louie won't talk to anybody until his lawyer arrives.

   Or:

   Louie won't talk to anyone until his lawyer arrives.

3. Now, I can't eat anything.

4. They could hardly finish their meal on time.

5. Ms. Packasandra hasn't ever been to HoHoKus before.

   Or:

   Ms. Packasandra has never been to HoHoKus before.

The Least You Need to Know

- ◆ Use an adjective to describe a noun or pronoun; use an adverb to describe a verb, adjective, or another adverb.
- ◆ Use the comparative degree to describe two items; use the superlative degree to describe three or more things.
- ◆ Some adjectives and adverbs are irregular. Just deal with it.
- ◆ Be careful when you use an adjective after a linking verb.
- ◆ Double negatives are never not wrong.

Chapter 9

Reaching an Agreement: Matching Sentence Parts

In This Chapter

◆ Define agreement

◆ Learn how to make subjects and verbs agree

◆ Learn how to make pronouns and antecedents agree

So a man said to his dentist, "Doctor, my teeth are yellow. What should I do?"

"Wear a brown tie," the dentist suggested.

That's all that *agreement* is about: matching. In this chapter, you learn how to match subjects and verbs, pronouns and antecedents, and maybe even a few outfits. You find out how agreement works with collective nouns and indefinite pronouns, too. Agreement is a biggie, because it occurs at least once a sentence. By the end of this chapter, your subjects and verbs will go together like Romeo and Juliet, Ben and Jerry, and Bert and Ernie.

Anyone Got a Match?

Agreement means that sentence parts match. Subjects must agree with verbs and pronouns must agree with antecedents. Otherwise, your sentences will sound awkward and jarring, like yellow teeth with a red tie.

The basic rule of sentence agreement is really quite simple:

A subject must agree with its verb in number. (*Number* means amount. The number can be *singular*—one—or *plural*—more than one.) Here's how it works.

You Could Look It Up

Agreement means that sentence parts match. Subjects must agree with verbs, and pronouns must agree with antecedents. Singular subjects need singular verbs; plural subjects need plural verbs.

In grammar, **number** refers to the two forms of a word: singular (one) or plural (more than one).

Singular Subjects and Verbs

The following guidelines make it easy to match singular subjects and verbs.

1. A singular subject takes a singular verb. For example:

   ◆ *He* who hesitates <u>is</u> probably right.

   The singular subject *he* agrees with the singular verb *is*.

   ◆ *Isaac Asimov* <u>was</u> the only author to have a book in every Dewey Decimal System category.

   The singular subject *Isaac Asimov* requires the singular verb *was*.

2. Plural subjects that function as a single unit take a singular verb. For instance:

   ◆ *Spaghetti and meatballs* <u>is</u> my favorite dish.

   The singular subject *spaghetti and meatballs* agrees with the singular verb *is*.

   ◆ *Ham and eggs* <u>was</u> the breakfast of champions in the 1950s.

   The singular subject *ham and eggs* agrees with the singular verb *was*.

3. Titles are always singular. It doesn't matter how long the title is, what it names, or whether or not it sounds plural. As a result, a title always takes a singular verb. Here are two examples:

   ◆ *Moby Dick* <u>was</u> a whale of a tale.

The singular title *Moby Dick* agrees with the singular verb *was*.

♦ *The Valachi Papers* <u>is</u> a good read.

The singular title *The Valachi Papers* agrees with the singular verb *is*—even though the title appears plural, it is singular. That's because all titles are singular.

4. Singular subjects connected by *either/or, neither/nor,* and *not only/but also* require a singular verb. That's because the connecting words show that you are choosing only one item.

♦ *Either* the witness or the defendant <u>was</u> lying.

Only *one* person is lying: the witness or the defendant. Therefore, the subject is singular. And the singular subject (*the witness* or *the defendant*) matches the singular verb (*was*).

Plural Subjects and Verbs

Matching plural subjects and verbs is a snap with these simple guidelines: Here's the #1 rule:

1. A plural subject takes a plural verb.

♦ The rejected New Mexico state motto: *Lizards* <u>make</u> excellent pets.

The plural subject *lizards* matches the plural verb *make*.

♦ *Mosquitoes* <u>are</u> attracted to blue more than any other color.

The plural subject *mosquitoes* matches the plural verb *are*.

Think of the conjunction *and* as a plus sign. Whether the parts of the subject joined by *and* are singular or plural (or both), they all add up to a plural subject and so require a plural verb.

♦ *Anwar and Hosni* <u>are</u> going to the movies.

The plural subject *Anwar and Hosni* agrees with the plural verb *are*.

♦ *Teddy Roosevelt and Abraham Lincoln* <u>were</u> great presidents.

The plural subject *Teddy Roosevelt and Abraham Lincoln* agrees with the plural verb *were*.

2. If the subject is made up of two or more nouns or pronouns connected by *or, nor, not only,* or *but also,* the verb agrees with the noun closest to the pronoun.

♦ *Neither* the contract nor the *page proofs* <u>are</u> arriving in time to meet the deadline.

The plural subject *proofs* agrees with the plural verb *are*.

 ◆ Neither the page proofs nor the *contract* <u>is</u> arriving in time to meet the deadline.

The singular subject *contract* agrees with the singular verb *is*.

3. Ignore words or phrases that come between the subject and the verb. A phrase or clause that comes between a subject and its verb does not affect subject-verb agreement.

 ◆ The *purpose* of working out for several hours <u>is</u> to get fit and buff.

The singular subject *purpose* matches the singular verb *is*. Ignore the intervening prepositional phrase "of working out for several hours."

 ◆ *Downward mobility*—a quick ride down the social and economic ladders—<u>poses</u> a serious problem.

The singular subject *downward mobility* agrees with the singular verb *poses*. Ignore the intervening appositive "a quick ride down the social and economic ladders."

Seventh-Inning Stretch

Take a second to get these first few rules down pat. Circle the correct verb in each sentence. Feel free to look back at the rules you just read.

1. A typical Radio City Music Hall Rockette (is/are) between 5 feet and 5 feet 9 inches tall.

2. An apple or a pear (contains/contain) about 75 calories each.

3. The supply of stupid drivers (increase/increases) during holidays.

4. Residents of our country (spend/spends) more than $31 billion a year on fast food.

5. Bill Cosby's cartoon characters (includes/include) Fat Albert and Weird Harold.

6. In winter, camels (is/are) able to go without water for eight weeks.

7. Contrary to popular thinking, camels (does/do) not store water in their humps.

8. The average person (breathes/breathe) 7 quarts of air per minute.

9. Camels also (urinates/urinate) very little, compared to other animals of roughly the same size.

10. Every year the Washington Monument (sink/sinks) an average of 6 inches into the ground.

Answers

1. is	6. are
2. contains	7. do
3. increases	8. breathes
4. spend	9. urinate
5. include	10. sinks

Collective Nouns

Collective nouns are singular in form but plural in sense. Here are some examples of collective nouns:

assembly	committee	faculty	herd
audience	crew	family	jury
class	crowd	flock	team

For purposes of agreement, collective nouns can be singular or plural, depending on how they are used in a sentence. Collective nouns used as one unit take a singular verb; collective nouns that indicate many units take a plural verb.

1. Singular collective nouns

   Singular collective nouns include molasses (one kind of syrup) and chicken pox (one kind of disease). Other examples include measles, civics, social studies, mumps, news, cast, social studies, economics, and mathematics.

   ◆ The play's *cast* <u>is</u> rehearsing for today's show.

   The singular subject *cast* takes the singular verb *is*. The members of the cast are functioning as a single unit.

   ◆ The *jury* <u>returns</u> a unanimous verdict.

   The singular subject *jury* requires the singular verb *returns*; the members of the jury are working together as one unit.

You Could Look It Up

A **collective noun** names a group of people or things. Examples of collective nouns include *class, committee, flock, herd, team, audience, assembly, team, club,* and so on.

2. Plural collective nouns

A collective noun is treated as plural when the group it names is considered to be made up of individuals. Because members of the group can act on their own, the word is considered plural.

◆ The play's *cast* <u>are</u> rehearsing their lines.

The plural subject *cast* requires the plural verb *are* because the members of the cast are functioning as individual people doing separate things.

◆ The *jury* often <u>have</u> different reactions to the evidence they hear.

The plural subject *jury* requires the plural verb *have* because the members of the jury are being considered as individuals.

Indefinite Pronouns

Indefinite pronouns, like collective nouns, can be singular or plural, depending on how they are used in a sentence. Singular indefinite pronouns take a singular verb; plural indefinite pronouns take a plural verb. Here are some guidelines to follow:

◆ Indefinite pronouns that end in *-one* are always singular. These words include *anyone, everyone, someone,* and *one*.

You Could Look It Up

Indefinite pronouns refer to people, places, objects, or things without pointing to a specific one. See Chapter 4 for a complete description of indefinite pronouns.

◆ Indefinite pronouns that end in *-body* are always singular. These words include *anybody, somebody, nobody*.

◆ The indefinite pronouns *both, few, many, others,* and *several* are always plural.

◆ The indefinite pronouns *all, any, more, most, none,* and *some* can be singular or plural, depending on how they are used.

Flag this chart for ready reference.

Indefinite Pronouns

Singular	Plural	Singular or Plural
another	both	all
anyone	few	any
each	many	more

Singular	Plural	Singular or Plural
everyone	others	most
everybody	several	none
everything		some
much		
nobody		
nothing		
other		
someone		
anybody		
anything		
either		
little		
neither		
no one		
one		
somebody		
something		

Check out these examples:

♦ *One* of the Elvis impersonators <u>is</u> missing.

The singular subject *one* requires the singular verb *is*.

♦ *Both* of the Elvis impersonators <u>are</u> missing, thank goodness.

The plural subject *both* requires the plural verb *are*.

CAUTION

Danger, Will Robinson

The indefinite pronoun *many a* is always singular, as in "*Many a* person <u>is</u> sick and tired of eating sautéed antelope on melba toast."

Take My Word for It _____

British English follows the same rules of agreement, but there are subtle differences in usage. For example, our neighbors across the pond consider the words *company* and *government* plural rather than singular nouns.

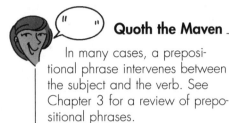

Quoth the Maven

In many cases, a prepositional phrase intervenes between the subject and the verb. See Chapter 3 for a review of prepositional phrases.

♦ *All* the sautéed rattlesnake <u>was</u> devoured.

The singular subject *all* requires the singular verb *was*.

♦ *All* the seats <u>were</u> occupied.

The plural subject *all* requires the plural verb *were*.

The Pause That Refreshes

Circle the correct verb in each sentence.

1. Economics (depends/depend) heavily on mathematics.

2. The light at the end of the tunnel (are/is) the headlight of an approaching train.

3. News of a layoff (causes/cause) many people to get worried.

4. Millions of Americans watched the high-speed chase and most (was/were) mesmerized by the event.

5. Some people believe that TV rots your brain; others, in contrast, (believes/believe) that TV can teach us important social lessons.

6. Both of those cities (were/was) on my vacation route.

7. The commuters wait at the bus stop. A few (sleep/sleeps) standing up.

8. One of our satellites (is/are) lost in space.

9. The supply of beta-endorphins in the brain (is/are) increased during exercise.

10. Too many onions in a stew often (causes/cause) an upset stomach.

Answers

1. depends   6. were

2. is   7. sleep

3. causes   8. is

4. were   9. is

5. believe   10. cause

Walk This Way

Now you know the main rules of agreement, so the rest of this business must be a piece of cake. Not so fast. Follow these three steps to check whether subjects and verbs in your sentences *really* agree:

1. Find the sentence's subject.

2. Figure out if the subject is singular or plural.

3. Select the appropriate verb form to match the form of the subject.

Here's where the problems occur:

1. Figuring out what is the subject.

2. Figuring out if the subject is singular or plural.

3. Selecting the appropriate verb form to match the form of the subject.

Let's look at each step in the process.

Hide and Seek

Some subjects can be harder to find than Judge Crater, Bigfoot, or Jimmy Hoffa. Foremost among these hard-to-find subjects is the subject that has the nerve to come after the verb. Inverted word order can make it difficult to find the true subject. But wherever the subject is, it still must agree in number with its verb, as these examples show:

◆ On the top of the hill <u>are</u> two Elvis *impersonators*.

The plural subject *impersonators* agrees with the plural verb *are*.

◆ There <u>are</u> still several *agitators* in the audience.

The plural subject *agitators* requires the plural verb *are*.

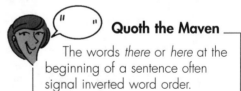

Quoth the Maven

The words *there* or *here* at the beginning of a sentence often signal inverted word order.

Strictly Speaking

Remember that a *predicate nominative* is a noun or pronoun that follows a linking verb. It renames or identifies the subject.

Another tricky agreement situation occurs with linking verbs. As with all other verbs, a linking verb always agrees with its subject. Problems crop up when the subject and the linking verb (the predicate nominative) are not the same number. For example, the subject can be plural but the linking verb can be singular. Here's an example:

Danger, Will Robinson

Most measurements are singular—even though they look plural. For example: "*Half a dollar* <u>is</u> more than enough" (not "*are* more than enough") or "*Ten inches* <u>is</u> more than enough" (not "*are* more than enough").

♦ Speeding *trucks* <u>are</u> one reason for the abundance of fresh produce in our grocery stores.

The plural subject *trucks* agrees with the plural verb *are*. Don't be tricked by the singular predicate nominative *reason*.

♦ One *reason* for the abundance of fresh produce in our grocery stores <u>is</u> speeding trucks.

Here, the singular subject *reason* agrees with the singular verb *is*. Here, the plural noun *trucks* is the predicate nominative.

Playing the Numbers

As you learned in the beginning of this chapter, in grammar, *number* refers to the two forms of a word: *singular* (one) or *plural* (more than one). With nouns, number is relatively easy to figure out. That's because most nouns form the plural by adding *-s* or *-es*. Here are some examples.

Singular Nouns	Plural Nouns
stock report	stock reports
interest rate	interest rates
debt	debts

You learned the few exceptions in Chapter 3 (*deer, oxen, men, women, feet,* and so on). There are more tricky plural words listed in Chapter 18.

Matchmaker, Matchmaker, Make Me a Match

Forget everything you learned about nouns when you start dealing with verbs. That's because we add *-s* or *-es* to the third-person singular form of most verbs. This is opposite to the way we form singular nouns. For example:

	Singular Verbs	Plural Verbs
1st and 2nd Person	3rd Person	1st, 2nd, 3rd Person
I start	he starts	we start
I do	he does	we do

The helping verbs are even nastier because they aren't regular. The following chart shows the forms of *to be*.

Singular *Be* Verbs	Plural *Be* Verbs
(I) am	(we) are
(he, she, it) is	(they) are
(I, he, she, it) was	(we, they) were
(he, she, it) has been	(they) have been

As a result, subject-verb agreement is most tricky in the present tense.

Mix and Match

You know the drill, so sharpen your pencils and get crackin' with the following 10 items. In each case, choose the verb that agrees with the subject.

1. There (is/are) a method to this madness.

2. The hostess trilled: "The Bengels (are/is) here!"

3. One reason for her success (was/were) her sunny personality.

4. The many mistakes made by the tour guide in giving directions (was/were) the reason we fired her.

5. (Does/Do) fig trees grow in this region?

6. (Is/Are) some the pie still in the refrigerator?

7. (Here's/Here are) more freeloaders for the open-house.

8. There (was/were) two good reasons for his decision.

9. Another example of Juan's fine leadership (is/are) the excellent roads.

10. Here (is/are) two gifts I'd especially like to receive: a wheelbarrow filled with cash and a diamond as big as the Ritz.

Answers

1. is	5. Do	9. is
2. are	6. Is	10. are
3. was	7. Here are	
4. were	8. were	

Agree to Disagree

Like subjects and verbs, pronouns and antecedents (the words to which they refer) must agree. A pronoun replaces a noun. To make sure that your writing is clear, always use the noun before using the pronoun. Follow these rules to make sure that your pronouns and antecedents get on well:

1. A pronoun agrees (or matches) its antecedent in *number, person,* and *gender.*

   ◆ *Number* is amount: singular or plural.

   ◆ *Person* refers to the first person, second person, or third person (the person speaking, the person spoken to, or the person spoken about).

   ◆ *Gender* refers to masculine, feminine, or neuter references. *He* and *him* are masculine in gender, *she* and *her* are feminine, and *it* and *its* are neuter.

Danger, Will Robinson

Not all verbs add *-s* or *-es* when they become plural. For example words that end in *-y,* such as *fry,* change the *-y* to *-i* before adding *-es.* So I *fry* becomes he *fries.* Be on the lookout for the different ways that verbs form their plurals.

For example:

Louise gave <u>her</u> paycheck straight to the orthodontist.

Both the antecedent *Louise* and the pronoun *her* are singular, in the third person, and feminine in gender.

   ◆ Errors often occur when there are incorrect shifts in person and gender. For example:

   Error: Herman will screen the video teleconference, which *you* need to stay timely.

   Correct: Herman will screen the video teleconference, which *he* needs to stay timely.

2. Use a singular personal pronoun with a singular indefinite pronoun.

   ◆ If *anyone* questions the amount, refer *him* or *her* to payroll.

The singular pronouns *him* or *her* refer to the singular pronoun *anyone.*

   ◆ *Each* police officer and firefighter has to watch *his or her* figure.

Use a singular pronoun if the nouns are preceded by *each* or *every.*

3. Use a plural pronoun when the antecedents are joined by *and*. This is true even if the antecedents are singular.

   ♦ Toody *and* Muldoon maintain *their* svelte figures by eating bean sprouts rather than donuts.

   Because the two singular antecedents *Toody* and *Muldoon* are joined by *and*, use the plural pronoun *their*.

4. Antecedents joined by *or*, *nor*, or correlative conjunctions such as *either/or*, *neither/nor* agree with the antecedent closer to the pronoun.

   ♦ Neither Toody nor the other *officers eat* <u>their</u> jelly donuts on duty.

   Use the plural pronoun *their* to agree with the plural antecedent *officers*.

   ♦ Neither the other officers *nor Toody eats* <u>his</u> donuts on duty.

   Use the singular pronoun *his* to agree with the singular antecedent *Toody*. Notice that the verb *eats* must also match.

5. Be sure that the pronoun refers directly to the noun. Confusion occurs when the pronoun can refer to more than one antecedent. If you end up with this mishmash, rewrite the sentence.

   Confusing: Raul saw an ad in last week's newspaper, but he can't seem to find *it*.

   What is it that Raul can't find: the ad or the newspaper?

   Correct: Raul can't find the ad he saw in last week's newspaper.

6. Avoid sexist language. Traditionally, the pronouns *he* and *his* were used to refer to both men and women. Not any more. The current correct usage is *he* and *she* or *she* and *he*.

   Error: An *employee* should turn in *his* timesheet every Friday.

   Correct: An *employee* should turn in *his or her* timesheet every Friday.

   If the pronoun pairing necessary to avoid sexist language is cumbersome (and you better believe that it will be), try these options:

   ♦ Recast the sentence into third person, *they* or *them*. For example: Employees should turn in their timesheets every Friday.

◆ Recast the sentence into the second person, *you*. For example: You should turn in your timesheet every Friday.

◆ Try to eliminate the pronoun altogether. For example: Turn in timesheets every Friday.

There's more on sexist language in Chapter 25.

7. Always use common sense. When the sentence doesn't seem to fit the rules and you can't figure out how to shoehorn it in, don't improvise, revise! Rewrite the sentence to avoid the problem entirely.

Confusing: The executive director along with the marketing vice president (was, were?) at odds over the new scheduling system.

Better: The executive director and the marketing vice president were at odds over the new scheduling system.

Nose to the Grindstone

This one should be a snap, given all the facts you've learned about agreement. In each case, choose the verb that agrees with the subject.

Given by the people of France to the people of the United States as a symbol of a shared love of freedom and everlasting friendship, the Statue of Liberty (1 are/is) the largest freestanding sculpture ever created. It (2 weigh/weighs) 450,000 pounds and (3 rise/rises) 151 feet above its pedestal. More than 100 feet around, Ms. Liberty (4 boast/boasts) eyes 2½ feet wide, a mouth 3 feet wide, and a nose 4½ feet long. Her upraised right arm (5 extend/extends) 42 feet; her hand (6 are/is) nearly 17 feet long. Her fingers (7 are/is) close to 10 feet long. The statue (8 has/have) an interior framework of iron that (9 keep/keeps) it from toppling over. Tourists and guides enjoy (10 their/his/her) time with this stirring and symbolic landmark.

Answers

1.	is	3.	rises	5.	extends	7.	are	9.	keeps
2.	weighs	4.	boasts	6.	is	8.	has	10.	their

The Least You Need to Know

◆ Agreement means that sentence parts match.

◆ Subjects must agree with verbs and pronouns must agree with antecedents.

◆ Avoid sexist language.

Chapter 10

Dazed and Confused: Common Usage Dilemmas

In This Chapter

- ◆ Dangle participles
- ◆ Misplace modifiers
- ◆ Mix metaphors
- ◆ Split infinitives
- ◆ Resolve other perplexing grammar issues

Once upon a time, when writing styles were more formal than they are now, some people were very careful never to end a sentence with a preposition. Even then, however, there were stylistic mavericks who let their prepositions fall with abandon. Winston Churchill was one of these people. His secretary, appalled, always revised the drafts of Churchill's speeches to avoid ending sentences with a preposition. Exasperated, Churchill finally sent this message to his secretary: "This is the sort of English up with which I will not put."

In this chapter, you learn whether you should or shouldn't follow Churchill's lead and conclude a sentence with a preposition. You also find information on other sticky grammar issues, including dangling participles and misplaced modifiers. In addition, I bring you up to speed on the latest grammar "rulings" concerning splitting infinitives, using *hopefully*, and choosing between *like* or *as*.

Dangling Modifiers: Counterintelligence

What's wrong with the following sentence?

Coming up the hall, the clock struck 10.

As written, the sentence states that the clock was coming up the hall. An ambulatory clock is possible, but neither highly likely nor terribly desirable. This misunderstanding about the clock's power of locomotion occurs because the phrase "coming up the hall" has nothing to modify or describe. A phrase left twisting in the wind like this is called a *dangling modifier*.

You Could Look It Up

A **dangling modifier** is a word or phrase that describes something that has been left out of the sentence. A **clause** is a group of words with its own subject and verb. See Chapter 12 for a detailed description of clauses.

Remember that a *modifier* is a word or phrase that gives more information about the subject, verb, or object in a *clause*. A modifier is said to "dangle" when the word it modifies is not actually in the sentence. "Coming up the hall" is a dangling modifier because it cannot be attached to any word in the sentence.

Dangling modifiers confuse your readers and obscure your meaning. These errors don't jump out at you like a spelling blooper or a shark attack; rather, they sneak up on you like April 15 or middle age. And they can be just as deadly.

Help Is on the Way

Because the basic problem with a dangling modifier is a lack of connection, you must provide a noun or pronoun to which the dangling construction can be attached. There are two basic ways to do this:

1. Rewrite the modifier as a subordinate clause.

   Dangling: Confirming our conversation, the shipment will be ordered on Monday.

(According to this sentence, the shipment—not the speaker—confirmed the conversation.)

Correct: As I stated in the memo, the shipment will be ordered on Monday.

2. Rewrite the main clause so the subject or object can be modified by the now-dangling phrase.

Dangling: Confirming our conversation, the shipment will be ordered on Monday.

Correct: Confirming our conversation, I have arranged for the shipment to be ordered on Monday.

Man the Battle Stations

Time to play, so let's have some fun. Correct each of these dangling constructions by rewriting the modifier as a subordinate clause or rewriting the main clause so the subject or object can be modified by the now-dangling phrase.

1. Do not sit in the chair without being fully assembled.

   _____

2. Locked in a vault for 50 years, the owner of the coins decided to sell them.

   _____

3. Important facts might be revealed when leaving.

   _____

4. Making startling new discoveries in science, the Renaissance was a time of rebirth.

   _____

5. While driving down the highway, a bad collision was seen.

   _____

6. While eating dinner, a fly slipped into her soup.

   _____

7. The tomb of the Egyptian pharaoh commanded attention coming into the exhibit.

   _____

8. Sailing up the river, the Statue of Liberty was seen.

   _____

Answers

Possible responses:

1. You should not sit in the chair unless it is fully assembled.

2. The owner decided to sell his coins, which had been locked in a vault for 50 years.

3. You might reveal important facts when you leave.

4. The Renaissance was a time of rebirth when people made startling new discoveries in science.

5. While we were driving down the highway, we saw a bad collision.

6. While Cecile was eating dinner, a fly slipped into her soup.

7. The tomb of the Egyptian pharaoh commanded our attention as we came into the exhibit.

8. As we sailed up the river, we saw the Statue of Liberty.

Misplaced Modifiers: Lost and Found

You can lose your car keys, your temper, and even your head—but please, don't misplace your modifiers. It's as tacky as a pork chop at a bar mitzvah.

A *misplaced modifier* is just that: a phrase, clause, or word placed too far from the noun or pronoun it describes. As a result, the sentence fails to convey your exact meaning. But misplaced modifiers usually carry a double wallop: They often create confusion or imply something unintentionally funny. This is not a good thing when you want to make a competent impression with your writing. Here's an example of a misplaced modifier:

They bought a puppy for my sister *they call Fido.*

You Could Look It Up

A misplaced modifier is a phrase, clause, or word placed too far from the word or words it modifies.

As this sentence is written, it means that the sister, not the puppy, is named Fido. That's because the modifier "they call Fido" is in the wrong place in the sentence. To *correct* a misplaced modifier, move the modifier as close as possible to the word or phrase it is describing. Here's how the sentence should read:

They bought a puppy *they call Fido* for my sister.

It Says What?

Study this chart to see how a misplaced modifier can distort a writer's meaning. Then see how I moved the modifier so the sentence makes sense.

Sentence #1: The patient was referred to a psychologist with several emotional problems.

What the writer thinks it says: The patient has emotional problems.

What the sentence really says: The psychologist has emotional problems.

Correction: The patient with several emotional problems was referred to a psychologist.

Sentence #2: Sam found a letter in the mailbox that doesn't belong to her.

What the writer thinks it says: Sam found a letter that doesn't belong to her.

What the sentence really says: The mailbox doesn't belong to Sam.

Correction: Sam found a letter that doesn't belong to her in the mailbox.

Sentence #3: Two cars were reported stolen by the Farmingdale police yesterday.

What the writer thinks it says: The Farmingdale police reported two stolen cars.

What the sentence really says: The police stole the two cars.

Correction: Yesterday, the Farmingdale police reported that two cars were stolen.

Sentence #4: Please take time to look over the brochure that is enclosed with your family.

What the writer thinks it says: Look over the brochure with your family.

What the sentence really says: The brochure is enclosed with your family.

Correction: Please take time to look over the enclosed brochure with your family.

Sentence #5: Luis had driven over with his wife, Chris, from their home in a Chevy for the basketball game.

What the writer thinks it says: Luis and Chris drove in their Chevy to the game.

What the sentence really says: Luis and Chris live in a Chevy.

Correction: Luis had driven over in a Chevy with his wife, Chris, from their home for the basketball game.

> **Quoth the Maven**
>
> To avoid these embarrassing sentence errors, place a modifier as close as possible to the word it modifies or describes. And do something about that tie, please.

Quiz Show

It's show time! To see if you've got the hang of writing sentences with correctly placed modifiers, rewrite each of the following bollixed-up sentences.

1. The writer read from his new book wearing glasses.

   _____

2. You are welcome to visit the cemetery where famous Russian composers, artists, and writers are buried daily except Thursday.

   _____

3. As we begin, I must ask you to banish all information about the case from your mind, if you have any.

   _____

4. A superb and inexpensive restaurant; fine food expertly served by waitresses in appetizing forms.

   _____

5. Many of the trustees congratulated him for his speech at the end of the meeting and promised their support.

   _____

6. For sale: An antique desk suitable for a lady with thick legs and large drawers.

   _____

7. For sale: Several very old dresses from grandmother in beautiful condition.

   _____

8. Wanted: Man to take care of cow that does not smoke or drink.

   _____

9. For sale: Mixing bowl set designed to please a cook with a round bottom for efficient beating.

   _____

10. We almost made a profit of $10.

   _____

Answers

Did you get these nice clear revisions?

1. Wearing glasses, the writer read from his new book. (Or: The writer, wearing glasses, read from his new book.)

2. Daily, except Thursday, you are welcome to visit the cemetery where famous Russian and Soviet composers, artists, and writers are buried.

3. As we begin, I must ask you to banish any information about the case from your mind.

4. A superb and inexpensive restaurant; fine food in appetizing forms is served expertly by waitresses.

5. At the end of the meeting, many of the trustees congratulated him for his speech and promised their support.

6. For sale: An antique desk with thick legs and large drawers suitable for a lady.

7. For sale: Several very old dresses in beautiful condition from grandmother.

8. Wanted: Man that does not smoke or drink to take care of cow.

9. For sale: Mixing bowl set with round bottoms for efficient beating designed to please a cook.

10. We made a profit of almost ten dollars.

Mixed Metaphors: A Dollar Late and a Day Short

Figures of speech use words for more than their literal meaning. There are a number of different kinds of figures of speech, including *hyperbole, understatement, personification, analogies, similes,* and *metaphors.* Today, class, our focus is on the metaphor.

A *metaphor* is a figure of speech that compares two unlike things. The more familiar thing helps describe the less familiar one. Unlike their first cousins, similes, metaphors do not use the words *like* or *as* to make the comparison. "My heart is a singing bird" is an example of a metaphor.

You Could Look It Up

A **metaphor** is a figure of speech that compares two unlike things. The more familiar thing helps describe the less familiar one.

As you can tell from the preceding definition, metaphors are innocent creatures that never did harm to anyone. That being the case, how can we explain this abomination:

> "I don't want to say they lost sight of the big picture, but they have marched to a different drummer," Victor Fortuno, the general counsel of Legal Services Corporation, said of the individual lawyer's challenges. "Whether it will upset the apple cart, I don't know."

You Could Look It Up

A **mixed metaphor** is a combination of images that do not work well together.

Strictly Speaking

Mixed metaphors occur when writers string together clichés. Don't string together clichés and you won't get mixed metaphors. More on this in Chapter 24.

Like the title of this section, this passage is a *mixed metaphor*, a combination of images that do not work well together. It's like that old joke: "Keep your eye on the ball, your ear to the ground, your nose to the grindstone, your shoulder to the wheel: Now try to work in that position." Here are some other mixed metaphors:

♦ Milking the temp workers for all they were worth, the manager barked orders at them.

   (The first image suggests cows; the second, dogs. That's one animal too many.)

♦ Unless we tighten our belts, we'll sink like a stone.

   (Belts and a stone? I think not.)

♦ The fullback was a bulldozer, running up and down the field like an angel.

   (Only Ali could float like a butterfly and sting like a bee; this football bulldozer can't move like an angel.)

♦ The movie weaves a story that herds characters and readers into the same camp.

   (Let's not mix spiderwebs and cattle roundups.)

Like all comparisons, metaphors must contain elements that can be compared logically— even if not explicitly. The comparison must be consistent as well. Like my sister zooming to the sweaters at a department store super sale, stay focused on a single element when you create metaphors. Otherwise, you risk creating the dreaded mixed metaphor. Don't mix your drinks or your metaphors and you'll go far.

Here are two more suggestions to help you keep your metaphors straight:

♦ Use only a single metaphor per paragraph.

♦ Make sure the verb matches the action the subject of the metaphor might take. (For example: a bulldozer driving up the field.)

Split Infinitives: To Boldly Go Where Everyone Else Goes

As their motto proves, the crew of the USS *Enterprise* split their infinitives along with their atoms. The motto should read: "To Go Boldly …" They're not alone. You were introduced to *split infinitives* in Chapter 2. Remember that a split infinitive occurs when an adverb or adverbial phrase is placed between *to* and the verb.

People who feel strongly about their split infinitives *really* feel strongly about their split infinitives. A famous *New Yorker* cartoon shows Captain Bligh sailing away from the *Bounty* in a rowboat and shouting, "So Mr. Christian! You propose *to unceremoniously cast me* adrift?" The caption beneath the cartoon reads: "The crew can no longer tolerate Captain Bligh's ruthless splitting of infinitives."

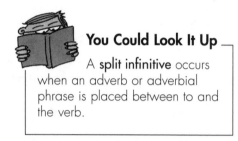

You Could Look It Up

A **split infinitive** occurs when an adverb or adverbial phrase is placed between to and the verb.

Even though some people get their pencils bent out of shape over this matter, there is no authoritative grammar and usage text that expressly forbids it. Famous writers have been splitting their infinitives with abandon for centuries. George Bernard Shaw, the brilliant Irish playwright, once sent this letter to the *Times* of London: "There is a busybody on your staff who devotes a lot of time to chasing split infinitives: I call for the immediate dismissal of this pedant. It is of no consequence whether he decides to go quickly or to quickly go or quickly to go. The important thing is that he should go at once."

What should you do? While I do not advocate that you go around town splitting infinitives with abandon, there's no point in mangling a sentence just to avoid a split infinitive. Good writers occasionally split infinitives to create emphasis, achieve a natural word order, and avoid confusion. If splitting an infinitive makes it possible for you to achieve the precise shade of meaning you desire, you have my blessing to split away.

Take My Word for It

The twentieth-century writer and cartoonist James Thurber had this to say to the editor who rearranged his infinitive: "When I split an infinitive, it is going to damn well stay split!"

The Good, the Bad, the Ugly

Fortunately for me as the grammar maven, English grammar and usage has many confusing issues. And fortunately for you, only a handful of them come up with any frequency. Let's take a look at these hot issues in the grammar news: how to use *hopefully*, whether to use *like* or *as*, and ending sentences with a preposition.

Hopefully

Since the eighteenth century, *hopefully* has been used to mean "in a hopeful manner," as in Robert Louis Stevenson's saying, "To travel hopefully is better than to arrive." But during the past generation, the adverb has come to mean "it is to be hoped." Today, it is also applied to situations as well as to people, as in "His fried eel will hopefully turn out well." In addition, rather than modifying (describing) a specific verb, as in Stevenson's example, *hopefully* is now used to modify an entire sentence.

Except for a few lone holdouts (and if you're one of them, please don't contact me), most people and dictionaries now accept *hopefully* as meaning "it is to be hoped." So don't sweat this one.

Like/As

The *like/as* debate is another potential minefield. About 50 years ago, a cigarette company started a new ad campaign whose centerpiece was this jingle: "Winston tastes good like a cigarette should." When English teachers, grammarians, and various pundits reacted with horror at the misuse of "like" for "as," the company came back with this rejoinder: "What do you want—good grammar or good taste?" Thanks to all the free publicity Winston received, the marketing executives no doubt laughed all the way to the bank.

Here's the generally accepted *like/as* rule:

1. Use *like* or *as* as a preposition to join a noun, as in these examples:

   ♦ Cleans *like* a blizzard

   ♦ Blind *as* a bat

2. Do not use *like* as a conjunction to introduce an adverb clause, as in this example:

   Incorrect: Nobody can do it *like* McDonald's can.

   Correct: Nobody can do it *as* McDonald's can.

Here's my advice: Write sentences that sound good like a sentence should. Don't create awkward-sounding sentences to conform to this (or any) rule.

Ending with a Preposition

Some prissy scholars have tried (with a great deal of success) to foist a bunch of phony Latin grammar rules into English grammar, especially concerning the issue of not ending a sentence with a preposition. To be *correct*, you could say, "This off me ticks." To sound smooth, you could end with the preposition and say, "This ticks me off."

My advice? Try to avoid ending a sentence with a preposition when possible, but never twist a sentence like something out of the *Kama Sutra* to avoid it. Make your sentences sound natural and graceful. If a few sentences end with a preposition, you'll be just fine. I give you permission to write "This ticks me off" rather than "This off me ticks."

The Least You Need to Know

- A dangling modifier is a word or phrase that describes something that has been left out of the sentence. Fix it by adding what's missing.

- A misplaced modifier is placed too far from the word or words it modifies. Put all modifiers as close as possible to the words they describe.

- Don't string together clichés and you won't get writing that's as dull as dishwater.

- The jury's out on split infinitives and ending a sentence with a preposition.

Part 3

Usage and Abusage

Then there's the story about the man who appeared at the Pearly Gates. St. Peter asked him, "Who goes there?"

"It is I," answered the man.

"Oh, no," moaned St. Peter. "Not another English teacher."

In this part, you get the lowdown on the building blocks of writing: phrases, clauses, and sentences. If you ever meet St. Peter, you'll know what to say—and how to say it!

Chapter 11

Phrases: Prime-Time Players

In This Chapter

◆ Probe prepositional phrases

◆ Admire appositives

◆ Visit verbals

In this chapter, we start the construction of your writing with the phrase, one of the key building blocks of the sentence. There are several different kinds of phrases, including prepositional phrases (with the subcategories adjectival phrases and adverbial phrases), appositives, and verbals. In this chapter, you learn them all. First, I teach you the individual parts of each different phrase and then ease you into the phrases themselves.

Phrases of the Moon

A *phrase* is a group of words that functions in a sentence as a single part of speech. A phrase does not have a subject or a verb. As you write, you use phrases to …

◆ Add detail by describing.

◆ Make your meaning more precise.

◆ Fold in additional information.

The following table shows the different types of phrases.

Different Types of Phrases

Type of Phrase	Definition	Example
Prepositional	Begins with a preposition and ends with a noun or pronoun	… *by* the *lake*
Adjectival	Prepositional phrase that functions as an adjective	She has a fish *with red gills*.
Adverbial	Prepositional phrase that functions as an adverb.	We cheered *with loud voices*.
Appositive	Noun or pronoun that renames another noun or pronoun.	Lou, *a Viking*, enjoys plunder.
Verbal	A verb form used as another part of speech.	(See the following three entries.)
Participle	Verbal phrase that functions as an adjective.	*Eating slowly*, the child was finally quiet.
Gerund	Verbal phrase that functions as a noun	*Partying hearty* requires great endurance.
Infinitive	Verbal phrase that functions as a noun, adjective, or adverb.	*To sleep late on Sunday* is a real treat.

Prepositional Phrases: The Big Daddy of Phrases

A *prepositional phrase* is a group of words that begins with a preposition and ends with a noun or a pronoun. This noun or pronoun is called the "object of the preposition."

Here are some sample prepositional phrases:

◆ By the ocean

◆ Near the window

- Over the cabinet
- With us
- In your ear
- Under your hat

You can connect two or more prepositional phrases with a coordinating conjunction. The seven coordinating conjunctions are *for, and, nor, but, or, yet,* and *so.* For example:

- The resort is *beside the mountain* <u>and</u> *by the lake.*

  The coordinating conjunction is *and.*

- You can usually find Macho Marvin *in the steam room, on the exercise bike,* <u>or</u> *under the barbells.*

  The coordinating conjunction is *or.*

You Could Look It Up

A **prepositional phrase** is a group of words that begins with a preposition and ends with a noun or a pronoun.

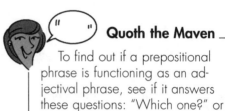

Quoth the Maven

To find out if a prepositional phrase is functioning as an adjectival phrase, see if it answers these questions: "Which one?" or "What kind?"

Offspring 1: Adjectival Phrases

When a prepositional phrase serves as an adjective, it's called an *adjectival phrase.* (That was a no-brainer, eh? Who says you don't get a break in this English biz?)

An adjectival phrase, as with an adjective, describes a noun or a pronoun. Here are some examples:

- The <u>manager</u> *with the pink slips* terrorized the employees.

  The adjectival phrase "with the pink slips" describes the noun "manager."

- The <u>price</u> *of the promotion* was much too steep.

  The adjectival phrase "of the promotion" describes the noun "price."

- <u>Something</u> *in the corner of the desk* was moving.

  The adjectival phrase "in the corner" describes the noun "something"; the adjectival phrase "of the desk" describes the noun "corner."

You Could Look It Up

An **adverbial phrase** is a prepositional phrase that modifies a verb, an adjective, or an adverb.

Offspring 2: Adverbial Phrases

Like Meryl Streep or Kevin Kline, the prepositional phrase is a versatile creature, able to slip into different roles. Depending on how it is used in a sentence, a prepositional phrase can function as an *adverbial phrase* by modifying a verb, an adjective, or an adverb. For example:

◆ She <u>lost</u> her head *at the retro love-in.*

The adverbial phrase "at the retro love-in" describes the verb "lost."

◆ The salesperson <u>skimmed</u> *over the product's real cost.*

The adverbial phrase "over the product's real cost" modifies the verb "skimmed."

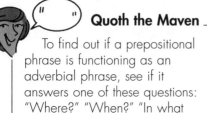

Quoth the Maven

To find out if a prepositional phrase is functioning as an adverbial phrase, see if it answers one of these questions: "Where?" "When?" "In what manner?" "To what extent?"

◆ The boss was <u>thrilled</u> *at their attitude.*

The adverbial phrase "at their attitude" modifies the adjective "thrilled."

◆ The rock climbers arrived <u>late</u> *at night.*

The adverbial phrase "at night" modifies the adverb "late."

Appositives: Something More for Your Money

An *appositive* is a noun or a pronoun that renames another noun or pronoun. Appositives are placed directly after the noun or pronoun they identify. For example:

◆ Bob's car, *a wreck*, died a grisly death by the side of the interstate.

The appositive "a wreck" renames the noun, "car."

◆ Spot, *a cat*, should understand my moods.

The appositive "a cat" renames the noun, "Spot."

◆ She, *my sister*, is always late.

The appositive "my sister" renames the pronoun "she."

You Could Look It Up

An **appositive** is a noun or pronoun that renames another noun or pronoun.

Some appositives are essential to the meaning of the sentence; others are not. Be sure to use commas carefully to establish meaning with essential and nonessential appositives. Otherwise your sentences will not make sense, as these examples show:

Confusing: Do you know my friend Bill?

Is Bill the friend or is the speaker talking to Bill?

Clear: Do you know my friend, Bill?

Appositive Phrases

Appositive phrases are nouns or pronouns with modifiers. Appositive phrases provide additional information and description to the sentence. As with solitary appositives, appositive phrases are placed near the noun or pronoun they describe. For example:

- Columbia University, the second-largest landowner in New York City (*after the Catholic Church*), is part of the Ivy League.

You Could Look It Up

Appositive phrases are nouns or pronouns with modifiers. In grammar lingo, nonessential appositives are called "nonrestrictive."

- David Prowse, *the guy in the Darth Vader suit in the* Star Wars *movies,* did not find out that his lines were going to be dubbed over by James Earl Jones until he saw the screening of the movie.

Appositives are great stylistic devices because they allow you to eliminate unnecessary words and put more information in one sentence. They can also help you ...

- Create more graceful sentences.

- Eliminate repetition.

- Create a beat or rhythm in your writing.

- Make your writing more interesting.

Here's an example:

Two sentences: Phineas T. Barnum was a great American showman. Barnum was near death in 1891 when a New York newspaper asked if he'd like to have his obituary published while he could still read it.

One sentence: Phineas T. Barnum, a great American showman, was near death in 1891 when a New York newspaper asked if he'd like to have his obituary published while he could still read it.

More on this and other stylistic devices in Part 5.

The Moment of Truth

As with appositives, appositive phrases come in two varieties: essential and nonessential. Don't set off essential appositives with commas, but be sure to set off nonessential appositives with commas.

Danger, Will Robinson

Don't set off essential appositives with commas.

Essential appositive: The famous British mystery writer Agatha Christie disappeared in 1924 and was missing for 10 days.

Nonessential appositive: Agatha Christie, *the famous British mystery writer,* disappeared in 1924 and was missing for 10 days.

One of the most common writing errors concerns misuse of commas with appositives and appositive phrases. Writers sometimes set off essential appositives with commas, but neglect those poor nonessential ones. You would never do that, would you? To make sure you're not guilty of that comma abuse, let's take a minute to practice, shall we? Add commas as needed to each of the following sentences.

1. Isadora Duncan a great American dancer of the early twentieth century has become almost as famous for her death as her dancing.

2. John Styth Pemberton an Atlanta pharmacist created the original Coca-Cola in 1886.

3. Richard Nixon is the only American president who was forced to resign his office.

4. King Louis XIV of France a ballet dancer from the time he was a teenager established the Royal Ballet Company.

5. Robert Benchley the American humorist and critic was a member of the Algonquin table of noted wits.

6. Nellie Melba a famous Australian soprano of the late nineteenth and early twentieth century gave her name to a snack food called "melba toast."

7. The centaur a mythological creature is said to feast on raw flesh and prodigious amounts of liquor.

8. Alexander the Great died of a fever.

9. Ferrets a domesticated variety of polecats were first tamed in 1500 B.C.E. by the Egyptians.

10. Some people consider the number 13 unlucky.

Answers

1. Isadora Duncan, a great American dancer of the early twentieth century, has become almost as famous for her death as her dancing.

2. John Styth Pemberton, an Atlanta pharmacist, created the original Coca-Cola in 1886.

3. No punctuation change needed.

4. King Louis XIV of France, a ballet dancer from the time he was a teenager, established the Royal Ballet Company.

5. Robert Benchley, the American humorist and critic, was a member of the Algonquin table of noted wits.

6. Nellie Melba, a famous Australian soprano of the late nineteenth and early twentieth century, gave her name to a snack food called "melba toast."

7. The centaur, a mythological creature, is said to feast on raw flesh and prodigious amounts of liquor.

8. No punctuation change needed.

9. Ferrets, a domesticated variety of polecats, were first tamed in 1500 B.C.E. by the Egyptians.

10. No punctuation change needed.

Take My Word for It

Appositives, as with other parts of a sentence, can be compound. To create a compound appositive, connect the appositives with a correlative conjunction: *and, but, or, for, so, nor,* and *yet.*

Verbal Phrases: Talk Soup

A *verbal* is a verb form used as another part of speech. Like Gaul, verbals come in three varieties: *participles, gerunds,* and *infinitives.* Each type has a different function in a sentence:

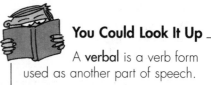

You Could Look It Up

A **verbal** is a verb form used as another part of speech.

- *Participles* function as adjectives.

- *Gerunds* function as nouns.

- *Infinitives* function as nouns, adjectives, or adverbs.

Although a verbal doesn't function as a verb in a sentence, it does retain two qualities of a verb:

- ◆ A verbal can be described by adverbs and adverbial phrases.

- ◆ A verbal can add modifiers to become a *verbal phrase.*

Let's get to know the three verbals a little better.

Part and Participle

A *participle* is a form of a verb that functions as an adjective. There are two kinds of participles: *present participles* and *past participles.*

You Could Look It Up

A **participle** is a form of a verb that functions as an adjective.

- ◆ Present participles end in *-ing* (*jumping, burning, speaking*).

- ◆ Past participles usually end in *-ed, -t,* or *-en* (*jumped, burnt, spoken*).

In the mood to add some participle action to your sentences? Here's how you do it:

- ◆ The *howling* <u>children</u> disturbed the neighbors.

  The present participle "howling" describes the noun "children."

- ◆ Fred Flintstone gave Barney Rubble a *crumbling* <u>rock</u>.

  The present participle "crumbling" describes the noun "rock."

- ◆ The *frozen* <u>candy bar</u> broke her $900 bridgework.

  The past participle "frozen" describes the noun "candy bar."

- ◆ *Annoyed,* <u>Rita</u> ate dinner by herself in the bathroom.

  The past participle "annoyed" describes the noun "Rita."

Don't confuse participles and verbs. Participles aren't preceded by a helping verb, as these examples show:

- ◆ The *sputtering* car jerked down the road. (participle)

- ◆ The car was *sputtering* down the road. (verb)

Participle phrases contain a participle modified by an adverb or an adverbial phrase. The whole kit and caboodle acts as an adjective, as these examples show:

- *Swimming slowly*, I didn't notice the shark on my tail.

    The participle phrase "swimming slowly" describes the pronoun "I."

- *Annoyed by its heavy breathing*, I told it to get lost.

The participle phrase "Annoyed by its heavy breathing" describes the pronoun "I." However, the participle phrase can also be placed after the word it describes. In that case, it is usually set off by commas, as in this example:

- "My sister, *burning the toast*, looked distracted."

Like appositives, participles and participle phrases are an indispensable part of the writer's bag of tricks because they allow you to create concise and interesting sentences. Use them to combine information from two or more sentences into one sentence. Notice how much more punch the following sentence has when it is combined by using a participle:

Two sentences: Noel Coward made a slight but pointed adjustment to an old cliché. He once described another writer as every other inch a gentleman.

One sentence: Making a slight but pointed adjustment to the old cliché, Noel Coward once described another writer as every other inch a gentleman.

Gerund Phrases

A *gerund* is a form of a verb used as a noun. Remember the following two guidelines when you hunt for gerunds:

- Gerunds always end in *-ing*.
- Gerunds always act as nouns.

Gerunds can function as subjects, direct objects, indirect objects, objects of a preposition, predicate nominatives, and appositives. Here are some examples of gerunds:

- Leroy expanded his skills by *studying*.

    The gerund "studying" is the object of the preposition "by."

- At the age of 10, Irving started *running*.

    The gerund "running" is a direct object.

You Could Look It Up

A **gerund** is a verb form used as a noun.

◆ My mother's sole occupation, *kvetching*, makes her tedious company.

The gerund "kvetching" (an especially virulent form of complaining) is an appositive in this sentence.

Like a participle, a gerund can be part of a phrase. In that case, the whole package is called a *gerund phrase*. (Got you with that one, didn't I?) Here are some gerund phrases busy at work in their sentences:

◆ *The quiet, steady rowing* soothed him.

The gerund phrase is "the quiet, steady rowing."

◆ My evening routine features *jogging slowly around the block*.

The gerund phrase is "jogging slowly around the block."

◆ Thousands of "Dead Heads" show their dedication to their departed leader by *following what's left of The Grateful Dead around the country*.

The gerund phrase is "following what's left of The Grateful Dead around the country."

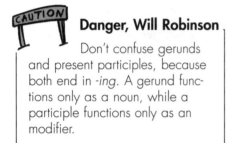

Danger, Will Robinson

Don't confuse gerunds and present participles, because both end in *-ing*. A gerund functions only as a noun, while a participle functions only as an modifier.

Infinitive Phrases: The Final Frontier

Last but not least we have the *infinitive*, a form of the verb that comes after the word *to* and acts as a noun, adjective, or adverb. Versatile little babies, infinitives can fill as many roles as gerunds, with the addition of adjectives and adverbs. Here are some examples:

◆ *To succeed* takes courage, foresight, and luck.

The infinitive is "to succeed," and it functions as the subject.

◆ Alone in her cubicle, all she wanted was *to survive*.

The infinitive is "to survive," and it functions as the direct object.

◆ Afraid *to move*, she froze in terror.

The infinitive is "to move," and it modifies the adverb "afraid."

You Could Look It Up

The **infinitive** is a verb form that comes after the word *to* and functions as a noun, adjective, or adverb.

An infinitive can be used as a phrase. An infinitive phrase, as with the other verbal phrases, contains modifiers that together act as a single part of speech. Following are some examples:

♦ His goal, *to break into Fort Knox*, was never achieved.

   The infinitive phrase is "to break into Fort Knox" and modifies the noun "goal."

♦ The pilgrim's hope was *to reach the shrine before sundown*.

   The infinitive phrase "to reach the shrine before sundown" describes "hope."

Danger, Will Robinson

Don't confuse infinitives with prepositional phrases that begin with *to*. Remember that a prepositional phrase always ends with a noun or a pronoun; an infinitive always ends with a verb.

The Least You Need to Know

♦ A phrase is a group of words, without a subject or a verb, that functions as a single part of speech. Phrases cannot stand alone as independent units.

♦ Prepositional phrases begin with a preposition and end with a noun or pronoun; they can function as adjectival phrases and adverbial phrases.

♦ Appositives rename another noun or pronoun; appositive phrases include modifiers.

♦ Verbals are verb forms used as another part of speech. Participles function as adjectives, gerunds function as nouns, infinitives function as nouns, adjectives, or adverbs.

♦ This sounds a lot more difficult than it is.

Chapter 12

Clauses: Kickin' It Up a Notch

In This Chapter

- Learn about independent clauses
- Discover dependent clauses
- Explore adverb, adjective, and noun clauses

You know all about Santa Claus, retractable claws, and Claus von Bulow. There's no reason to be claustrophobic: Clauses are your friends.

In this chapter, you meet *independent* and *dependent* clauses, including adverb, adjective, and noun clauses. Along the way, you learn how to use clauses to add description, show relationships between ideas, and eliminate unnecessary words.

Clauses: Phrases on Steroids

You've got words, you've got phrases, and now you've got *clauses*. The progression suggests that clauses are pumped up phrases. Indeed, clauses tend to be beefier than phrases. That's because a clause is a group of words with its own subject and verb.

Like phrases, clauses enrich your written and oral expression by adding details and making your meaning more exact. Clauses also allow you to combine ideas to show their relationship. This adds logic and cohesion, very good things when you're trying to communicate.

You Could Look It Up

A **clause** is a group of words with its own subject and verb. An **independent (main) clause** is a complete sentence; a **dependent (subordinate) clause** is part of a sentence. A dependent clause cannot stand alone.

There are two types of clauses: *independent clauses* (main clauses) and *dependent clauses* (subordinate clauses and relative clauses).

♦ An independent clause is a complete sentence; it can stand alone.

♦ A dependent (subordinate) clause is part of a sentence; it cannot stand alone.

Here are some examples of each type of clause.

Dependent Clause	Independent Clause
Until Captain Cooke returned from his voyage to Tahiti,	Tattooing was not known in the Western world.
Although they had the worst batting average in baseball,	The New York Mets won the World Series in 1969.
Because his salary in 1930 and 1931 was $80,000,	Babe Ruth was the best-paid athlete in the world at the time.

Strictly Speaking

Why is there a period at the end of each independent clause? Because they are complete sentences. Note that there's no period at the end of each dependent clause. That's because they're not complete sentences.

Independent Clauses: Top Dogs

An independent clause contains a subject and a predicate. It can stand alone as a sentence because it expresses a complete thought. The three independent clauses shown on the previous chart all contain a subject and a verb and express a complete idea.

The following table shows some independent clauses divided into their subjects and predicates.

Subject	Predicate
The door	opened.
Dancing	burns up 200 to 400 calories per hour.
Elvis's twin	died at birth on January 8, 1935.
Don Larsen	pitched the only perfect game in World Series history.
It	was the fifth game of the 1956 Series.

Dependent Clauses: I Get by with a Little Help from My Friends

Dependent clauses add additional information to the main clauses, but they are not necessary to form a complete thought. They do not form a complete thought by themselves. Although each of the dependent clauses shown on the first chart in this chapter has a subject and a verb, it does not express a complete thought. As a result, it cannot stand alone. A dependent clause is like a child; it's unable to support itself but able to cause a lot of problems if crossed.

A dependent clause often starts with a word that makes the clause unable to stand alone. Look back at the three dependent clauses on the first chart. The words used here are *until*, *although*, and *because*, respectively. These words are subordinating conjunctions, as you learned in Chapter 3. We'll review subordinating conjunctions in a few minutes.

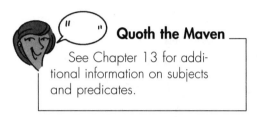

Quoth the Maven

See Chapter 13 for additional information on subjects and predicates.

I Know 'Em When I See 'Em

Before we go on, make sure you can identify independent and dependent clauses. In the space provided, write I for independent clauses and D for dependent clauses.

_____ 1. The first movie version of *Frankenstein* came out in 1910.

_____ 2. Which was produced by Thomas Edison.

_____ 3. Robert Zimmerman grew up in Minnesota.

_____ 4. Before he changed his name to Bob Dylan.

_____ 5. Pearl Bailey enrolled as a freshman at Georgetown University.

_____ 6. After she enjoyed a long career in show business.

Answers

1. I	3. I	5. I
2. D	4. D	6. D

Subordinating Conjunctions Link 'Em Together

Subordinating conjunctions link an independent clause to a dependent clause. Each subordinating conjunction expresses a relationship between the meaning of the dependent clause and the meaning of the independent clause.

Danger, Will Robinson _____

Don't use length as your yardstick when determining if a clause is independent or dependent. Either type of clause can be very long or very short—or somewhere in between. Skilled writers often vary the length of their clauses to achieve rhythm, balance, and meaning in their writing.

For example, some conjunctions show time order; others, result or effect. The following table shows the most common subordinating conjunctions and the relationships they express.

Subordinating Conjunctions

Relationship	Examples
Condition	unless, provided that, if, even if
Reason	because, as, as if
Choice	rather than, than, whether
Contrast	though, although, even though, but
Location	where, wherever
Result, effect	in order that, so, so that, that
Time	while, once, when, since, whenever, after, before, until, as soon as

Looking for Love in All the Right Places

Linking the right ideas can be nearly as gratifying as linking the right people. Okay, it might not be as satisfying, but it can be a whole lot easier.

Give it a whirl. Join each dependent clause with its independent clause by using the subordinating conjunction that expresses the most suitable meaning. Make your choice from the preceding chart. Write your answer on the lines provided.

1. Police in Wichita, Kansas, arrested a 22-year-old man at the airport hotel _____ he tried to pass two counterfeit $16 bills.

2. You know it's going to be a bad day _____ you see a *60 Minutes* news team outside your office.

3. Cats have more than 100 vocal sounds, _____ dogs have only about 10.

4. _____ she were life-size, Barbie's measurements would be 39-23-33.

5. _____ avoid an attack by a vampire, you should eat as much garlic as possible, keep a crucifix close by, and avoid cemeteries.

6. A man in Johannesburg, South Africa, shot his 49-year-old friend in the face, seriously wounding him, _____ the two practiced shooting beer cans off each other's head.

7. Ice cream will actually make you warmer rather than colder _____ it contains so many calories.

8. A Los Angeles man who later said he was "tired of walking," stole a steamroller and led police on a 5 mph chase _____ an officer stepped aboard the steamroller and brought the vehicle to a stop.

9. The writer Oscar Wilde made this statement about Niagara Falls: "Every American bride is taken there, and the sight must be one of the earliest, _____ not the keenest, disappointments of married life."

10. _____ two service station attendants in Ionia, Michigan, refused to hand over the cash to an intoxicated robber, the robber threatened to call the police. They still refused, _____ the robber called the police himself and was promptly arrested.

Answers

Possible responses:

1. after	6. while
2. when	7. because
3. while, or although	8. until
4. If	9. if
5. In order to	10. When, so

Quoth the Maven

When a dependent clause introduced by a subordinating conjunction comes before the independent clause, the clauses are usually separated by a comma. For example: *If you are to keep your respect for sausages and governments, it is best not to know what goes into either.*

There are three different kinds of subordinate clauses: *adverb clauses, adjective clauses,* and *noun clauses.* Let's examine each one and see how it can help you beef up your writing and speech.

Adverb Clauses: Hot Shots

Dependent clauses can function as adverbs. In this case, they are called *adverb clauses*. (Bet I didn't surprise you with that one.) An adverb clause is a dependent clause that describes a verb, adjective, or another adverb. As with regular old garden-variety adverbs, an adverb clause answers these questions:

- ◆ Where?
- ◆ Why?
- ◆ When?
- ◆ To what extent?
- ◆ Under what condition?
- ◆ In what manner?

You Could Look It Up

An **adverb clause** is a dependent clause that describes a verb, adjective, or another adverb.

All adverb clauses start with a subordinating conjunction. You reviewed some of the most common subordinating conjunctions in the previous section; here are a few more that you can use to link ideas and show how they are related:

- ◆ As long as
- ◆ As soon as
- ◆ As though
- ◆ In

Follow the Leader

You can place an adverb clause in the beginning, middle, or end of a sentence. Refer to these examples of adverb clauses as you fashion your own.

Quoth the Maven

Set off adverb clauses that occur at the beginning of sentences with commas.

- ◆ *Wherever she goes*, she <u>leaves</u> a piece of luggage behind.

  The adverb clause "wherever she goes" modifies the verb "leaves."

- ◆ Bob enjoyed the movie <u>more</u> *than I did*.

  The adverb clause "than I did" modifies the adverb "more."

◆ Prince <u>wanted</u> to change his name *because too many dogs answered when he was called.*

The adverb clause "because too many dogs answered when he was called" modifies the verb "wanted."

Shape Up Your Sentences

You sweat for rock-hard abs, firm pecs, and a tight, uh, southern hemisphere. Why not give your sentences a good workout to make them as healthy as your bod? Adverb clauses can help you eliminate sentence flab. For instance:

Two sentences: Sean Connery had worked as both a bricklayer and a truck driver. This was before he became the original James Bond.

One sentence: Before he became the original James Bond, Sean Connery had worked as both a bricklayer and a truck driver.

Check out Part 5 for other ways to use clauses to achieve sentence style.

Adjective Clauses: Paint by Numbers

Here's another type of clause: the *adjective clause.* Like adverb clauses, adjective clauses are of the dependent variety.

Adjective clauses describe nouns and pronouns. They add detail to sentences by functioning as adjectives. Obviously, you can tell an adjective clause by its function, but there's also another little clue: Most adjective clauses start with the pronouns *who, whom, whose, which, that, when,* or *where.* Adjective clauses that begin with one of the relative pronouns are also called *relative clauses.*

Here are some other pronouns that can start an adjective clause:

◆ Whoever

◆ Whomever

◆ Whichever

◆ What

◆ Whatever

◆ Why

You Could Look It Up

Adjective clauses describe nouns and pronouns.

You can identify an adjective clause because it answers the adjective questions: "Which one?" or "What kind?"

Here are some examples of adjective clauses:

♦ The only <u>one</u> of the seven dwarfs *who does not have a beard* is Dopey.

The adjective clause "who does not have a beard" describes the noun "one."

Danger, Will Robinson

Place an adjective clause as close as possible to the word it describes or risk driving your readers mad with confusion.

♦ I found a quiet, secluded <u>place</u> *where we can meet*.

The adjective clause "where we can meet" describes the noun "place."

♦ It never rains on <u>days</u> *when my garden needs watering*.

The adjective clause "when my garden needs watering" describes the noun "days."

Relative Clauses: It's All Relative

Adjective clauses that begin with one of the relative pronouns are also called *relative clauses*. Here are the relative pronouns: *who, whom, whose, which,* and *that*.

As you learned in Chapter 4, relative pronouns connect (or "relate"—get it?) an adjective clause to the word the clause describes. In addition, relative pronouns function within the clause as an adjective, subject, direct object, or object of a preposition. For instance:

1. Relative pronoun as an adjective:

♦ The <u>boy</u> *whose book I borrowed* is very hunky.

The relative clause "whose book I borrowed" describes the noun "boy."

Strictly Speaking

Remember to use *who, whom* (and all variations such as *whoever* and *whomever*) to refer to people. Reserve *which* and *that* if the antecedent is a thing or an animal.

2. Relative pronoun as a subject:

♦ The bird *that is soaring in the sky* is a seagull.

The relative clause "that is soaring in the sky" functions as a subject.

3. Relative pronoun as a direct object:

♦ The book *that <u>you</u> panned* is really very good.

The relative clause "that you panned" is the direct object of the subject "you."

4. Relative pronoun as the object of a preposition:

   ◆ The woman of *whom you spoke* is my boss.

   The relative clause "whom you spoke" is the object of the preposition "of."

Clauses Make the Sentence

As with adverb clauses, you can use adjective clauses to link ideas, combine information, and create more effective sentences. In addition to adding description to sentences, adjective clauses allow you to create relationships between ideas. Here's an example:

Two sentences: "Rock Around the Clock" was released by Bill Haley and the Comets in 1955. "Rock Around the Clock" is often called the first big rock-and-roll hit.

One sentence: "Rock Around the Clock," which is often called the first big rock-and-roll hit, was released by Bill Haley and the Comets in 1955.

There's more on creating an effective writing style with clauses in Part 5.

Noun Clauses: What's in a Name?

Not to be left out of the fun, nouns also have their own clause. Just as you would expect, a *noun clause* is a dependent clause that functions as a noun. Because it functions as a noun, this clause can be a subject, direct object, indirect object, object of a preposition, predicate nominative, or appositive. For instance:

◆ No one understands *why experience is something you don't get until just after you need it.*

   The noun clause "why experience is something you don't get until just after you need it" functions as a direct object.

◆ *Where the candy bar is hidden* remains a mystery.

   The noun clause "where the candy bar is hidden" functions as the subject of the sentence.

◆ The instructor gave *whoever got their papers in early* extra credit.

   The noun clause "whoever got their papers in early" functions as an indirect object.

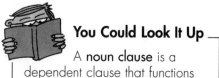

You Could Look It Up

A **noun clause** is a dependent clause that functions as a noun.

Connect the Dots

Clauses can also be used to express comparisons. When such clauses imply some of the words rather than state them outright, you have created an *elliptical clause*. The name "elliptical" comes from the word *ellipsis*, which means "omission." For example:

You Could Look It Up

Elliptical clauses intentionally omit words for conciseness.

- The other members of the demonstration were as angry as I.

  Insert the missing word *was* after "I."

- The social climber feared the judgment of the decorator more than the cost of the project.

  Insert the missing subject and verb "he (or she) feared" after the word *than*.

Elliptical clauses come in different flavors: adverb, adjective, and noun. Here's how you can recognize them.

Type of Clause	What's Omitted
Adverb clause	Subject, verb, or either one
Adjective clause	The words *that, which, whom*
Noun clause	Subject, verb, or the second half of the comparison

Danger, Will Robinson

Because elliptical clauses are missing words, there's a danger that they might not convey your meaning. As you write, say the word or words you are leaving out to make sure your clauses are clear.

The mark of punctuation called an *ellipsis* is three spaced dots (…). It's used to show that something has been intentionally omitted from a sentence. Elliptical clauses don't use the three spaced dots of the ellipsis; instead, the elliptical clause just swipes the name of the ellipsis and adopts its function in the way it structures a sentence by omitting certain words.

Elliptical clauses help create concise writing and speech. In these days when many people have a lot to say but say little, we want to support the use of the elliptical clause as much as possible.

Getting Down and Dirty

Time for fun, Gentle Reader. Knowing how to identify clauses is important, but it's even more important that you know how to use them to create precise and graceful sentences. Try it now. Combine each pair of clauses to eliminate unnecessary words and express the meaning more clearly. There are several different ways to combine each sentence. If you're stumped, I've given you a hint in parenthesis at the end of each pair of sentences.

1. I found the book. I need the book. (that)

   _____

   _____

2. "Rock Around the Clock" was released by Bill Haley and the Comets in 1955.
   It is often called the first big rock-and-roll hit. (which)

   _____

   _____

3. Many people believe that skyscrapers can sway eight feet or more in a strong wind.
   That is not true. (although or but)

   _____

   _____

4. Charlie Chaplin was widely copied.
   He once entered a Charlie Chaplin look-alike contest and came in third. (who)

   _____

   _____

5. You recommended a movie.
   It is no longer playing. (that)

   _____

   _____

6. Dopey does not have a beard.
   He is the only one of the seven dwarfs without a beard. (who)

   _____

   _____

7. I received a postcard from a friend.

   The friend is working in Bora-Bora. (from whom)

   _____

   _____

8. He travels all over.

   He collects bizarre souvenirs. (wherever)

   _____

   _____

9. Thomas Jefferson returned from Naples to American with four crates of "mac-carony."

   He never guessed that someday his countrymen would be eating more than 150 types of pasta. (when)

   _____

   _____

10. Pasta has the reputation of being fattening.

    It is not necessarily fattening. (despite)

    _____

    _____

Answers

1. I found the book that I need.

2. "Rock Around the Clock," which is often called the first big rock-and-roll hit, was released by Bill Haley and the Comets in 1955.

3. Although many people believe that skyscrapers can sway eight feet or more in a strong wind, that is not true.

4. Charlie Chaplin, who was widely copied, once entered a Charlie Chaplin look-alike contest and came in third.

5. The movie that you recommended is no longer playing.

6. The only one of the seven dwarfs who does not have a beard is Dopey.

   Or:

   Dopey is the only one of the seven dwarfs who does not have a beard.

7. The friend from whom I received a postcard is working in Bora-Bora.

8. Wherever he travels, he collects bizarre souvenirs.

9. When Thomas Jefferson returned from Naples to American with four crates of "maccarony," he never guessed that someday his countrymen would be eating more than 150 types of pasta.

10. Despite its reputation, pasta is not necessarily fattening.

The Least You Need to Know

- An independent (main) clause is a complete sentence.

- A dependent (subordinate) clause is part of a sentence; it cannot stand alone.

- Adverb clauses, adjective clauses, and noun clauses are types of dependent clauses.

- Elliptical clauses intentionally omit words.

Chapter 13

Sentence and Sensibility

In This Chapter

- ◆ Define the sentence
- ◆ Learn about the four kinds of sentences
- ◆ Discover the four sentence functions
- ◆ Correct run-ons and fragments

If someone asked you to define a sentence, do you think you could? You might be tempted to say, "No way!" I bet you *do* know a sentence when you see it. Prove me right; pick out the sentence from these four groups of words:

- ◆ Throughout people's ears grow entire their lives.
- ◆ Grow throughout people's entire ears lives their.
- ◆ Entire throughout lives ears grow people's their.
- ◆ People's ears grow throughout their entire lives.

Each of the four groups contains exactly the same words, but only one is a sentence: the last one. You were able to pick out the sentence so easily because you have an innate knowledge of how English works—knowledge you have absorbed from reading, speaking, listening, and watching.

But perhaps you need a little more work on sentences. Maybe you're not sure about the different kinds of sentences and how they're used. That's what this chapter is all about. First, you learn about the two main parts of the sentence: the subject and the predicate. Then I teach you the four different types of sentences: simple, compound, complex, and compound-complex. Next come the four different sentence functions. Along the way, you learn how to fix the two most common sentence errors: fragments and run-ons.

You Could Look It Up

A **sentence** is a group of words that express a complete thought.

I Know It When I See It: The Sentence

Sentence: Stop!

Sentence: You stop!

Sentence: You better stop right now.

Each of these three word groups is a sentence. That's because they each meet the three requirements for a sentence. To be a sentence, a group of words must ...

Strictly Speaking

How can "Stop!" be a sentence, when it's clearly lacking a subject? It is a sentence because the subject, *you*, is understood rather than stated outright. A one-word command is the shortest possible English sentence.

◆ Have a *subject* (noun or pronoun).

◆ Have a *predicate* (verb or verb phrase).

◆ Express a complete thought.

A sentence has two parts: a *subject* and a *predicate*. The subject includes the noun or pronoun that tells what the subject is about. The predicate includes the verb that describes what the subject is doing. Here are some examples of complete sentences.

Subject	Predicate
You	stop!
New York City	is called the "Big Apple."
The forward with the knee brace	made 10 baskets.

Seek and Ye Shall Find

Being able to recognize the subject and the verb in a sentence will help you make sure that your own sentences are complete and clear. To check that you've included the subject and verb in your sentences, follow these steps:

1. To find the subject, ask yourself, "Self, what word is the sentence describing?"

2. To find an action verb, ask yourself, "Self, what did the subject do?"

3. If you can't find an action verb, look for a linking verb. For example: Herman *is* the winner. "Is" is the linking verb.

Hidden Treasures

Some sentences are not that cooperative about the placement of their subject and verb, however. In most sentences, the subject will come before the verb. Not so with questions. In a question, the verb often comes before the subject. Here are some examples:

◆ Is the frog in the freezer?

The subject of the sentence is "frog."

◆ Are you traveling this weekend?

The subject of the sentence is "you."

To find the subject in a question, rewrite the question as a statement. The question "Is the frog in the freezer?" becomes "The frog is in the freezer." Now the subject, *frog*, is in the usual position before the verb.

It can be equally tricky to find the subject in sentences that start with *here* or *there*. Remember that *here* or *there* never function as the subject of a sentence. For example:

◆ Here is your frozen frog.

The subject of the sentence is "frog."

◆ There goes the frog, all nicely defrosted.

The subject of the sentence is still Mr. Frog.

To find the subject in a sentence that starts with *here* or *there*, use the same strategy you learned for questions: Rewrite the sentence to place the subject first.

Sentence Structure: The Fab Four

In Chapter 12, you learned that there are two types of clauses: independent and dependent. Recall that independent clauses are complete sentences because they have a subject and verb and express a complete thought. Dependent clauses, in contrast, cannot stand alone because they do not express a complete thought—even though they have a subject and a verb. Independent and dependent clauses can be used in a number of ways to form the four basic types of sentences: simple, compound, complex, and compound-complex. Time to make their acquaintance.

Simple Sentences: Simple Isn't as Simple Does

A *simple sentence* has one independent clause. That means it has one subject and one verb—although either or both can be compound. In addition, a simple sentence can have adjectives and adverbs. What a simple sentence can't have is another independent clause or any subordinate clauses. For example:

- Americans eat more bananas than they eat any other fruit.

  one subject, one verb

- David Letterman and Jay Leno host talk shows.

  compound subject, one verb

- My son toasts and butters his bagel.

  one subject, compound verb

You Could Look It Up

A **simple sentence** has one independent clause.

Don't shun the simple sentence—it's no simpleton. The simple sentence served Ernest Hemingway well; with its help, macho man Ernie snagged a Nobel Prize in Literature. In the following excerpt from *The Sun Also Rises*, Hemingway uses the simple sentence to convey powerful emotions:

The driver started up the street. I settled back. Brett moved close to me. We sat close against each other. I put my arm around her and she rested against me comfortably. It was very hot and bright, and the houses looked sharply white. We turned out onto the Gran Via.

"Oh, Jake," Brett said, "we could have had such a damned good time together."

Ahead was a mounted policeman in khaki directing traffic. He raised his baton. The car slowed suddenly pressing Brett against me.

"Yes," I said. "Isn't it pretty to think so?"

Okay, so it's a real downer. You think they give Nobels for happy talk?

Compound Sentences: Compound Interest

A *compound sentence* consists of two or more independent clauses. The independent clauses can be joined in one of two ways:

◆ With a coordinating conjunction: *for, and, nor, but, or, yet, so*

◆ With a semicolon (;)

You Could Look It Up

A compound sentence consists of two or more independent clauses.

As with a simple sentence, a compound sentence can't have any subordinate clauses. Here are some compound sentences for your reading pleasure.

Independent Clause	Conjunction or Semicolon	Independent Clause
Men are mammals	and	women are femammals.
Mushrooms grow in damp places	so	they look like umbrellas.
The largest mammals are found in the sea	;	there's nowhere else to put them.

You might also add a conjunctive adverb to this construction, as in this example: The largest mammals are found in the sea; after all, there's nowhere else to put them.

Complex Sentences: Not So Complex at All

A complex sentence contains one independent clause and at least one dependent clause. The independent clause is called the "main clause." These sentences use subordinating conjunctions to link ideas. As you check out these examples, see if you can find the subordinating conjunctions.

◆ Parallel lines never meet (*independent clause*) until (*subordinating conjunction*) you bend one of them (*dependent clause*).

◆ Many dead animals of the past changed to oil (*independent clause*) while (*subordinating conjunction*) others preferred to be gas (*dependent clause*).

◆ Even though (*subordinating conjunction*) the sun is a star (*dependent clause*), it knows how to change back to the sun in the daytime (*independent clause*).

The subordinating conjunctions are *until, while,* and *even though.*

Compound-Complex Sentences: The Big Kahuna

A compound-complex sentence has at least two independent clauses and at least one dependent clause. The dependent clause can be part of the independent clause. For instance:

◆ When the heat comes, the lakes dry up,

    dependent clause   *independent clause*

    and farmers know the crops will fail.

    independent clause

◆ I planned to drive to work, but I couldn't

    independent clause   *independent clause*

    until the mechanic repaired my car.

    dependent clause

The Choice Is Yours

Decisions, decisions: Now that you know you have four different sentence types at your disposal, which ones should you use? Effective communication requires not only that you write complete sentences, but also that you write sentences that say exactly what you mean. Try these six guidelines as you decide which sentence types to use and when:

Danger, Will Robinson

Don't join the two parts of a compound sentence with a comma—you'll end up with a type of run-on sentence called a *comma splice*. More on this later in this chapter.

◆ Every sentence should provide clear and complete information.

◆ Most effective sentences are concise, conveying their meaning in as few words as possible.

◆ Effective sentences stress the main point or the most important detail. In most cases, the main point is located in the main clause to make it easier to find.

◆ Your choice of sentences depends on your *audience*. For example, you would use simple sentences and short words if your *readers* were children, while an audience of engineers would call for more technical language and longer sentences.

◆ Always consider your *purpose* for writing before you select a sentence type.

◆ The rhythm and pacing of your writing is determined by your sentences.

Before you shift into panic mode, you should know that most writers use a combination of all four sentence types to convey their meaning. Even Ernest Hemingway slipped a compound sentence or two in among all those simple sentences. Besides, there's much more on this topic in Chapter 14. By the time you finish this book, you'll be picking sentence types as easily as you pick up the daily newspaper.

You Could Look It Up

Your **readers** make up your audience.

Face the Music

But now it's time to see what's what, who's who, and where you're at with this sentence stuff. To do so, label each of the following sentences as simple, compound, complex, or compound-complex.

_____ 1. If at first you don't succeed, destroy all evidence that you tried.

_____ 2. The hardness of the butter is proportional to the softness of the bread.

_____ 3. You never really learn to swear until you learn to drive.

_____ 4. It takes about half a gallon of water to cook spaghetti, and about a gallon of water to clean the pot.

_____ 5. Monday is an awful way to spend one-seventh of your life.

_____ 6. Genetics explains why you look like your father and if you don't, why you should.

_____ 7. To succeed in politics, it is often necessary to rise above your principles.

_____ 8. Two wrongs are only the beginning.

_____ 9. When oxygen is combined with anything, heat is given off, a process known as "constipation."

_____ 10. To steal ideas from one person is plagiarism; to steal from many is research.

Answers

1. complex

2. simple

3. complex

4. compound

5. simple

6. compound-complex

7. complex

8. simple

9. compound-complex

10. compound

Sentence Functions: The Four Tops

In addition to classifying sentences by the number of clauses they contain, you can pigeonhole sentences according to their functions. There are four sentence functions in English: *declarative, exclamatory, interrogative,* and *imperative.*

1. *Declarative sentences* state an idea. They end with a period. For example:

   ◆ The first toilet ever seen on television was on *Leave It to Beaver.*

   ◆ The problem with the gene pool is that there's no lifeguard.

2. *Exclamatory sentences* show strong emotions. They end with an exclamation mark. For example:

   ◆ What a mess this room is!

   ◆ The cake is ruined!

3. *Interrogative sentences* ask a question. As you would expect, they end with a question mark. For instance:

   ◆ How you gonna keep 'em down on the farm when they've seen Paris?

   ◆ Why is it possible to tickle someone else but not to tickle yourself?

4. *Imperative sentences* give orders or directions, and so end with a period or an exclamation mark. For instance:

   ◆ Sit down and listen!

   ◆ Fasten your seatbelts when the sign is illuminated.

> **Strictly Speaking**
>
> Which type of sentence often omits the subject? Imperative sentences, because the subject is often understood, as shown in these examples: "Clean up this mess" or "Help!"

Alley Oops

Why learn the different types of sentences and their functions? So you can write correct ones, bubba. When your sentences aren't correct, no one will know what the dickens you're saying. This is not a good thing.

There are two basic types of sentence errors: *fragments* and *run-ons.* These problems with sentence construction cause clumsy, unpolished writing and speech. Let's look at each of these sentence errors in detail so you'll be able to fix them with ease.

Fragments: Lost in Place

As its name suggests, a *sentence fragment* is a group of words that do not express a complete thought. Most times, a fragment is missing a subject, a verb, or both. Other times, a fragment may have a subject and a verb but still not express a complete thought. Fragments don't discriminate: They can be phrases as well as clauses.

There are three main ways that fragments occur. And here they are:

- Fragments occur when a dependent clause masquerades as a sentence. For example:

  - Because Lincoln Logs were invented by Frank Lloyd Wright's son.

  - Because the most common name in the world is Mohammed.

- Fragments also happen when a phrase is cut off from the sentence it describes. For instance:

  - Used to cure fleas and ticks.

  - Hoping to keep the ceiling from collapsing.

- You can also create a fragment if you use the wrong form of a verb. For example:

  - The writer *gone* to the office.

  - The pearl being the main ingredient in many love potions.

You Could Look It Up

A **sentence fragment** is a group of words that does not express a complete thought. A fragment is the same as a dependent clause.

Danger, Will Robinson

Don't be misled by a capital letter at the beginning of a word group. Starting a group of words with a capital letter doesn't make the word group a sentence any more than putting a comb on a hen makes her a rooster.

Quoth the Maven

Experienced writers often use fragments to create realistic-sounding dialogue. They know that few people ever speak in complete sentences, regardless of what we'd like to think.

You can correct a fragment two ways:

- Add the missing part to the sentence

  Fragment: In the cabinet over the bookshelf.

  Complete: I keep extra supplies in the cabinet over the bookshelf.

♦ Omit the subordinating conjunction or connect it to another sentence.

   Fragment: When you go to the party.

   Complete: When you go to the party, be sure to head straight for the shrimp and caviar and chow down.

Run-Ons and Comma Splices: It Could Be a Stretch

A *run-on sentence* is two incorrectly joined independent clauses. A *comma splice* is a run-on with a comma where the two independent clauses run together. When your sentences run together, your ideas are garbled. For instance:

♦ Most people who drink coffee don't know where it comes from it is actually the fruit of an evergreen tree.

♦ Robert Wadlow was the tallest person who ever lived he was 8 feet 11 inches tall when he died in 1940.

So far, so good, but there are two important facts to realize about run-ons:

♦ Run-ons are not necessarily long. Some can be quite short, in fact. For instance:

   ♦ She walked he ran.

   ♦ Birds chirp cows moo.

♦ The second clause of a run-on often begins with a pronoun.

   ♦ Godzilla wants to sleep he is exhausted from destroying Tokyo.

You Could Look It Up

A **run-on sentence** is two incorrectly joined independent clauses. A **comma splice** is a run-on with a comma where the two sentences run together.

You can correct a run-on sentence in one of four ways. Let's use Godzilla as our example.

♦ Separate the run-on into two sentences with end punctuation such as periods, exclamation marks, and question marks.

   ♦ Godzilla wants to sleep. He is exhausted from destroying Tokyo.

♦ Add a coordinating conjunction (*and, nor, but, or, for, yet,* or *so*) to create a compound sentence.

   ♦ Godzilla wants to sleep, *for* he is exhausted from destroying Tokyo.

◆ Add a subordinating conjunction to create a complex sentence.

  ◆ Godzilla wants to sleep, *because* he is exhausted from destroying Tokyo.

◆ Use a semicolon to create a compound sentence.

  ◆ Godzilla wants to sleep; he is exhausted from destroying Tokyo.

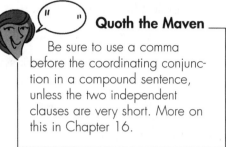

Quoth the Maven

Be sure to use a comma before the coordinating conjunction in a compound sentence, unless the two independent clauses are very short. More on this in Chapter 16.

Seventh-Inning Stretch

Take a few minutes to fix the fragments and run-ons in these two anecdotes.

1. In the late 1900s, the man who was shot out of the cannon every day. At the Barnum and Bailey Circus decided to quit his wife had asked him to find a less risky way of making a living P. T. Barnum hated to lose a good man. So he sent him a message, "I beg you to reconsider—men of your caliber are hard to find."

2. In 1946, Winston Churchill traveled to Fulton, Missouri, to deliver a speech. Which turned out to be his famous Iron Curtain address. And to be present at the dedication of a bust in his honor. After his speech, a rather attractive and ample woman approached the wartime prime minister of England and said, "Mr. Churchill, I traveled more than a hundred miles this morning. For the unveiling of your bust." Churchill, who was known far and wide for his quick wit, replied, "Madam, I assure you, in that regard I would gladly return the favor."

Answers

Possible responses:

1. In the late 1900s, the man who was shot out of the cannon every day at the Barnum and Bailey Circus decided to quit because his wife had asked him to find a less risky way of making a living. P. T. Barnum hated to lose a good man, so he sent him a message, "I beg you to reconsider—men of your caliber are hard to find."

2. In 1946, Winston Churchill traveled to Fulton, Missouri, to deliver a speech, which turned out to be his famous Iron Curtain address, and to be present at the dedication of a bust in his honor. After his speech, a rather attractive and ample woman approached the wartime prime minister of England and said, "Mr. Churchill, I traveled more than a hundred miles this morning for the unveiling of your bust." Churchill, who was known far and wide for his quick wit, replied, "Madam, I assure you, in that regard I would gladly return the favor."

The Least You Need to Know

◆ A sentence has a subject and verb and expresses a complete thought.

◆ There are four types of sentences: simple, compound, complex, and compound-complex.

◆ There are four sentence functions: declarative, exclamatory, interrogative, and imperative.

◆ Fragments are parts of sentences; run-ons are incorrectly joined independent clauses.

Chapter 14

Coordination and Subordination: What to Say When the Cops Come

In This Chapter

◆ Learn how to coordinate ideas

◆ Explore subordination

◆ Achieve parallel structure

When you write effective sentences, you move beyond mere correctness to writing with style and grace. It's like moving from Martha Washington to Madonna, or from a Ford to a Ferrari. This chapter introduces you to the nitty-gritty of writing well. First you learn how to coordinate and subordinate clauses to communicate relationships between two or more ideas. Then I show you how to use parallel structure to make sure your ideas are expressed in a logical way.

Coordination: All the Right Moves

You coordinate your outfits, home furnishings, and dance moves. So why not coordinate your sentences to give them some style as well? In the previous chapter, you learned how to connect the parts of a sentence. There, I touched on coordinating independent clauses. Let's kick it up a notch and get into the nitty-gritty of coordinating independent clauses.

Sometimes you want to show that two or more ideas are equally important in a sentence. In such cases, you're looking to coordinate. Sentence *coordination* links ideas of equal importance. This process gives your writing harmony by bringing together related independent clauses. There are four main ways to coordinate independent clauses. You can use:

You Could Look It Up

Sentence **coordination** links ideas of equal importance.

Quoth the Maven

Remember to use a comma between coordinating conjunctions that join two independent clauses, unless the clauses are very short.

- Coordinating conjunctions
    - for
    - and
    - nor
    - but
    - or
    - yet
    - so

- Correlative conjunctions
    - either … or
    - neither … nor
    - not only … but also
    - both … and

- Semicolons and conjunctive adverbs. As you learned in Chapter 4, there are many different conjunctive adverbs. Here are some examples:
    - ; furthermore,
    - ; therefore,
    - ; for example,
    - ; however,

- A semicolon

Mix and Match

Coordination isn't just slapping on a black tie with a white shirt or putting some parsley on a leg of lamb. No siree; coordination involves using the right word or mark of punctuation to show different relationships between ideas. For example, each of the coordinating conjunctions has a different meaning, as the following table shows.

Coordinating Conjunctions and Their Shades of Meaning

Coordinating Conjunction	Meaning	Function
for	because	to show cause
and	also	to link ideas
nor	negative	to reinforce negative
but	however	to contrast ideas
or	choice	to show possibilities
yet	however	to contrast
so	therefore	to show result

Correlative conjunctions convey balance, while semicolons and conjunctive adverbs indicate relationships such as *examples, continuation,* and *contrast.* A semicolon alone shows that the ideas are of equal importance.

> **Strictly Speaking**
>
> A coordinate sentence is also known as a compound sentence. You learned all about compound sentences in Chapter 13.

Dancing Cheek-to-Cheek

Follow these steps when you coordinate independent clauses:

1. Decide which ideas can and should be combined.

2. Select the method of coordination that shows the appropriate relationship between ideas.

Each way to form compound sentences establishes a slightly different relationship between ideas. Often, there's no "right" answer when you're choosing which conjunctions and punctuation to use to coordinate ideas. With practice, you'll discover that some sentences sound smoother and more logical than others. Here are some examples to help you get your ear in tune:

Uncoordinated: Years ago most baseball players were recruited right out of high school or from the minors. Today, most play college baseball and then move on to the major leagues.

Coordinated: Years ago most baseball players were recruited right out of high school or from the minors, *but* today most play college baseball and then move on to the major leagues.

Coordinated: Years ago most baseball players were recruited right out of high school or from the minors; *however,* today most play college baseball and then move on to the major leagues.

But and *however* are used to show contrast.

> **Danger, Will Robinson**
>
> Be careful not to connect unrelated ideas, establish a vague connection among ideas, or connect too many ideas in one sentence. The first and second errors confuse your readers; the third causes "stringy sentences."

Uncoordinated: Star Trek was very successful in syndication. It was not a big hit during its original run from 1966 to 1969.

Coordinated: Star Trek was very successful in syndication, *yet* it was not a big hit during its original run from 1966 to 1969.

Coordinated: Star Trek was very successful in syndication; *nevertheless,* it was not a big hit during its original run from 1966 to 1969.

Yet and *nevertheless* are used to show comparison.

Don't String Me Along

What happens if you go coordination crazy? You end up with a *stringy sentence.* A *stringy sentence* contains too many ideas connected by coordinating conjunctions or *then.* Repetitious and hard-to-follow, stringy sentences are as annoying as stringy celery or stringy cheese. Here's an example of a stringy sentence:

♦ Mount Everest is in the Himalayas *and* it is the world's tallest mountain *and so* climbing it is very difficult *so* Edmund Hillary and Tenzing Horgay first climbed it in 1963 *and* everyone applauded their achievement.

To correct a stringy sentence, place closely related ideas in one sentence, and less closely related ideas in their own sentences. Here's a variation that achieves logic as well as emphasis of ideas:

♦ Because Mount Everest, in the Himalayas, is the world's tallest mountain, climbing it is very difficult. It was not until 1963 that the first explorers, Edmund Hillary and Tenzing Horgay, conquered the mountain to great acclaim.

Why Not Give It a Shot?

Take a few minutes to link the following simple sentences by adding coordinating conjunctions, correlative conjunctions, conjunctive adverbs and semicolons, or semicolons alone.

1. In the Great Fire of London in 1666 half of London was burnt down. Only six people were injured.

   _____

   _____

2. New York stockbroker Bill Wilson and Ohio surgeon Robert Smith both had a drinking problem. They joined forces and started Alcoholics Anonymous.

   _____

   _____

3. Most people don't keep their New Year's resolutions for more than a few weeks. They don't make resolutions in the first place.

   _____

   _____

4. The oldest female elephant in the herd usually leads the other elephants. The other female elephants are ranked below her in age.

   _____

   _____

5. The puppy pulled all the slippers from under the bed. She shredded all the toilet paper.

   _____

   _____

Answers

Possible responses:

1. In the Great Fire of London in 1666 half of London was burnt down, *but* only six people were injured. (shows contrast)

2. New York stockbroker Bill Wilson and Ohio surgeon Robert Smith both had a drinking problem, *so* they joined forces and started Alcoholics Anonymous. (shows result)

3. Most people don't keep their New Year's resolutions for more than a few weeks *or* they don't make resolutions in the first place. (shows choice)

4. The oldest female elephant in the herd usually leads the other elephants; the other female elephants are ranked below her in age. (semicolon shows closely linked ideas)

5. The puppy pulled all the slippers from under the bed, *and* she shredded all the toilet paper. (coordinating conjunction shows ideas of equal importance)

Subordination: What I Did for Love

Coordination shows the relationship among equal independent clauses; subordination, in contrast, shows the relationship between ideas of unequal rank. *Subordination* is connecting two unequal but related clauses with a subordinating conjunction to form a complex sentence. When you subordinate one part of a sentence to another, you make the dependent clause develop the main clause. Subordination can help your sentence in many ways. Here are three biggies:

You Could Look It Up

Subordination is connecting two unequal but related clauses with a subordinating conjunction to form a complex sentence.

- ◆ To trace ideas unfolding

- ◆ To show specific relationships among ideas

- ◆ To stress one idea over another

As a result, subordination can give your writing and speech greater logic, coherence, and unity.

As with sentence coordination, sentence subordination is more than random switcheroos. Subordination requires logic and thought. Follow these four steps to subordinate sentence ideas:

Quoth the Maven

As you learned in Chapter 3, subordinating conjunctions link an independent clause to a dependent clause. There are many subordinating conjunctions, including *after, although, because, before, if, though, since, when, till, unless, wherever,* and *where.* A more complete list appears in Chapter 12.

1. Decide which idea or clause is the most important. It will be the information you most want to emphasize in the reader's mind.

2. Designate this as the "main clause."

3. Select the subordinating conjunction that best expresses the relationship between the main clause and the dependent clause.

4. Arrange the clauses to achieve logic, coherence, rhythm, and polish.

Strictly Speaking

Conjunctions and conjunctive adverbs can also be called transitions because they signal connections between ideas.

The following table shows some of the most common subordinating conjunctions and the relationships that they show between ideas.

Relationship	Subordinating Conjunctions
Cause, reason	as, because
Choice	whether, rather than
Condition	even if, if, unless, provided that
Contrast	though, even though, although
Effect, result	so, so that, in order that, that
Location	wherever, where
Time	once, whenever, since, until, when, while, after, before

Follow the Leader

Here are some examples of effective sentence subordination:

Not subordinated: You lick a postage stamp. You consume one tenth of a calorie.

Subordinated: When you lick a postage stamp, you consume one tenth of a calorie.

Starting the dependent clause with the subordinating conjunction "when" gives a reason for the main clause.

Not subordinated: You are a typical American man. You spend four hours a year tying your tie.

Subordinated: If you are a typical American man, you spend four hours a year tying your tie.

Starting the dependent clause with the subordinating conjunction "if" gives a reason for the main clause.

Danger, Will Robinson

Be careful not to switch the main clause and the dependent clause when you subordinate. If you put the main idea in a dependent clause, your sentence will not be logical, as this example shows: *Because the TV camera focused on him, Todd wore a bright blazer.* The sentence should read: *Because Todd wore a bright blazer, the TV camera focused on him.*

Dice 'n' Slice

Choppy sentences are a series of short sentences that create an annoyingly abrupt rhythm. Because there is no subordination in a series of choppy sentences, each idea is given equal emphasis. Like a date from the dark side, choppy sentences are abrupt, boring, and repetitious. For instance:

◆ Director John Ford banned the use of makeup while he filmed *The Grapes of Wrath*. John Ford also banned artificial lighting. He also banned special camera effects. He wanted to stay true to the realistic nature of Steinbeck's novel.

Try some sentence combining and subordination of ideas to achieve meaning, emphasis, and rhythm.

◆ In an attempt to stay true to the realistic nature of *The Grapes of Wrath*, director John Ford banned the use of makeup, artificial lighting, and special camera effects while he filmed Steinbeck's novel.

Double Dare

It's time to put up or shut up. Use subordinating conjunctions to link the ideas in each of the following sentence pairs. First decide which clause will be dependent and which one will be independent. Write your answers in the spaces provided.

1. You put a ton of Jell-O in the swimming pool. You still can't walk on water.

   _____

   _____

2. The word *trousers* is an uncommon noun. It is singular at the top and plural at the bottom.

   _____

   _____

3. Milk stays fresh. Keep it in the cow.

   _____

   _____

4. You have 3 quarters, 4 dimes, and 4 pennies. You have $1.19, the largest amount of money in coins without being able to make change for a dollar.

   _____

   _____

5. Thomas Jefferson was broke when he died. He was one of America's brilliant presidents.

_____

_____

Answers

Possible responses:

1. Even if you put a ton of Jell-O in the swimming pool, you still can't walk on water.

2. The word *trousers* is an uncommon noun because it is singular at the top and plural at the bottom.

3. So that milk will stay fresh, keep it in the cow.

4. If you have 3 quarters, 4 dimes, and 4 pennies, you have $1.19, the largest amount of money in coins without being able to make change for a dollar.

5. Although Thomas Jefferson was broke when he died, he was one of America's most brilliant presidents.

Duke It Out: Coordination Versus Subordination

When to coordinate? When to subordinate? Most often, the logic of the ideas dictates the placement of those ideas in main clauses or dependent clauses. Here's the rule of thumb:

◆ Coordinate when you want to link related independent clauses.

◆ Subordinate when you want to put the most important idea in the main clause and give less importance to the idea in the dependent clause.

Here are some examples that show each sentence strategy at work:

Two clauses: The sky became a frightening gray. The mood was ominous.

Coordinated: The sky became a frightening gray, *and* the mood was ominous.

Subordinated: As the sky became a frightening gray, <u>the</u> <u>mood</u> *was ominous*.

With this construction, the mood is the focus.

Subordinated: As the mood became ominous, <u>the</u> <u>sky</u> <u>became</u> <u>a</u> *frightening gray*.

With this construction, the sky is the focus.

Parallel Structure: Trod the Straight and Narrow

Parallel structure means putting ideas of the same rank in the same grammatical structure. Your writing and speech should have parallel words, phrases, and clauses. Parallel structure gives your writing many admirable strengths, including the following:

You Could Look It Up

Parallel structure means putting ideas of the same rank in the same grammatical structure. You can have parallel words, phrases, and clauses.

- ◆ Rhythm
- ◆ Emphasis
- ◆ Balance
- ◆ Impact
- ◆ Crispness
- ◆ Conciseness

Here's how to create parallel words, phrases, and clauses:

- ◆ *Parallel words* share the same part of speech (such as nouns, adjectives, or verbs) and tense (if the parallel words are verbs).

  - ◆ My date was *obnoxious, loud,* and *cheap;* no doubt he thought I was *gorgeous, personable,* and *witty.*

  - ◆ We *pleaded, begged,* and *prayed*—to no avail.

- ◆ *Parallel phrases* create an underlying rhythm in your speech and writing, as these examples show:

  - ◆ "For taking away our Charters, abolishing our laws, and altering the Forms of our Government ..." (Declaration of Independence)

  - ◆ "Now the trumpet summons us again—not as a call to bear arms, though arms we need—not as a call to battle, though embattled we are—but a call to bear the burden of a long twilight struggle ..." (John F. Kennedy's inauguration speech)

- ◆ *Parallel clauses* can give your writing balance as well. For instance:

  - ◆ "Let every nation know, whether it wishes us well or ill, that we shall pay any price, bear any burden, meet any hardship, support any friend, oppose any foe to assure the survival and success of liberty." (John F. Kennedy's inauguration speech)

  - ◆ "Our chiefs are killed; Looking-Glass is dead; Ta-Hool-Shute is dead." (Chief Joseph's surrender speech, 1877)

Take My Word for It _____

Some of the world's most famous documents and speeches derive power from parallel structure. In his famous 1963 speech on the steps of the Lincoln Memorial, for example, Dr. Martin Luther King Jr. created an enduring statement with these parallel phrases: "I have a dream that one day every valley shall be exalted, every hill and mountain shall be made low, the rough places will be made plains, and the crooked places will be made straight, and the glory of the Lord shall be revealed, and all flesh shall see it together."

Make It So

Be sure to brush after every meal, wear clean underwear in case you are in a car accident, and use matching forms to create parallel structure. Here are some examples to show how creating parallel structure can improve your oral hygiene, raise your social status, and make your writing better:

Not parallel: To avoid getting hit by lightning, never seek protection under a tree, lying down on wet ground, or not staying on a bike.

Parallel: To avoid getting hit by lightning, never seek protection under a tree, lie down on wet ground, or stay on a bike.

Because the phrases "match," the sentence sounds smoother and more logical.

Not parallel: During a thunderstorm, people who are inside should not talk on the telephone, standing near open windows, and using large appliances.

Parallel: During a thunderstorm, people who are inside should not talk on the telephone, stand near open windows, or use large appliances.

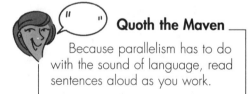

Quoth the Maven _____

Because parallelism has to do with the sound of language, read sentences aloud as you work.

Now that it's parallel, this sentence is balanced and less wordy.

Time to Face Old Sparky

Revise each of the following sentences so the elements are parallel. Write your answers on the lines provided.

1. Groucho Marx said to one of his leading ladies: "Martha, dear, there are many bonds that will hold us together through eternity: your savings bonds, the bonds that are called Liberty bonds, and the bonds you get from the government."

   _____

   _____

2. In addition to being a puppeteer, the late Jim Henson was also a painter, an artist skilled with animation, and someone who liked to sculpt clay.

   _____

   _____

3. Contrary to legend, Ringo Starr never sang, "She's 16, she has beauty, and she belongs to me."

   _____

   _____

4. The typical member of the Book-of-the-Month Club is well educated, his or her age is about 40, a Democrat (moderate variety).

   _____

   _____

5. If you happen to be stranded at sea with a group and you see a shark, bunch together to form a tight circle, warned to be using shark repellent, staying dressed, and be sure to float as a good way to save energy.

   _____

   _____

Answers

Possible responses:

1. Groucho Marx said to one of his leading ladies: "Martha, dear, there are many bonds that will hold us together through eternity: your savings bonds, Liberty bonds, and government bonds."

2. In addition to being a puppeteer, the late Jim Henson was also a painter, animator, and sculptor.

3. Contrary to legend, Ringo Starr never sang, "She's 16, she's beautiful, and she's mine."

4. The typical member of the Book-of-the Month Club is well educated, about 40 years old, and a moderate Democrat.

5. If you happen to be stranded at sea with a group and you see a shark, bunch together to form a tight circle, use shark repellent, stay dressed, and float to save energy.

The Least You Need to Know

◆ Sentence coordination links ideas of equal importance.

◆ Sentence subordination connects two unequal but related clauses with a subordinating conjunction to form a complex sentence.

◆ Parallel structure means putting ideas of the same rank in the same grammatical structure.

◆ Use 'em all to create logical, concise, and graceful writing.

Part 4

Tools of the Trade

If you need to get a nail into a wall, you'll probably reach for a hammer rather than a tire iron, toaster, or socket wrench. A jack is the tool of choice when you're changing a tire; cleavers work great to dice celery. Most tools are so simply labeled that there's no choice at all: Even I know that a screwdriver goes with screws, for instance.

Life is not as simple for writers and their tools, however. Not only are there many different writing tools to choose from, but the ones you select can have a great influence on the quality and style of your writing.

In addition to pens and computers, writers work with punctuation, capitalization, abbreviations, and spelling rules. That's what this part is all about.

The Writer's Tools: Round Up the Usual Suspects

In This Chapter

◆ Learn how to use a dictionary

◆ See what a thesaurus can offer you

◆ Check out computerized writing aids

Most people write with a pen, many write with a computer, and a few holdouts still write with a typewriter. All good writers use dictionaries and reference books. How can each of these help you to write better? That's what you find out in this chapter. So let's go shopping for some essential writing equipment.

Pencil Pusher

The Canterbury Tales, The Count of Monte Cristo, and *Candide* were written longhand. So were *Dracula, Don Quixote,* and the *Divine Comedy.* Pen-and-paper writers have a long and illustrious history. How can you tell if writing with a pen and paper is for you? Fill out this easy questionnaire by putting a check next to each answer that describes your writing style.

_____ 1. You type 2,500,000 words per minute—blindfolded.

_____ 2. You have many fingers. Unfortunately, they are all thumbs.

_____ 3. You can assemble a nuclear reactor, intercept messages from Venus on your short-wave radio, and program a VCR.

_____ 4. You can sharpen a pencil.

_____ 5. You can sit at a workstation and type for so long that your rear end assumes the shape of the chair.

_____ 6. You can write in a bubble bath until you turn into a prune.

_____ 7. Your friends call you a computer nerd.

_____ 8. Your friends call you a Luddite.

_____ 9. You own an espresso machine the size of a compact car, a car that cost more than the GNP of a small Latin American country, and a watch that shows the time on Pluto (in binary).

_____ 10. You have a rotary phone.

Answers

If you checked 1, 3, 5, 7, and 9: Beam me up, Scottie.

If you checked 2, 4, 6, 8, and 10: Bet you still bake from scratch, too.

What do your answers to this quiz reveal? As much as possible, you should tailor your choice of writing tools to your personal needs and society's conventions. Many people are less willing to self-edit their writing when they use a pencil or pen because it takes a long time by hand and "looks messy." If you have any proficiency with typing, computers allow much greater variation in style (not to mention the advantage of spell checkers). But if you're intimidated by a computer, using one might inhibit your writing—especially if a computer has ever swallowed one of your documents!

Good manners still dictate that letters of condolence, congratulation, or other personal messages be handwritten; business documents, in contrast, must be prepared on a computer. Select the method that works for you, within the constraints of society's conventions and your job.

Using the Dictionary: You Could Look It Up

Life was simpler in the past. Grandma had orthopedic shoes, not Rollerblades; bacon was considered a healthful food. Children were seen but not heard. Okay, okay—so what if the only residents of this mythical land were Wally and the Beaver?

Life might never have been that simple, but English was certainly less complex a few generations ago. The emergence of English as a global language has accelerated the speed with which it changes. Thank goodness for dictionary editors, those wonderful folks who help us understand the most current usage of words in the language. Actually, dictionaries give us a lot more than a list of words and their meanings. A good dictionary can be as useful as a good shrink, only a whole lot cheaper.

Who You Gonna Call?

Here's the information you can get from a dictionary:

- Spelling

- Word division (syllabication)

- Pronunciation

- Part of speech

- Word histories

- Meaning

- Examples of the word in context

- Synonyms

- Antonyms

- Idioms that include the word

- Usage labels

> **Quoth the Maven**
>
> A good dictionary will give spelling variations, especially British versus American spelling.

word division
(syllabification) pronunciation

spelling | part of speech

word meanings — al*pha (al'f ə), n. 1. the first letter of the Greek alphabet (A,a). 2. the first; beginning. 3. (*cap.*) *Astron.* the brightest star in a constellation. 4. *Chem.* a. one of the possible positions of an atom or group in a compound. b. one of two or more isometric compounds. [< L < Gk < a Phoenician word; cf. Heb. *alph* ox]

history

An entry in a good dictionary tells you much more than the definition of a word.

Let's look at a typical dictionary entry and what it offers. This entry provides much of the information previously listed.

Read the Labels

A dictionary's usage labels explain how, where, and when a word has been used in speech and writing. As you learned in Chapter 1, there are different levels of usage, including formal and informal, standard and nonstandard.

You should always use the words that suit your audience and purpose. Look at the different usage labels you'll find in the dictionary.

Label	Meaning	Example
Colloquial	Used in conversation and informal writing	*dad* (for *father*)
Slang	Not standard usage	*rad, phat*
Obsolete	No longer used	*owe* used to mean "to possess" This meaning is now obsolete.
Archaic	No longer used except in a special phrase	*quick* used to mean "living"; now it's used that way only in the phrase "the quick and the dead"
Dialect	Restricted to certain geographic groups	*ain't*
Poetic	used in literature, not everyday speech	*o'er* (for *over*)

Shop 'Till You Drop

Fortunately, buying a dictionary is nowhere as difficult as buying a well-fitting pair of jeans or a reliable gigolo. It's also a lot cheaper.

To make your shopping trip easier, here are five of the standard *abridged dictionaries* you might want to consider. Compare them to see which one best suits your needs.

- ◆ *Webster's New World Dictionary of the American Language.* This dictionary has a contemporary American emphasis. Here's what this volume contains:

  - ◆ Definitions listed in chronological order, the earliest first

  - ◆ Extensive word histories, synonyms, and usage notes

  - ◆ Proper names, place names, abbreviations, and foreign phrases in the main listings

◆ ***Webster's New Collegiate Dictionary (latest edition).*** This dictionary includes about 160,000 entries and emphasizes what it calls "standard language." It contains the following features:

  ◆ Full word histories, with the most recent meaning listed last

  ◆ Extensive lists of synonyms and illustrative quotations

  ◆ Foreign words and phrases, biographical and geographical names

  ◆ A manual of style

◆ ***The American Heritage Dictionary.*** This dictionary includes about 200,000 entries. It differs from most dictionaries in that it presents the most contemporary meaning of the word first, rather than arranging the meanings historically. Here are some other special features:

  ◆ Extensive usage notes that reflect the opinions of a panel of language experts

  ◆ Many photographs, illustrations, and maps

  ◆ Foreign words

  ◆ Names of mythological and legendary figures

Take My Word for It

You will find that several dictionaries claim the name *Webster's*, after the early American lexicographer Noah Webster. Because his name is in the public domain and not copyrighted, it's fair game for one and all.

◆ ***The Concise Oxford Dictionary of Current English.*** Here's what it includes along with the standard features:

  ◆ Current usage and illustrative quotations

  ◆ Many scientific and technical terms

  ◆ Colloquial and slang expressions

  ◆ British as well as American spellings

Danger, Will Robinson

An old dictionary is like pictures of your high school sweeties—nice to have around but of little practical use. Unless you're a dictionary collector, replace your dictionary every 10 years—if not sooner.

There are no pictures.

◆ ***The Random House College Dictionary.*** With more than 150,000 entries, this is a very complete reference. The most common usage of the word is listed first. Here are the special features:

   ◆ Informal and slang usage

   ◆ Synonyms and antonyms

   ◆ Technical words

   ◆ A brief manual of style in the back of the book

Take My Word for It _____

The Oxford English Dictionary is the standard unabridged dictionary. It contains more than 500,000 entries. Don't rush right out to buy one to stash in your briefcase, however; it attempts to record the birth and history of every printed word in the language since about 1000 C.E. to the current date of publication. The *OED* now contains about 60 million words in 20 volumes.

Specialized Dictionaries: Everyone's an Expert

The standard abridged and *unabridged dictionaries* can provide you with a ton of information. But there are times when you need a bit of specialized language and writing information. Help is only a book away—try the following specialized dictionaries.

Take My Word for It _____

An **unabridged dictionary** is complete. An **abridged dictionary** is shortened. It is fine for everyday purposes, like looking up words and silencing howling cats. You'll want the unabridged dictionary if you're interested in knowing everything there is to know about a word or filling an entire bookshelf. (An unabridged dictionary looks like a set of encyclopedias!)

◆ Dictionaries of usage

   ◆ *A Dictionary of Contemporary Usage*, ed. Bergan Evans and Cornelia Evans

   ◆ *Dictionary of Modern English Usage*, ed. H. W. Fowler

   ◆ *Modern American Usage*, ed. Jacques Barzun

◆ Dictionaries of word origins

   ◆ *Dictionary of Word and Phrase Origins*, ed. William Morris and Mary Morris

   ◆ *Origins: A Short Etymological Dictionary of Modern English*, ed. Eric Partridge

- Dictionaries of slang and usage
  - *The New Dictionary of American Slang*, ed. Robert Chapman
  - *Dictionary of Slang and Unconventional English*, ed. Eric Partridge
- Dictionaries of regional and foreign terms
  - *Dictionary of American Regional English*, ed. Frederic Cassidy
  - *Dictionary of Foreign Phrases and Abbreviations*, ed. Kevin Guinagh

You Could Look It Up

Etymologies are word histories.

Computer Spell Checkers: Marvels of Technology

Computer *spell-check programs* call attention to any words that they cannot match to their own dictionary. As a result, the programs are a great help in spotting typos. They are included with nearly all word processing packages.

But like all good things, these spell-check programs have limits. They are useless with homonyms, for example. If you intended to type "there" but instead wrote "they're," the spell checker does not pick this up as an error because you spelled "they're" correctly. Therefore, you must still proofread your documents carefully to make sure that you used the words you intended to use. The following poem illustrates my point:

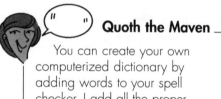

Quoth the Maven

You can create your own computerized dictionary by adding words to your spell checker. I add all the proper nouns I use regularly, for example.

> Who wood have guest
> The Spell Chequer would super seed
> The assent of the editor
> Who was once a mane figure?
> Once, awl sought his council;
> Now nun prophet from him.
> How suite the job was;
> It was all sew fine …
> Never once was he board
> As he edited each claws,
> Going strait to his deer work
> Where he'd in cyst on clarity.
> Now he's holy unacceptable,

Take My Word for It

Computerized grammar-check programs can catch many of these "spelling" problems, however. Of course, these grammar programs are not without their own problems. More on the advantages and disadvantages of computerized grammar-check programs in the next section of this chapter.

Useless and knot kneaded …
This is know miner issue,
For he cannot urn a wage.
Two this he takes a fence,
Butt nose naught watt too due.
He's wade each option
Of jobs he mite dew,
But nothing peaks his interest
Like making pros clear.
Sum will see him silly
For being sew upset,
But doesn't good righting
Go beyond the write spelling?

Electronic Grammar Software: Help Is Only a Button Away

Dishwashers, Dustbusters, electric vibrators: What *will* they think of next? How about computerized grammar checkers?

Computerized grammar checkers are software programs that flag errors or doubtful usage in a passage so that you can correct these writing problems. They will catch errors in voice, sentence boundaries (run-ons and fragments), and so on. The best programs average about 36 percent accuracy. This low accuracy rate means they're not good enough to substitute for a thorough knowledge of the rules of grammar and usage.

Different grammar programs catch different errors, so you'll get better results using two separate programs together. But even the best programs flag as errors some things that are not, in fact, wrong. This is especially true with documents that have a less formal tone, such as this book. A grammar checker would go berserk with some of the words, phrases, and sentence constructions used here.

My advice: If your knowledge of grammar and usage is very shaky, use at least two good grammar programs to catch the whoppers. However, be very much aware that no grammar program now available is an effective substitute for knowing your stuff.

Danger, Will Robinson

Be careful with computerized grammar programs because they can homogenize your style, stripping away individuality. For instance, many of these programs strive to eliminate the passive voice. Now, in general, the passive voice is about as welcome as bad breath, but the passive voice does have some definite advantages in some instances. So does bad breath. See Chapter 5 for more on passive voice.

The Thesaurus: War of the Words

Aching to increase your vocabulary? Want to learn more words to express yourself with greater ease and accuracy? I know you do, because you realize that accuracy of word choice is a big part of perfecting your writing style. The more precisely you use words, the more clearly you can express yourself, in speech as well as writing.

Using a *thesaurus* is an invaluable aid in your quest to learn more words. It's just as useful for helping you correctly use the words you already know. A thesaurus is especially helpful when you're looking for a word with just the right shade of meaning: its denotation and connotation.

All words carry *denotations*, their dictionary meaning. Some words, however, also carry *connotations*, emotional overtones that shade the word's meaning. For example, *thrifty* has a positive connotation, but *parsimonious* has a negative connotation. However, both words have the same denotation: "careful with money." *House* does not have a connotation, but *home* (which has the same denotation as house), carries connotations of warmth and welcome.

You Could Look It Up

A **thesaurus** is a dictionary of synonyms and antonyms. A word's **denotations** are its dictionary meanings. A word's **connotations** are its emotional overtones. All words have denotations; only some words have connotations.

Take this simple quiz to see how good you are at finding a word's connotation. Write + if the word has a positive connotation, – if the word has a negative connotation, and 0 if the word has no connotation.

Word	Connotation
_____	1. thin
_____	2. slender
_____	3. emaciated
_____	4. plump
_____	5. obese
_____	6. bold
_____	7. intrepid
_____	8. insolent
_____	9. proud
_____	10. noble

Answers

Did you get these answers?

1. thin 0

2. slender +

3. emaciated –

4. plump +

5. obese –

6. bold +

7. intrepid +

8. insolent –

9. proud +

10. noble +

Let's Go Shopping

As you use a thesaurus, be sure that you select words that have the connotations that you want. That said, here are two standard dictionaries of synonyms:

◆ *The New Roget's Thesaurus of the English Language in Dictionary Form*

◆ *Webster's Dictionary of Synonyms*

Whiz-Bang Thesaurus Programs

As with a print thesaurus, computerized thesaurus programs present a list of synonyms and antonyms for your consideration. In many instances these are useful programs, but the list of choices is limited. I've never found computerized thesaurus programs to be an adequate replacement for a nice big fat print thesaurus. Until the computer brains come out with a computerized thesaurus that resembles a dinner menu, I'm still browsing through my printed thesaurus.

The Least You Need to Know

◆ Writers need tools, including a dictionary and a thesaurus.

◆ You might want to use some computerized sources, too.

Chapter 16

Punctuation: Commas Are Our Friends

In This Chapter

- Get the nuts and bolts of punctuation
- Finally distinguish between semicolons and colons
- Learn that a hyphen is not a dash and parentheses are not brackets

Using the correct punctuation is more than following the grammar rules—correct punctuation enables your audience to understand your ideas more clearly. Like traffic signals, punctuation keeps your ideas flowing in the right direction.

Hey, you already know all this—you just want to know how to tell the difference between a dash and a hyphen, what on earth you do with an ellipsis, and what relationship a semicolon has to J. Lo. (No, they were never married … at least not yet.) So sharpen your pencil; we're ready to boogie.

Punctuation Matters

The following two letters contain the same exact words—but the punctuation differs sharply. Which letter would you rather receive?

Dear John:

I want a man who knows what love is all about. You are generous, kind, thoughtful. People who are not like you admit to being useless and inferior. You have ruined me for other men. I yearn for you. I have no feelings whatsoever when we're apart. I can forever be happy—will you let me be yours?

Harriet

Dear John:

I want a man who knows what love is. All about you are generous, kind, thoughtful people, who are not like you. Admit to being useless and inferior. You have ruined me. For other men, I yearn. For you, I have no feelings whatsoever. When we're apart, I can forever be happy. Will you let me be?

Yours,

Harriet

These letters tell us a lot about John and Harriet—but they tell us even more about the importance of punctuation. Change a comma here, move a period there … and the entire document is different. *That's* why punctuation matters; it creates meaning as much as words do.

Show Me the Money

I'll bet that you know a lot more than you think about the correct way to use standard punctuation. To prove it, I'm going to ask you to take this simple quiz. In each case, write C if the punctuation is correct or W if the punctuation is incorrect. Answers and explanations follow.

Two men (1) ___ , sentenced to die in the electric chair on the same day (2) ___ , were led to the room in which they would meet their maker. The priest had given the last rites (3) ___ the warden had given the formal speech, and the participants had said a final prayer.

The warden, turning to the first man, solemnly asked (4) ___ "Son (5) ___ , do you have a last request (6) ___ ?"

The man replied, "Yes sir, I do (7) ___ . I love dance music. Could you please play the Chicken Dance for me one last time?"

(8) ___ Certainly (9) ___ ," replied the Warden. He turned to the other man and asked, "Well (10) ___ , what about you, son? What is your final request?"

"Please kill me first," replied the other man.

Answers

1. C (use a comma to set off nonessential information)

2. C (use a comma to set off nonessential information)

3. W (comma needed to set off introductory clause)

4. W (comma needed before a direct quotation)

5. C (use a comma to set off a word of direct address)

6. C (use a question mark to indicate a question; place it inside the quotation marks)

7. C (use a period to indicate the end of a statement)

8. W (use quotation marks to set off dialogue)

9. C (use a comma to set off dialogue)

10. C (use a comma to set off interrupting expressions)

So how did you do?

8 to 10 correct	Were you a proofreader in a past life?
5 to 7 correct	There's no reason to hide under the bed when you see a semicolon.
4 to 6 correct	I can help you, baby, I really can.
1 to 3 correct	You love the Chicken Dance, you say?

Period, Question Mark, Exclamation Mark: The End of the Line

The period, question mark, and exclamation mark are the Three Musketeers of punctuation: all for one and one for all. Here's why:

♦ They are all end marks; that is, they are used at the end of a sentence.

♦ All three marks of punctuation have the same function: to indicate a full stop.

♦ They all show the end of a complete thought.

♦ They can all prevent run-on sentences, as you learned in Chapter 14.

Okay, so maybe they're not the Three Musketeers, but at least they're not the Three Stooges, Three Amigos, or the Three Bears. Let's look at these three end marks more closely.

The Period: Do Not Pass Go, Do Not Collect $200

The period is the workhorse of punctuation. Like a great dessert, it's always welcome at the end. Here's how to use periods:

- Use a period after a complete sentence.

  Example: A hangover is the wrath of grapes.

- Use a period after a command.

  Example: Please close the door behind you.

- Use a period after most abbreviations.

  Examples: Dr., Ms., Jr.

- Don't use a period after the individual letters in an acronym. For example, write NATO, not N.A.T.O.

- Use a period after an initial.

  Example: John F. Kennedy

- Use a period after each Roman numeral, letter, or number in an outline.

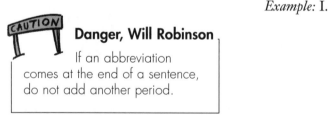

Example: I.

Danger, Will Robinson

If an abbreviation comes at the end of a sentence, do not add another period.

A.

B.

1.

2.

- Always place a period inside a quotation mark that ends a sentence.

  Example: The sign read, "A pest is a friend in need."

The Question Mark: Inquiring Minds Want to Know

You know the rules for life: Never wear white shoes after Labor Day, brush after every meal, and avoid making rude noises in public. Here, then, are the rules for using question marks.

◆ Use a question mark after a question.

Example: Isn't the Mason-Dixon line what separates y'all from youse guys?

◆ Place the question mark inside of closing quotation marks if it *is* part of the quotation.

Example: In a dream, I heard someone asking, "Isn't atheism a nonprophet organization?"

◆ Place the question mark outside of the closing quotation marks if it *is not* part of the quotation.

Example: Was it your mother who said, "The Lord prefers common-looking people; that's the reason he made so many of them"? (In such a circumstance, it's okay to drop the period from the quotation.)

Exclamation Marks: Gosh and Golly!

In speech, exclamations are used freely, especially in moments of high passion, as when the dishwasher overflows at 11 P.M. on a Saturday night. In writing, however, it is far more convincing to create emphasis by the force of your words rather than the force of your punctuation. But there will be occasions to use exclamation marks, so here are some guidelines to follow.

◆ Use an exclamation mark after an exclamatory sentence.

Example: "Apparent" is a large, old bossy person who tortures youth!

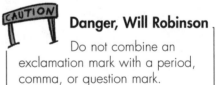

Danger, Will Robinson

Do not combine an exclamation mark with a period, comma, or question mark.

The Pause That Refreshes

Following are some questions and answers submitted to an advice columnist. The advice is confusing because the periods, question marks, and exclamation marks are missing. Add them as needed.

1. I've been going steady with this man for six years We see each other every night He says he loves me, and I know I love him, but he never mentions marriage Do you think he's going out with me just for what he can get

   Signed, Baffled in Boston.

2. Dear Baffled: I don't know What's he getting

3. Are birth control pills deductible

   Signed, Confused in Cleveland

4. Dear Confused: Only if they don't work

5. Is it possible for a man to be in love with two women at the same time

   Signed Perplexed in Pittsburgh

6. Dear Pittsburgh: Yes, and also dangerous

7. Our son was married in June Five months later his wife had a 10-pound baby girl They said the baby was premature Tell me, can a baby this big be that early

   Wondering in Walla-Walla

8. Dear Wondering: The baby was on time, but the wedding was late

Answers

1. I've been going steady with this man for six years. We see each other every night. He says he loves me, and I know I love him, but he never mentions marriage. Do you think he's going out with me just for what he can get?

   Signed, Baffled in Boston.

2. Dear Baffled: I don't know. What's he getting?

3. Are birth control pills deductible?

   Signed, Confused in Cleveland

4. Dear Confused: Only if they don't work.

5. Is it possible for a man to be in love with two women at the same time?

   Signed, Perplexed in Pittsburgh

6. Dear Pittsburgh: Yes, and also dangerous.

7. Our son was married in June. Five months later his wife had a 10-pound baby girl. They said the baby was premature. Tell me, can a baby this big be that early?

   Wondering in Walla-Walla

8. Dear Wondering: The baby was on time, but the wedding was late.

The Comma: A Major Player

Punctuation helps readers identify clusters of words between and within sentences. Between sentences, the most common mark of punctuation is the period; within sentences, the most common mark is the comma.

Commas tell us how to read and understand sentences because they tell us where to pause. A correctly placed comma helps move readers from the beginning of a sentence to the end. A misplaced comma can create more confusion than a conversation with a teenager.

Here are the guidelines that govern comma use.

First Impressions Count

Use a comma after introductory and concluding expressions:

- Use a comma after an introductory prepositional phrase. In each sentence, the introductory phrase is underlined.

  Example: <u>Along the route from the house to the woods</u>, Hansel and Gretel left a trail of old lottery tickets.

- Use a comma after an introductory participial phrase.

  Example: <u>Excited by their approach</u>, the witch called her agent and decided to take a meeting.

- Use a comma after an introductory subordinate clause.

  Example: <u>When Hansel and Gretel arrived</u>, they were astonished to find the TV contract already prepared.

- Use a comma after the greeting of an informal letter.

  Examples: Dear Sammi, Dear Mudface,

- Use a comma after phrases that show contrast.

  Example: The neighbors return home at all hours, <u>often drunk as skunks</u>.

- Use a comma at the close of any letter.

  Examples: Yours truly, Sincerely, Yours until Niagara falls,

 Quoth the Maven

Basically, commas are like spicy chilies or little children: A little goes a long way. The last thing you want are excess commas hovering over your writing like the Goodyear blimp over the Orange Bowl.

Sentence Interruptus

Use a comma after interrupting words and expressions.

◆ Use a comma to set off interrupting words and expressions. The interrupting words are underlined in the following example.

Example: Windows, <u>as you know</u>, is the best $89 solitaire game you can buy.

◆ Use a comma to set off *words of direct address* (words that tell to whom a remark is addressed). The words in direct address are underlined in the following example.

Example: <u>Mr. Happy</u>, did you know that "kitty litter" is throwing cats out a car window?

◆ Use a comma with names and titles.

Example: Mr. Gary Goldstein, Editor

You Could Look It Up

Words in apposition give additional information about the preceding or following word or expression.

Danger, Will Robinson

Never use commas to set off an essential clause, a clause that cannot be omitted. For example: Philosophy is the science that lets us be unhappy more intelligently.

Take My Word for It

The comma before *and* in a series of items is optional.

◆ Use a comma to set off *words in apposition* (words that give additional information about the preceding or following word or expression). The words in apposition are underlined in the following examples.

Example: <u>A light sleeper</u>, my landlord is the first to awake when he hears the chains rattle.

Example: My landlord, <u>a light sleeper</u>, is the first to awake when he hears the chains rattle.

◆ Use a comma to set off a *nonessential clause* (a clause that can be omitted without changing the sentence's basic meaning). The nonessential clause in underlined in the following example.

Example: Philosophy, <u>a science that lets us be unhappy more intelligently</u>, is being offered this semester at the local university.

◆ Use a comma to separate items in a series.

Example: We bought marshmallows, graham crackers, and chocolate to make those delicious campfire treats.

In Media Res

Use a comma to set off parts of a sentence:

- Use a comma to separate parts of a compound sentence. Use the comma before the coordinating conjunction. Remember: The coordinating conjunctions are *and*, *but*, *or*, *nor*, *for*, *so*, and *yet*. The coordinating conjunction is underlined in the following example.

  Example: The faucet stopped working, <u>and</u> the sink leaks.

 Danger, Will Robinson

Do not use a comma before the ZIP Code in an address. Also, on an envelope, the Post Office prefers no comma after the city, either. Just two spaces between both the city/state and state/ZIP.

- Use a comma to set off a direct quotation.

  Example: He said, "Lawyers are the larval form of politicians."

  Example: "Lawyers," he said, "are the larval form of politicians."

- Use a comma to separate the parts of an address.

  Example: She lives at 763 Main Street, Farmingdale, New York 11735.

Dazed and Confused

Use commas to prevent misreading:

- Use a comma to clarify any potentially confusing sentences.

  Huh: To get through a tunnel must be dug.

  Revised: To get through, a tunnel must be dug.

Of course, you're usually much better off just revising the sentences so there is no possibility of a chowderhead misreading your words.

Bean Counters

Use commas with numbers:

- Use a comma between the day of the month and the year.

  Examples: December 7, 1941, July 20, 1969

 **Danger, Will Robinson**

Do not use commas when writing telephone numbers, page numbers, or years.

♦ Use commas to show thousands, millions, and so on.

Examples: 1,000; 10,000; 100,000; 1,000,000

Constant Commas

Add commas as necessary in the following sentences.

1. Even though it is not among the top rated shows shown on a single night *The Wizard of Oz* is generally considered the most successful single program in TV history.

2. My friend Stephan a very picky eater refuses to eat any vegetables at all.

3. A child who is under the age of eight should not be left alone without a sitter.

4. A mature child of 10 or 11 however can usually be trusted home alone.

5. Among the top man-made attractions in the United States are the Golden Gate Bridge Mount Rushmore the Statue of Liberty and Hoover Dam.

6. Let's find a fast cheap restaurant.

7. The Academy Awards were first telecast on March 19 1953.

8. No you can't pile up 10000 bricks and try to climb to the roof.

Answers

1. Even though it is not among the top rated shows shown on a single night, *The Wizard of Oz* is generally considered the most successful single program in TV history.

2. My friend Stephan, a very picky eater, refuses to eat any vegetables at all.

3. No commas at all.

4. A mature child of 10 or 11, however, can usually be trusted home alone.

5. Among the top man-made attractions in the United States are the Golden Gate Bridge, Mount Rushmore, the Statue of Liberty, and Hoover Dam.

6. Let's find a fast, cheap restaurant.

7. The Academy Awards were first telecast on March 19, 1953.

8. No, you can't pile up 10,000 bricks and try to climb to the roof.

The Semicolon: Love Child of the Comma and the Period

People are irrationally frightened of semicolons. I can understand being terrified of your mother and Pee Wee Herman, but semicolons? Pleeeze. These little guys wouldn't hurt a flea, even if they fell on it.

◆ Use a semicolon between closely related independent clauses.

  Example: Bigamy is one wife too many; monogamy is the same idea.

◆ Use a semicolon between main clauses when the coordinating conjunction has been left out.

  Example: She planned to dye her hair purple; however, the store was out of grape Jell-O so she decided to pierce her navel instead.

◆ Use a semicolon to join independent clauses when one or both clauses contains a comma.

  Example: After the sheep was cloned, the cows tried calling the tabloids; but they didn't get through.

◆ Use a semicolon between main clauses connected by conjunctive adverbs such as *however, nevertheless, moreover, for example,* and *consequently.*

  Example: Cloning sheep is a good idea; however, cloning ex-spouses, English teachers, or Freddy Kruger is not.

Take My Word for It

Place semicolons outside closing quotation marks. For example: We read "Tell-Tale Heart"; we refuse to sleep alone again.

The Colon: What a Party Animal

Even though the semicolon and the colon walk alike and talk alike, they are not alike. Unlike those annoying twins Patty and Cathy, the colon and the semicolon are not interchangeable. Here's how to use the colon.

◆ Use a colon before a list.

  Example: The new ice-cream parlor offered a choice of the following flavors of the month: chicken fat ripple, pork and beans, and prime rib chip.

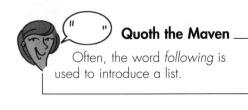

Quoth the Maven

Often, the word *following* is used to introduce a list.

Take My Word for It

Place colons outside closing quotation marks.

◆ Use a colon before a long quotation, especially a formal one.

Example: Abraham Lincoln said: "Four score and seven years ago our fathers brought forth upon this continent a new nation, conceived in liberty and dedicated to the proposition that all men are created equal."

◆ Use a colon before part of a sentence that explains what has just been stated.

Example: Life is a series of rude awakenings: It is what happens to you while you are making other plans.

◆ Use a colon after the salutation of a business letter.

Examples: Dear Mr. President:, To Whom It May Concern:

◆ Use a colon to distinguish chapter from verse in a biblical citation, hours from minutes, titles from subtitles.

Example: Song of Songs 4:15

Semi-Tough

Add semicolons and colons as needed to complete each sentence.

1. Old postal carriers never die they just lose their zip.

2. Documented sightings of UFOs go back a long time in fact, the first sightings were reported in 1896.

3. Woodrow Wilson appears on the $100,000 bill Grover Cleveland appears on the $1,000 bill.

4. There are four dimensions width length depth and time.

5. Old magicians never die they just lose their hare.

6. Here's a fascinating fact about the writer Mark Twain Halley's Comet appeared when he was born in 1835 and again when he died, in 1910.

Answers

1. Old postal carriers never die; they just lose their zip.

2. Documented sightings of UFOs go back a long time; in fact, the first sightings were reported in 1896.

3. Woodrow Wilson appears on the $100,000 bill; Grover Cleveland appears on the $1,000 bill.

4. There are four dimensions: width, length, depth, and time.

5. Old magicians never die; they just lose their hare.

6. Here's a fascinating fact about the writer Mark Twain: Halley's Comet appeared when he was born in 1835, and again when he died, in 1910.

Quotation Marks: Quote/Unquote

Nothing spices up your writing like a few juicy quotations. Just consider what a letter would be like without a little dialogue—as dry as rice cakes. Here's how to use these cute little partners in crime.

♦ Use quotation marks to set off a speaker's exact words.

  Example: "Is that person a man or a woman?" we asked.

♦ Use quotation marks to set off the titles of short works such as poems, essays, songs, short stories, and magazine articles.

  Example: "The Rime of the Ancient Mariner"

♦ Use single quotation marks to set off quoted material or the titles of short works within a quotation enclosed by double quotation marks.

  Example: As the wit said, "'Health' is the slowest possible rate of dying."

♦ Use quotation marks to set off a definition.

  Example: The word *karaoke* means "So you think you can sing? Think again."

 Quoth the Maven

Place periods and commas inside of the end quotation mark; place colons and semicolons outside of the end quotation mark. Question marks and exclamation marks go inside or outside of the end quotation mark, depending on the meaning.

A Little Dabba Do Ya

Add quotation marks and commas as needed to make sense of the following joke:

There once was a farmer who was raising three daughters on his own. He was very concerned about their well-being and always did his best to watch out for them.

On one particular evening, all three girls were going out on dates. The farmer greeted each young suitor at the door holding his shotgun to show who was boss. The doorbell rang and the first of the boys arrived. The farmer answered the door and the lad said

Hi my name's Joe

I'm here to see Flo.

We're going to the show.

Is she ready to go?

The father looked him over and sent the kids on their way. The next lad arrived and said

My name's Eddie.

I'm here to see Betty.

We're gonna get some spaghetti.

Do you know if she's ready?

The father felt this one was okay so off the two kids went. The final young man arrived and the farmer opened the door. The boy began

Hi my name's Chuck … and the farmer shot him.

Answer

There once was a farmer who was raising three daughters on his own. He was very concerned about their well-being and always did his best to watch out for them.

On one particular evening, all three girls were going out on dates. The farmer greeted each young suitor at the door holding his shotgun to show who was boss. The doorbell rang and the first of the boys arrived. The farmer answered the door and the lad said,

"Hi, my name's Joe,

I'm here to see Flo.

We're going to the show.

Is she ready to go?"

The father looked him over and sent the kids on their way. The next lad arrived and said,

"My name's Eddie.

I'm here to see Betty.

We're gonna get some spaghetti.

Do you know if she's ready?"

The father felt this one was okay, so off the two kids went. The final young man arrived and the farmer opened the door. The boy began,

"Hi, my name's Chuck ..." and the farmer shot him.

Not Separated at Birth: The Dash and the Hyphen (and Let's Add the Ellipsis for Fun)

The dash and the hyphen are like Arnold Schwarzenegger and Danny DeVito: confused so often they are taken for each other. But like these two fine actors, the dash and the hyphen are not the same, no sireee.

- A *hyphen* is one click on the keyboard: –

- A *dash* is two clicks on the keyboard: —

- An ellipsis is three spaced periods: …

Therefore, the dash is twice as long as the hyphen. That's not all; the dash and hyphen have totally different uses. Not to mention the ellipsis.

> **Strictly Speaking**
>
> You could make it through life fine and dandy without a dash, but you'd be the poorer for it. Like argyle socks, the dash shows flair and style. It creates rhythm and emphasis in your writing.

The Dash: Long and Lean

Basically, the dash is used to show emphasis. Here's how:

- Use a dash to show a sudden change of thought.

   Example: An archaeologist—of course I don't mean you—is a person whose career lies in ruins.

◆ Use a dash before a summary of what is stated in the sentence.

Example: Avoiding work, getting liposuction, becoming a finalist in the George Hamilton Cocoa Butter Open—everything depends on that trust fund.

The Hyphen: Short and Sweet

The hyphen, in contrast, is used to show a break in words.

◆ Use a hyphen to show a word break at the end of a line.

Example: When you finish *The Complete Idiot's Guide to Grammar and Style, Second Edition*, your written work will be as sharp as your appearance.

◆ Use a hyphen in certain compound nouns.

Example: great-grandmother

◆ Use hyphens in fractions and in compound numbers from twenty-one to ninety-nine.

Examples: one-half, sixty-six

The Ellipsis: Dot, Dot, Dot

The ellipsis, in contrast, indicates a break in continuity.

◆ Use an ellipsis to show that you have deleted words or sentences from a passage you are quoting.

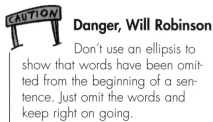

Danger, Will Robinson

Don't use an ellipsis to show that words have been omitted from the beginning of a sentence. Just omit the words and keep right on going.

Example: Abraham Lincoln said: "Four score and seven years ago our fathers brought forth ... a new nation, conceived in liberty and dedicated to the proposition that all men are created equal."

◆ Use an ellipsis to show a pause or interruption.

Example: "No," I said. "I ... I need my space."

Parentheses and Brackets: Bosom Buddies

Like hot dogs and heartburn, parentheses and brackets always come in pairs. But unlike tube steaks and burps, parentheses and brackets are not at all the same.

◆ These are parentheses: ( )

◆ These are brackets: [ ]

You use parentheses much more often than you use brackets. Follow these rules for using these marks of punctuation correctly.

(Parentheses)

Use parentheses to set off nonessential information. In essence, the information in the parentheses is a nonessential modifier; it gives the reader additional information that's by no means crucial.

◆ Use parentheses to enclose additional information in a sentence.

Example: Isn't a *thesaurus* an ancient reptile with an excellent vocabulary (see Chapter 16)?

◆ Use parentheses to enclose numbers or letters.

Example: Recipe for a great day: (1) Drive to the mall; (2) Whip out the charge card; (3) Shop 'til you drop.

[Brackets]

Use brackets for editorial clarification. And editorial clarification only.

◆ Use brackets to enclose a comment that interrupts a direct quotation.

Example: She said, "I helped Richard with his memos [in fact, she wrote them all] when he was pressed for time."

Slash and Burn

This is a slash (/). It's like a *Green Acres* TV marathon; you don't need it often, but when you do, nothing else will fit the bill.

◆ Use slashes to separate lines of poetry. Leave a space before and after the slash to show when the line of poetry ends.

Example: The opening of Robert Frost's poem "Stopping by Woods on a Snowy Evening" goes like this: "Whose woods these are / I think I know, / His house is in the village, though. / He will not see me stopping here / To watch his woods fill up with snow."

◆ Use slashes to show choice.

Example: Be sure to use the right temperature scale (Fahrenheit/Centigrade).

◆ Use slashes in fractions or formulas.

Example: ½, ¾

Apostrophes

The apostrophe (') is used in three ways:

◆ To show possession (ownership)

◆ To show plural forms

◆ To show where a letter or number has been omitted

This is a snap in speech, but in writing it does present difficulties. This is especially true where the three different uses of the apostrophe overlap. The worst offenders are butchers who sell "pork chop's" or "hamburger's." It's still another reason to become a grammarian or a vegetarian.

In the meantime, here are the rules for using apostrophes.

1. Use an apostrophe to show possession.

   ◆ With singular nouns *not* ending in *s*, add an apostrophe and *s*.

   Examples: girl, girl's manuscript; student, student's ideas

   ◆ With singular nouns ending in *s*, add an apostrophe and *s*.

   Examples: Charles, Charles's book; hostess, hostess's menu

   If the new word is hard to say, leave off the *s*. For example: James' book, Louis' menu. You won't get arrested by the grammar police for using your brain.

   ◆ With plural nouns ending in *s*, add an apostrophe after the *s*.

   Examples: girls, girls' manuscript; students, students' ideas

   ◆ With plural nouns *not* ending in *s*, add an apostrophe and *s*.

   Examples: women, women's books; mice, mice's tails

2. Use an apostrophe to show plural forms.

   ◆ Use an apostrophe and *s* to show the plural of a letter.

   Example: Mind your p's and q's.

   ◆ Use an apostrophe and *s* to show the plural of a number.

   Example: Computers will be even more important in the late 1990's.

   ◆ Use an apostrophe and *s* to show the plural of a word referred to as a word.

   Example: There are too many distracting like's and um's in her speech.

3. Use an apostrophe to show where a letter or number has been omitted.

   ◆ To show that letters have been left out of contractions.

   Examples: can't, won't, I'll

   ◆ To show that numbers have been left out of a date.

   Examples: the '70s, the '90s

You Could Look It Up

Contractions are two words combined. When you contract words, add an apostrophe in the space where the letters have been taken out.

Example: does + not = doesn't

Danger, Will Robinson

Don't confuse contractions with possessive pronouns. Study this list.

Contraction	Possessive Pronoun
it's (it is)	its
you're (you are)	your
they're (they are)	their
who's (who is)	whose

Once More, Dear Friends

Rewrite each phrase to use an apostrophe.

Example: the mood of my sister   my sister's mood

1. the talents of Matt Damon   _____

2. the courage of the police officer   _____

3. the liberation of women _____

4. the union of the steelworkers _____

5. the books of Laurie Rozakis _____

6. the wages of the waiters _____

Answers

1. Matt Damon's talents

2 the police officer's courage

3. women's liberation

4. steelworkers' union

5. Laurie Rozakis' books

6. waiters' wages

The Least You Need to Know

◆ Punctuation helps convey the meaning of your sentences to your readers.

◆ Between sentences, the most common mark of punctuation is the period; within sentences, the most common mark is the comma.

◆ Semicolons separate complete sentences; colons introduce lists.

◆ Hyphens separate word parts; dashes separate sentence parts or sentences.

◆ Godzilla is frightening; punctuation isn't.

Chapter 17

Capitalization and Abbreviations: Go to the Head of the Class

In This Chapter

◆ Get the capital idea

◆ Learn to abbrev. the rgt. wds.

The next time you're in Rome, stop by an ancient building or two and check out the inscriptions. You might notice that on the oldest of the old buildings, every letter is capitalized. Eventually, however, the scribes realized that they could fit more on a building (or a page) if the letters were smaller. Their realization became the basis for our capital/lowercase letter system of writing. So we have the ancient Romans to thank for this chapter.

Capitalization: A Capital Idea

In addition to enabling us to fit more letters on a page, a system of capital and lowercase letters serves a far more important purpose: It allows writers to point out specific words within a sentence (such as proper nouns) and to signal the start of a new sentence.

Capital Punishment

How much do you already know about capital letters? I'll bet it's a lot more than you suspect. Take the following simple quiz to see where you stand. On the lines provided, write the words that should be capitalized. Some lines will have one word or more than one word; other lines won't have any words.

(1) There was an orioles fan with really lousy seats (2) at camden yards for the recent playoffs. Looking with (3) his binoculars, he spotted an empty seat right behind (4) the orioles' dugout. thinking to himself, "what a (5) waste," he made his way down to the empty seat. (6) when he arrived at the seat, he asked the man (7) sitting next to it, "is this seat taken?" the man replied, (8) "this was my wife's seat. she passed away. she was a big (9) orioles fan." (10) the other man replied, "i'm sorry to hear of your (11) loss. may i ask why you didn't give the ticket to a (12) friend or a relative?" (13) the man replied, "they're all at the funeral."

Answers

(1) _____

(2) _____

(3) _____

(4) _____

(5) _____

(6) _____

(7) _____

(8) _____

(9) _____

(10) _____

(11) _____

(12) _____

(13) _____

Answers

1. Orioles

2. Camden Yards

3. *none*

4. Orioles, Thinking, What

5. *none*

6. When

7. Is, The

8. This, She, She

9. Orioles

10. The, I'm

11. May, I

12. *none*

13. The, They're

Danger, Will Robinson

When you quote a fragment of dialogue, don't capitalize it, as this example shows: The boss told us the stock performed "like gangbusters."

Rules to Capitalize By

Time to review the rules for clear capitalization. The envelope, please.

◆ Capitalize the first word of:

  ◆ A sentence: It rains on the Spanish plain.

  ◆ A complete sentence after a colon: The fans all realized the same astonishing fact: No NFL team that plays its home games in a domed stadium has ever won a Super Bowl.

  ◆ A quotation, if it is a complete sentence: The child said, "Blood circulates through the body by flowing up one leg and down the other."

  But:

  "Blood," the child said, "circulates through the body by flowing up one leg and down the other."

  ◆ A line of poetry: I think that I shall never see
              A poem lovely as a tree

  ◆ The greeting of a letter: Dear Ms. Ramirez:

  ◆ The first word in the complimentary close of a letter: Sincerely yours, Yours very truly,

◆ Capitalize the first word of each item in an outline:

I. Introduction

    A. Topic sentence

    B. First major point

    C. Second major point

◆ Capitalize the titles of books, plays, newspapers, and magazines:

    ◆ A book title: *The Complete Idiot's Guide to Grammar and Style, Second Edition*

    ◆ A play: *If Pigs Could Fly*

    ◆ A newspaper: *The New York Times*

    ◆ A magazine: *The Atlantic Monthly*

◆ Capitalize titles before a person's name: Dr. Frankenstein, Ms. Steinem

Take My Word for It

When should you capitalize compass points such as *north, south, east,* and *west*? Here's the scoop. Capitalize a compass point when it identifies a specific area of the country, as in this example: "We live in the South." Don't capitalize a compass point when it refers to direction: "The breeze comes from the east."

Strictly Speaking

Should you always capitalize the names of countries and languages? Should it be *french fries* or *French fries*? *spanish omelet* or *Spanish omelet*? Dictionaries vary; no one's in agreement. Here's your rule of thumb: Pick one style and stick with it.

◆ Capitalize abbreviations that appear after a person's name: Dr. Martin Luther King Jr., Laurie Rozakis, Ph.D.

◆ Capitalize titles used in direct address: Doctor, I have a pain in my side.

◆ Capitalize titles of parents and relatives not preceded by a possessive word: We saw Mother kissing Santa Claus. I saw my father with my mother.

◆ Capitalize geographical places and sections of the country: Europe, Asia, United States of America, Lake Erie, Mars, the South

◆ Capitalize the names of specific historical events, eras, and documents: The Civil War, the Renaissance, the Magna Carta

◆ Capitalize the names of languages, nationalities, countries, and races:

    Languages: French, German, Russian

    Nationalities: American, Japanese

    Countries: America, England

    Races: African American, Asian

◆ Capitalize religions and references to the Supreme Being, including the pronouns referring to the Supreme Being:

    Religions: Judaism, Catholicism

    References: the Creator, Him, He, Heaven, His name

◆ Capitalize each part of a person's name: William Jefferson Clinton, Barbra Streisand

◆ Capitalize proper nouns and proper adjectives:

    Proper nouns: Shakespeare, Mexico

    Proper adjectives: Shakespearean, Mexican

In a hyphenated proper adjective, capitalize only the adjective: French-speaking residents

◆ Capitalize brand names and trademarks: Jell-O pudding, Kleenex tissues

◆ Capitalize the names of organizations, institutions, courses, and famous buildings:

    Organizations: The Girl Scouts of America

    Institutions: The United Nations

    Courses: French 101, Mathematics 203 (but not mathematics)

    Buildings: The Empire State Building

◆ Capitalize days, months, and holidays:

    Days: Monday, Tuesday, Wednesday

    Months: February, March, April

    Holidays: Thanksgiving

Danger, Will Robinson

Don't capitalize the prefix attached to a proper adjective unless the prefix refers to a nationality. For example: all-American, Anglo-Saxon.

Danger, Will Robinson

Don't capitalize the words *god* or *goddess* when they refer to ancient mythology, as these examples show: "the goddess Athena, the god Poseidon."

Quoth the Maven

If a last name begins with *Mc*, *O'*, or *St.*, capitalize the next letter as well: *McMannus*, *O'Neill*, *St. Claire*. If the name begins with *la*, *le*, *Mac*, *van*, *von*, *de*, or *D'*, the capitalization varies: *le Blanc* and *Le Blanc* are both correct, for example. Ask the person with that name for clarification.

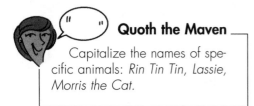

Quoth the Maven

Capitalize the names of specific animals: *Rin Tin Tin, Lassie, Morris the Cat.*

♦ Capitalize abbreviations for time: 6 A.M., 6 P.M.

♦ Capitalize the words "I" and "O": Quickly, I turned around. O! Did you see that?

Capital Investment

Now that you've learned the rules, take a few minutes to apply them to the following sentences. On the lines provided, write all the words that need to be capitalized. Correct the words that have been incorrectly capitalized.

1. how many dolly clones does it take to screw in a Lightbulb? as many as you'd like. as many as you'd like.

   _____

2. how many microsoft Executives does it take to screw in a lightbulb? none—bill gates will just redefine darkness as the Industry Standard.

   _____

3. how many Baby Boomers does it take to screw in a lightbulb? ten—six to talk about how great it is that they've all come together to do this, one to screw it in, one to film it for the News, one to plan a Marketing Strategy based on it, and one to reminisce about the mass naked bulb-screwing of the '60s.

   _____

4. how many surrealists does it take to screw in a lightbulb? fish

   _____

5. how many communists does it take to screw in a lightbulb? one, But it takes him about 30 years to realize that the old one has burned out.

   _____

6. how many ukrainians does it take to screw in a lightbulb? they don't need light bulbs—they glow in the Dark.

   _____

7. the graduate with a Science degree asks, "why does it work?"

   _____

8. the graduate with an Engineering degree asks, "how does it work?"

_____

9. the graduate with an Accounting degree asks, "how much will it cost?"

_____

10. the graduate with a Liberal Arts degree asks, "do you want fries with that?"

_____

Answers

1. How, lightbulb As, As

2. How, Microsoft, executives, None, Bill, Gates, industry standard

3. How, baby, boomers, Ten, news, marketing, strategy

4. How, Surrealists, Fish

5. How, Communists, One, but

6. How, Ukrainians, They, dark

7. The, science, Why

8. The, engineering, How

9. The, accounting, How

10. The, liberal, arts, Do

Abbreviations: Good Things Come in Small Packages

An _abbreviation_ is a shortened form of a word or phrase. Abbreviations start with a capital letter and end with a period. They're a handy way to save time and space when you're writing, but only if you use commonly accepted abbreviations. Otherwise, you'll just confuse your readers. Here's how to use abbreviations correctly.

♦ Abbreviate social titles and titles of rank, both before and after a person's name: Mr.; Mrs.; Ms.; Dr. Laurie Rozakis, Ph.D.

♦ Abbreviate academic degrees: Ramon Torres, B.A. (Bachelor of Arts); Hester Lewis, M.F.A. (Master of Fine Arts)

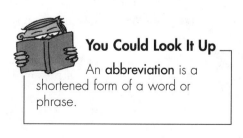

You Could Look It Up

An **abbreviation** is a shortened form of a word or phrase.

The following list shows some of the most commonly abbreviated degrees.

Abbreviations for Academic Degrees

Degree	Abbreviation
Bachelor of Science	B.S.
Bachelor of Arts	B.A.
Bachelor of Business Administration	B.B.A.
Master of Arts	M.A. or A.M.
Master of Science	M.S. or S.M.
Master of Business Administration	M.B.A.
Medical Doctor	M.D.
Doctor of Philosophy	Ph.D.
Doctor of Divinity	D.D.
Doctor of Dental Surgery	D.D.S.
Registered Nurse	R.N.

♦ Abbreviate time: A.M. or a.m. (before noon; *ante meridian*); P.M. or p.m. (after noon; *post meridian*)

Note: These abbreviations are acceptable with and without periods.

Danger, Will Robinson

Never combine the abbreviations *Mr., Mrs.,* or *Ms.* with an abbreviation for a professional or academic title. For example: Laurie Rozakis, Ph.D., *not* Ms. Laurie Rozakis, Ph.D.

Take My Word for It

Because of their Latin roots, abbreviations for many degrees can be written in either direction: M.A. or A.M. for Masters of Arts, for instance.

♦ Abbreviate some historical periods. In most—but not all—cases, the abbreviation is placed after the date:

Ancient times (2,000 years in the past)

B.C. (before the birth of Christ)

B.C.E. (before the Common Era)

Modern times (within the last 2,000 years)

C.E. (Common Era)

A.D. (*Anno Domini,* "in the year of the Lord," an abbreviation that comes before the date)

Here's how these abbreviations are used: Emperor Augustus lived from 63 B.C. (or B.C.E.) to A.D. 14 (or C.E.).

- Abbreviate words associated with addresses or location: I live on Sunset Ave.

- Abbreviate states. Use the official U.S. Postal Service (that's the official name of the good ol' "Post Office") ZIP Code abbreviations: NY (New York), CA (California)

Danger, Will Robinson

The ZIP Code abbreviations for states are not followed by periods. There's a list of all 50 abbreviations in your telephone book.

- Abbreviate some Latin expressions: e.g. (for example), et al. (and others)

- Abbreviate measurements: in. (inches), ft. (feet)

The following list shows some of the most common abbreviations for measurements:

Abbreviations for Measurements

Item	Abbreviation
yards	yd.
miles	mi.
teaspoon	tsp. or t
tablespoon	TB., Tbsp., or T
ounce	oz.
pound	lb.
pint	pt.
quart	qt.
Fahrenheit	F
Celsius	C
grams	g
kilograms	kg
millimeters	mm
liters	L
centimeters	cm
meters	m
kilometers	km

Danger, Will Robinson

Metric abbreviations are not followed by a period.

You Could Look It Up

An **acronym** is an abbreviation formed from the first letter of each word in the title.

◆ Abbreviate the titles of some organizations and things. These abbreviations are not followed by a period: UN (United Nations); FBI (Federal Bureau of Investigation)

◆ Use acronyms to abbreviate some organizations. An *acronym* is an abbreviation formed from the first letter of each word in the title. Because acronyms are used as words, they never take periods: NATO (North Atlantic Treaty Organization); NASA (National Aeronautics and Space Administration)

The Least You Need to Know

◆ Capital letters help determine meaning.

◆ Most abbreviations start with a capital letter and end with a period. Use only commonly accepted abbreviations.

Chapter 18

Guide to Spelling: Hooked on Phonics

In This Chapter

◆ Learn how to attach prefixes and suffixes

◆ Form contractions, plurals, and possessives

◆ Learn the rules!

> "Waiter, waiter!" said the irate patron in the fancy restaurant. What's this fly doing in my soup?"
>
> "Looks like the backstroke to me," replied the waiter.

Right or wrong, good or bad—you know that spelling matters. A fly in your soup doesn't do much for your appetite; likewise, a misspelled word can destroy the effect of an entire document. This chapter gives you some quick and dirty ways to learn to spell. (Getting rid of the fly is a subject for another book, however!)

Bee a Good Speller

Can you spell? I dare you to prove it! Take this pretest to see how well you spell. Use what you learn here to focus on the sections of this chapter that you need the most.

In each of the following groups of words, only one of the words is misspelled. For each group, select the misspelled word and spell it correctly. Write your answer in the space provided.

_____	1. arguering	knives	shepherd	thousandth
_____	2. baggy	unreleived	canine	vengeful
_____	3. contagious	obituary	lonliness	cadence
_____	4. millinery	sacrafice	caramel	burglarize
_____	5. publicity	promontory	sieze	patriarch
_____	6. bridle	loosely	breakage	symtom
_____	7. civillian	primeval	apologetic	truancy
_____	8. uncanny	statuesque	ajournment	aisle
_____	9. trigonometry	exhaust	Artic	visualize
_____	10. bewitches	satchel	vegetable	obstinite

Answers

1. arguing
2. unrelieved
3. loneliness
4. sacrifice
5. seize

6. symptom
7. civilian
8. adjournment
9. Arctic
10. obstinate

Score Yourself

8 to 10 correct	You can proofread my work anytime.
5 to 7 correct	You'll be okay with a good spell checker.
3 to 6 correct	Treading on thin ice, kiddo.
0 to 2 correct	Are you Mr. Potatoe, Dan Quayle?

If U Cn Reed This ...

Why don't we simply spell words the way they sound? You're not the first smart person to ask that question. In the year 1200, an Augustinian monk named Orm developed a phonetic spelling system. It didn't catch on, but that didn't stop others from following in his footsteps (in spelling, not monkhood). Among those who tried to overhaul our spelling system were Benjamin Franklin, Theodore Roosevelt, George Bernard Shaw, and Upton Sinclair. And look where it got *them*.

In *The Devil's Dictionary*, writer and wit Ambrose Bierce defines *orthography* as "the science of spelling by the eye instead of the ear. Advocated with more heat than light by the outmates of every asylum for the insane." So why haven't we gotten around to reforming spelling to bridge the chasm between *phonology* (the way we say words) and *orthography* (the way we write them)? And while we're at it, why haven't we worked out the kinks with Olestra, fixed the ozone layer, and done something about those Mets?

Here are some reasons why our spelling remains the way it is:

- ◆ Uniform spelling would rob English of its rich legacy of *homophones*.

- ◆ We'd also lose the fascinating and useful etymological history of many words.

- ◆ Creating a unified system of spelling is a job for Superman, and he's busy with evil Lex Luthor and luscious Lois Lane.

- ◆ We can't agree on a soft drink but we'll agree on a spelling system? Get a grip!

So now that you know you can run but you can't hide, let's get to work polishing your spelling.

> **You Could Look It Up**
>
> **Homophones** are words that are pronounced the same but spelled differently.

> **Take My Word for It**
>
> Spelling *is* important. The word *spell* itself underscores this importance. It derives from the Middle English word *spellen*, which means "to read out." The word *spelling* is related to an Old English word meaning "to talk."

Quick and Dirty Tricks of the Trade

Whatever your level of skill, you can benefit from the following eight time-tested spelling tricks. They're easy—and they work. Try them all, or pick and choose the ones that suit your needs.

1. **Classify errors.** Why not specialize? Figure out what words pose the most trouble for you and concentrate on those errors. For example, if you have a problem with words that contain *ie*, study the "ie" rule and concentrate on the words that follow the rules and the major exceptions.

2. **Break words down into smaller parts.** For example, to spell *bookkeeper*, break the word down to its two parts: *book* and *keeper*. Then you won't forget there's a double *k* in the middle of the word.

3. **Do word puzzles and games.** There are many different kinds to choose from, including crosswords, acrostics, Scrabble, and Boggle. Each type of word puzzle or game gives you practice in spelling. As a bonus, doing puzzles also teaches you vocabulary. So what if it includes some useless words? You want, maybe, everything?

4. **Use dictionaries.** I know, I know, looking up a word is a pain. So is exercise, but they both work. Using a dictionary will help you remember a word's spelling and its exact meaning.

5. **Try air writing.** No, it's not a New Age crystal thing; it's what Miss Nelson taught you in the fourth grade. To check the spelling of a word or to learn the spelling of an unfamiliar word, try writing it in the air.

6. **Guess and check.** It's a free country; you're allowed to guess. To check the spelling of a word, make a guess. Write it down and see how it looks. If the planets are aligned, you'll be able to see if you're right or wrong. You'll probably also be able to see where you went wrong: omitted letter, double letter, wrong letter.

7. **Use word cards.** Those flash cards you used in elementary school still work quite nicely with spelling, thank you very much. Try this three-step plan:

    ◆ As you read through this chapter, write each difficult-to-spell word on a 3×5 index card, one word per card.

Strictly Speaking

Compound words divide most easily into parts because they are made by combining individual words. For example: *cross-dressing, chambermaid, four-poster.*

Quoth the Maven

Print dictionaries don't run out of batteries; handheld computerized dictionaries are light and easy to carry. It's your call. Just be sure to use a dictionary.

Quoth the Maven

Mnemonics are memory tricks that help you remember everything from the order of the planets to your grocery list. For example, to remember how to spell *principal*, look at the last three letters: the principal is your *pal*. Principle, in contrast, ends in *le*, like rule (which is what principle means). Create your own mnemonics to conquer spelling demons.

- ◆ Study the cards every chance you get.

- ◆ Take them with you on the bus, train, and plane; hide them in your lap and sneak a peek during dull meetings.

8. **Visualize.** Think about how the word is spelled; get a clear mental picture of the word. This will help you remember the word and spell it correctly in the future.

Attaching Prefixes and Suffixes: Bits and Pieces

Prefixes are word parts you add to the beginning of a word to change its meaning; *suffixes* are word parts you add to the end of a word to change its meaning. Because many useful words are created by adding prefixes and suffixes to *root words*, you can save a lot of time wondering "Did I spell this sucker correctly?" by knowing how to add prefixes and suffixes. Let's take a look at the guidelines.

Attaching Prefixes: Front-End Collision

The rule here is simple: Don't add or omit a letter when you attach a prefix. Keep all the letters—every one of them. Here are some examples.

You Could Look It Up

Prefixes are word parts you add to the beginning of a word to change its meaning; **suffixes** are word parts you add to the end of a word to change its meaning.

Prefix		Word		New Word
dis	+	satisfied	=	dissatisfied
mis	+	spell	=	misspell
un	+	acceptable	=	unacceptable
re	+	election	=	reelection
inter	+	related	=	interrelated

Attaching Suffixes: Rear-End Collision

Keep all the letters when you add a suffix ... unless the word ends in a *y* or a silent *e*. We'll talk about *them* later. The following chart and guidelines show you how to master the suffix situation.

Word		Suffix		New Word
accidental	+	ly	=	accidentally
drunken	+	ness	=	drunkenness
ski	+	ing	=	skiing
foresee	+	able	=	foreseeable

1. If the letter before the final *y* is a consonant, change the *y* to *i* and add the suffix. Study these examples.

Word		Suffix		New Word
hurry	+	ed	=	hurried
greedy	+	ly	=	greedily

Hurry doesn't follow the rule: hurry + ing = hurrying. Here are some other exceptions: dryly, dryness, shyly, shyness, babyish, ladylike.

2. If the letter before the final *y* is a vowel, do not change the *y* before attaching a suffix.

Word		Suffix		New Word
play	+	ing	=	playing
destroy	+	ed	=	destroyed

Here are some exceptions: laid, paid, said, mislaid, underpaid, unsaid.

3. If the suffix begins with a vowel, drop the silent *e*. Here are some examples.

Word		Suffix		New Word
write	+	ing	=	writing
love	+	able	=	lovable
use	+	age	=	usage

When the word ends in *ce* or *ge*, keep the *e* if the suffix begins with *a* or *o*: *noticeable, manageable, advantageous.* Here are some common exceptions: *acreage, mileage, singeing, canoeing, hoeing.*

4. If the suffix begins with a consonant, keep the silent *e*. Here are some examples.

Word		Suffix		New Word
excite	+	ment	=	excitement
care	+	ful	=	careful
fierce	+	ly	=	fiercely

Of course there are some exceptions: *argument, duly, truly, wholly,* and *ninth.*

5. If the word ends in *ie*, drop the *e* and change the *i* to *y*. Check out these examples.

Word		Suffix		New Word
lie	+	ing	=	lying
die	+	ing	=	dying
tie	+	ing	=	tying

6. Add *ly* to change an adjective to an adverb. Here are some examples.

Word		Suffix		New Word
brave	+	ly	=	bravely
calm	+	ly	=	calmly

If the adjective ends in *ic*, add *al* before *ly*.

Word		Al		Suffix		New Word
drastic	+	al	+	ly	=	drastically
scientific	+	al	+	ly	=	scientifically

If the adjective ends in *ble*, change *ble* to *bly*.

Word	New Word
able	ably
noble	nobly

7. In a one-syllable word, double the final consonant before a suffix beginning with a vowel.

Word		Suffix		New Word
plan	+	er	=	planner
big	+	est	=	biggest

Don't double the final consonant if it comes after two vowels or another consonant. For example: *failed, stooped, warmer, lasting.*

8. In a word of two or more syllables, double the final consonant only if it is in an accented syllable before a suffix beginning with a vowel. Here are some examples:

Word		Suffix		New Word
defer	+	ed	=	deferred
resubmit	+	ing	=	resubmitting

Don't double the final consonant if it comes after two vowels or another consonant. For example: obtained, concealed, abducting, commendable.

9. If a words ends in *ic*, insert a *k* after the *c*.

Word		Suffix		New Word
mimic	+	ing	=	mimicking
traffic	+	ing	=	trafficking

10. There's only one hint for adding *able* or *ible:* an adjective usually ends in *-able* if you can trace it back to a noun ending in *-ation*. *Sensible* is the exception.

Noun	Adjective
adaptation	adaptable
commendation	commendable

But there are many words that don't fit this rule, so this isn't the rule to have tattooed on your palm.

Go for the Gusto

In the space provided, spell each misspelled word correctly.

1. dissorganized   _____
2. diservice   _____
3. disagreable   _____
4. lazyness   _____
5. acrage   _____
6. unatural   _____
7. suddeness   _____
8. costlyness   _____
9. mislayd   _____
10. truely   _____

Answers

1. disorganized   6. unnatural
2. disservice   7. suddenness
3. disagreeable   8. costliness
4. laziness   9. mislaid
5. acreage   10. truly

Contractions: Suck It In

Creating contractions is another useful skill, right up there with knowing how to work an ATM, execute a three-point turn, and rappel down a cliff. Fortunately, it's much easier to learn how to form contractions than it is to work an ATM or do a three-point turn. I'm not even going to discuss mountain-type stuff like rappelling.

Strictly Speaking
Traditionally, contractions are not used in formal writing, such as reports and letters.

Using contractions adds a more informal tone to your writing and reproduces the spoken word more accurately in your prose.

Danger, Will Robinson

Here's a key exception:
will + not = won't (not *willn't*).

The basic rule for forming a contraction is a snap: to combine two words, just insert an apostrophe in the space where the letter or letters have been omitted. Here are some examples.

Word #1		Word #2		Contraction
I	+	am	=	I'm
you	+	are	=	you're
he	+	is	=	he's
we	+	are	=	we're

Follow the Rules! Spelling Rules

Who can trust the rules of life? You really *can* go swimming right after you eat; men *do* buy the cow even after they've gotten the milk for free. Spelling, fortunately, has some valid rules. Here are three nifty ones that will serve you well.

1. The *-ceed/-cede* rule. There are only three verbs in English that end in *-ceed: succeed, proceed,* and *exceed.* All the other verbs with that sound end in *-cede.* For example:

   ◆ secede

   ◆ intercede

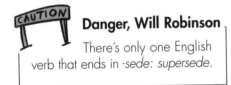

Danger, Will Robinson

There's only one English
verb that ends in *-sede: supersede.*

   ◆ concede

   ◆ accede

   ◆ cede

   ◆ precede

2. The *-ful* rule. Remember that the sound *full* at the end of a word is spelled with only one *l.* For example:

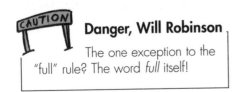

Danger, Will Robinson

The one exception to the
"full" rule? The word *full* itself!

   ◆ careful

   ◆ graceful

   ◆ healthful

   ◆ hopeful

3. *i* before *e* except after *c* … Remember this baby from the eighth grade? (Or were you too busy putting Clearasil on your nose and ogling the teacher to pay attention to something as mundane as spelling?) Here's the rule (and it even has a bouncy rhyme to it):

i before *e* except after *c* or when sounded as *a* as in *neighbor* and *weigh*

Here are some words that fit the rule.

i before *e*	except after *c*	sounded as *a*
achieve	conceit	neighbor
believe	ceiling	weigh
siege	receive	freight
relief	conceive	reign
grief	deceit	sleigh
chief	deceive	vein
fierce	perceive	weight
fiend	receipt	
piece	receive	
shriek		

And here are some words that don't:

♦ either

♦ neither

♦ foreign

♦ height

♦ leisure

♦ seize

♦ weird

(Hey, is anything perfect? I never promised you a rose garden, only some neat-o spelling rules.)

ieeeeeeeeeeee!

Add ie or ei to complete each word.

1. f____rce
2. s____ge
3. bel____ve
4. rec____pt
5. conc____t
6. dec____ve

7. n____ghbor
8. c____ling
9. for____gn
10. rel____f
11. w____rd
12. v____n

Answers

1. fierce
2. siege
3. believe
4. receipt
5. conceit
6. deceive

7. neighbor
8. ceiling
9. foreign
10. relief
11. weird
12. vein

See and Say

Some words are misspelled because they are often mispronounced. Sometimes extra letters are added; other times, letters are omitted. How many of the following words do you mispronounce?

1. **Leaving out a consonant:** February, recognize, surprise, government, library, eighth, Arctic, candidate, probably.

2. **Adding an unnecessary vowel:** forty, pronunciation, schedule, chimney, disastrous, umbrella.

3. **Leaving out an unstressed syllable:** accidentally, superintendent, incidentally.

4. **Leaving out an unstressed vowel:** temperature, vegetable, original, miniature, interesting, diamond, chocolate.

At other times, you're not at fault at all: The words are spelled differently from the way they sound. With such unphonetic words, you're working without a net. There are no rules, only spelling techniques like memorization and visualization. Of course, there are always dictionaries.

These unphonetic words fall into three main categories: *silent letters, tricky-dickie word endings*, and *y/i use*. And here they are …

Silent Letters

Never seem to meet the people you want to see, but can't get rid of the same old pests? The same is true of spelling words. Keeping this truism in mind, here are some words with silent letters that have no doubt been annoying you for years. Only now, you know why.

- Silent *b:* doubtable, subpoena, subtle, undoubtedly
- Silent *h:* exhaust, exhibit, exhilaration, ghastly, ghost, heir, rheumatism, rhyme
- Silent *g:* align, design, gnarled, diaphragm
- Silent *p:* cupboard, pneumatic, pneumonia, psalm, pseudonym, psychology, receipt
- Silent *t:* bankruptcy, listen, mortgage, wrestle
- Silent *c:* acquaint, acquire, acquit, ascertain, miscellaneous, ascend, fascinate, indict, muscle

Tricky-Dickie Word Endings

The following words confound even the best spellers because they don't end the way we think they should:

- Words that end in *-ar:* beggar, burglar, bursar, calendar, cellar, liar
- Words that end in *-cian:* electrician, musician, pediatrician, politician
- Words that end in *-ain:* Britain, captain, certain, mountain, porcelain

> **Quoth the Maven**
>
> *Homonyms* and *homophones* are especially tricky to spell and use correctly. See Chapter 24 for a complete list of these words.

Y/I Use

Here are some words that sound like they contain an *i*. No such luck; each has a *y* creating the *i* sound.

- abyss
- analyze
- cylinder
- hypocrisy
- paralysis
- syllable
- symmetry
- symphony
- synonym

Spelling Demons

How can you tell a spelling demon? They're the words that look wrong even when they're right.

I know you can spell *all right* because it's the opposite of *all wrong*. Maybe you were lucky enough to learn that *a lot* is two words, *rarefy* has that pesky *e*, and *sacrilegious* has a whole lot of letters.

There are still tons of words lying (laying?) in wait for you. Here are 10 common spelling demons that have no doubt been deviling you for years:

Ten Tough Spelling Words—and Ways to Make Them Tender

1. **traveler.** The British spell it with two *l*'s, but Americans don't double-up, except in accented syllables (such as *controlled*, *referral*, *propeller*).

2. **coolly.** Here, you're just adding the suffix to the root. (I know it still looks funny. But it's right. Trust me.)

3. **embarrass.** Two *r*'s and two *s*'s. But then again, we have *harass*.

4. **unparalleled.** Memorize this sucker. There's no other way around it.

5. **nickel.** Is there any justice in the world?

6. **glamour.** We can deal with this … but what about glam*o*rous?

7. **resuscitate.** That's why people learn CPR; they're too busy being heroes (not heros) to spell what they just did.

8. **genealogy.** Like its first cousins *mineralogy* and *analogy*, one of a few words that doesn't end with *-ology*.

9. **pavilion.** That's what we get for taking words from the French. *Cotillion* and *vermilion* also pose difficulty.

10. **dysfunction.** Because so many people have it, better learn how to spell it (maybe a cure is easier?).

Still game? Here's a list of spelling demons you're likely to encounter in daily life. Of course, there are many more, so don't write to me, e-mail me, or fax me your favorites. I'll give you a few lines at the bottom of the list where you can record your favorites.

abbreviate	cellophane	February	journal
abyss	debtor	fickle	journeying
academic	decided	gallery	juvenile
ache	defense	ghetto	keenness
adjacent	deferred	grammar	kindliness
allotted	delicious	guess	laboratory
bachelor	deluge	handicapped	larceny
balloon	ecstasy	heaviness	legend
bicycle	efficient	height	leisure
bigamy	eighth	heroes	maintain
budget	eligible	icing	marmalade
bureau	emperor	icy	marriage
capsule	emphasis	illegally	mathematics
career	fascinate	illogical	neutral
carnival	feasible	jeopardy	niece

ninety	opponents	rabid	sincerely
notary	pageant	rebelled	sugar
obnoxious	papal	rebuttal	treachery
obstinate	parallel	referee	turkeys
offensive	paralysis	_____	_____
_____	_____	_____	_____
_____	_____	_____	_____
_____	_____	_____	_____
_____	_____	_____	_____

The Least You Need to Know

◆ Know your spelling rules.

◆ Learn how to add prefixes and suffixes to improve your spelling.

◆ Use a dictionary and other hints, such as air writing and visualizing.

◆ Some words just don't follow the rules. These you must learn or look up.

Part 5

Style: All the Write Stuff

Chartreuse stilettos, Pop Tarts and Pez, The Wolfman—what do these items have in common? They all have style, that elusive *je ne sais quoi*, the "I know it when I see it." The Wicked Witch of the West had it; Good Witch Gilda didn't. Cary Grant, Fred Astaire, and Audrey Hepburn oozed style; pity poor Prince: Even with a symbol rather than a name, he has no style. Radioactive desert shrubs don't have style; Beemers, Batman, and boxers do.

In this part, you learn how to give your writing its own distinctive style. You learn ways to develop your own distinctive writing style, including using figurative language, tone, and diction.

What Is Style, and How Do I Get Some?

In This Chapter

- ◆ Define "style" in writing
- ◆ Explore the 3C's of all effective writing styles: consistency, coherence, and clarity
- ◆ Analyze different writing styles
- ◆ Explore myths about writing styles

"Every style that is not boring is good," wrote the French writer Voltaire. All good writing shares one common quality: It has *style*—no matter what form the writing takes. In this chapter, you explore the elements of writing style. Along the way, you analyze different writing styles to find the ones that work best for your purpose and audience.

Style: Write On!

A writer's *style* is his or her distinctive way of writing. Style is a series of choices—words, sentence length and structure, figures of speech, tone, voice, diction, and overall structure.

Think of style as the writer's voice or personality coming through the words. I use *The Complete Idiot's Guide to Grammar and Style* in my college classroom. I assign a big chunk of reading as the first night's homework. The next class, my students always say, "As I read your book, I felt like you were talking to me, Dr. Rozakis." That's because my style of writing in this book is very similar to my style of classroom teaching: personal, informal, and funny.

You Could Look It Up

A writer's **style** is his or her distinctive way of writing.

However, writers often change their style for different kinds of writing and to suit different audiences. In poetry, for example, a writer might use more imagery and figures of speech than he or she would use in prose. My style is very different when I write a letter of complaint, a letter of condolence, or a business memo, for example.

Some twentieth-century American writers celebrated for their lucid writing style include Truman Capote, James Thurber, Dorothy Thompson, Joan Didion, John McPhee, Tracy Kidder, and E. B. White. The late Mr. White, a long-time essayist and short story writer for *The New Yorker*, oozed so much style that he even co-authored a famous little writing manual called *The Elements of Style*. It's the *ne plus ultra* of writing style guides.

But good writing style is not restricted to professional writers. People like you get ahead in part because of your ability to write clearly and effectively. For example …

- Lawyers need to make their briefs logical.

- Accountants must write clear cover letters for audits.

- Retail workers often write letters of recommendation and promotion.

- Insurance brokers write letters soliciting business.

- Educators write observations of staff members and reports on students.

- Computer specialists write proposals.

- Marketing personnel write sales reports.

- Engineers must write reports, e-mails, and faxes.

- Stock and bond traders write letters and prospectuses.

And who among us doesn't write resumés, cover letters, memos, faxes, and business letters? We all need to develop good writing style.

The 3C's: Consistency, Coherence, Clarity

As I mentioned in the opening of this chapter, effective writers adapt their style to suit their audience and purpose for writing. You'll learn all about audience and purpose in Chapter 20. Now, let's start with the basics: All good writing shares the following three qualities: consistency, coherence, and clarity.

Consistency

Consistent writing delivers a single effect. The "effect" may be comedic or horrific, sorrowful or joyous, businesslike or personal. The document maintains the same tone or mood throughout. That tone suits the topic, too. The tone is also well suited to your readers. For example, you would use a friendly tone in a memo to a colleague about a meeting, but a more formal tone in a letter to a customer about a problem with a product.

Edgar Allan Poe (1809–1849) is famous because he created the modern short story, the modern detective story, and the modern horror story. (He was also a whiz-bang literary critic.) In a classic review, Poe gave some advice to short story writers that holds true for all writers. His advice concerns consistency in style and tone. Here's what Poe had to say:

> **Quoth the Maven**
>
> The more difficult your ideas, the easier you must make it for your reader to follow your ideas. Consider using shorter sentences, more transitions, and precise figures of speech (especially comparisons such as metaphors and similes). You can also define difficult words in context to help your readers more readily grasp abstract concepts.

A skillful literary artist has constructed a tale. If wise, he has not fashioned his thoughts to accommodate his incidents; but having conceived, with deliberate care, a certain unique or single *effect* to be wrought out, he then invents such incidents—he then combines such events as may best aid him in establishing this preconceived effect. If his very initial sentences tend not to the outbringing of this effect, then he has failed in his first step. In the whole composition there should be no word written, of which the tendency, direct or indirect, is not to the one pre-established design. ... Undue brevity is just as exceptional here as in the poem, but undue length is yet more to be avoided.

—From Poe's review of Hawthorne's *Twice-Told Tales*, May 1842

Take My Word for It _____

It's true that Edgar Allan Poe was found dead in a gutter, battered, wearing someone else's clothes. It's also true that he was orphaned before he was three years old and adopted by John Allan, a wealthy businessman. Poe did indeed marry jailbait, his 13-year-old cousin Virginia Clemm. It's also likely that he ingested every illegal substance short of plutonium. These details paint the picture of an eccentric fella, maybe even a madman, but here's the truth: Edgar Allan Poe was more insecure than haunted, his life more destitute than mad.

Consistent writing also maintains the same point of view. The writer does not switch from the first-person *I* to the second-person *you*, for instance.

In 1850, James Pennington published "Escape: A Slave Narrative." The account describes his flight from slavery in Maryland to freedom in Pennsylvania. As you read the following except, decide what consistent "single effect" it conveys. As you analyze the passage, underline the words and phrases that Pennington used to create this consistent mood.

> I penetrated through the woods, thick and thin, and more or less wet, to the distance I should think of three miles. By this time my clothes were all thoroughly soaked through, and I felt once more a gloom and wretchedness, the recollection of which makes me shudder at this distant day …
>
> I was now out of the hands of those who had so cruelly teased me during the day; but a number of fearful thoughts rushed into my mind to alarm me. It was dark and cloudy, so that I could not see the north star. How do I know what ravenous beasts are in this wood? How do I know what precipices may be within its bounds? I cannot rest in this wood tomorrow, for it will be searched by those men from whom I have escaped; but how shall I regain the road? How shall I know when I am on the right road again?
>
> These are some of the thoughts that filled my mind with gloom and alarm.

Pennington creates a consistent effect of fear, and even terror. He accomplishes this in part by his choice of words. These include:

- ◆ "a gloom and wretchedness"
- ◆ "shudder"
- ◆ "fearful thoughts"

- ◆ "alarm me"

- ◆ "dark and cloudy"

- ◆ "ravenous beasts"

- ◆ "precipices"

- ◆ "gloom and alarm"

Strictly Speaking

Fashions in writing style change like fashions in clothes—but fortunately, there's no grammatical equivalent of thong undies. In the 1800s, it was common to construct long sentences with many subordinate clauses. Although some writers today do favor long, discursive sentences, in general the trend is toward shorter sentences.

Coherence

Coherent writing is logical and unified. Every single sentence helps clarify or support the main idea. You can follow the progression of ideas because the writer provides signposts or clues. These clues include the following:

- ◆ Transitions

- ◆ Pronouns

- ◆ Repetition

- ◆ Parallel structure

A *transition* can be a whole paragraph of text or simply a transitional expression, a word or phrase that shows a logical relationship between ideas. Different transitional expressions signal to the reader how one idea is linked to others. Using the appropriate transitions helps you convey your ideas smoothly and clearly. You learned all about transitions in Chapter 15.

You've learned all about these puppies earlier, so you can use them to make your writing unified as well. To make sure we're all on the same page, here's a quick reminder.

The following table provides examples of techniques for creating coherence. The examples are underlined in each excerpt.

Techniques for Creating a Coherent Style

Stylistic Device	Examples
Transitions	The small items sold well, <u>but</u> Strauss found himself stuck with the rolls of canvas because it was not heavy enough to be used for tents. <u>While</u> talking to one of the miners, Strauss learned that sturdy pants that would stand up to the rigors of digging were almost impossible to find.
Pronouns	When a <u>circus</u> came, <u>it</u> left us all burning to become clowns …" —Mark Twain, *Life on the Mississippi*
Repetition	<u>He has</u> refused his Assent to Laws the most wholesome and necessary for the public good. <u>He has</u> forbidden his Governors to pass Laws of immediate and pressing importance, unless suspended in their operation until his Assent should be obtained; and, when so suspended, he has utterly neglected to attend to them. <u>He has</u> refused to pass other Laws for the accommodation of large districts of people, unless those people would relinquish the rights of Representation in the Legislature; a right inestimable to them, and formidable to tyrants only … —Thomas Jefferson, "The Declaration of Independence"
Parallel structure	"<u>With malice toward none</u>; <u>with charity for all</u>; <u>with firmness in the right</u>, as God gives us to see the right, let us strive on <u>to finish</u> the work we are in, <u>to bind</u> up the nation's wounds; <u>to care</u> for him who shall have borne the battle, and for his widow and orphan—<u>to do</u> all which may achieve and cherish a just and lasting peace <u>among ourselves</u>, and <u>with all nations</u>." —Abraham Lincoln, Second Inaugural Address, March 4, 1865

You can use one or more of these techniques to create coherence. In the following passage, I used transitions, parallel structure, and pronouns to link ideas:

> Long-time Boston residents still talk about the molasses flood that engulfed the city's north end on January 15, 1919. Crowds of people were sitting near the Purity Distilling Corporation's 50-foot-high molasses tank enjoying the unseasonably warm day. The tank was filled with over 2 million gallons of molasses— and it was about to burst apart. First, molasses oozed through the tank's rivets. Then the metal bolts popped out, the seams burst, and tons of molasses burst

out in a surge of deadly goo. The first wave, over 25 feet high, smashed buildings, trees, people, and animals like toys. Residents were carried into the Charles River, which was soon a gooey brown sludge. However, the molasses was not the only threat. In addition, sharp pieces of the tank sliced through the air, injuring scores of people. After the initial destruction, molasses continued to clog the streets for days. Many survivors had to have their clothing cut off: Dried molasses turned clothing into cement. People were stuck to sidewalks and benches; molasses glued telephone receivers to ears and hands. The smell of molasses stayed in the air for months. The disaster left over 20 people dead and more than 50 hurt.

You Could Look It Up

Repetition is using the same sound, word, phrase, line, or grammatical structure to link related ideas, create rhythm, and emphasize key points. Only repeat the words that contain a main idea or that use rhythm to focus attention on a main idea.

Quoth the Maven

Pay special attention to your writing style when you have to write especially difficult messages, such as letters that convey bad news.

Clarity

"Clarity" means the writing is easy to understand. Mark Twain, a master stylist much admired for his clear writing, laid out the rules for mastering a great style. Twain was moved to write these rules for the same reason we usually lay down the law: Someone had just pushed him too far. That "someone" was James Fenimore Cooper, author of the *Leatherstocking Tales*. (The most famous volume in the series is *The Last of the Mohicans*, immortalized in our day in a staggeringly tedious movie distinguished only by some really great hair.) Twain thought Cooper was a terrible writer, vastly over-rated, and so he wrote "Fenimore Cooper's Literary Offenses" to trash the competition.

Twain's rules serve as great guidelines for all writers today. Here are some that you'll find most useful for producing clear prose:

1. That a tale shall accomplish something and arrive somewhere. …

2. They require that the episodes of a tale shall be necessary parts of the tale, and shall help develop it …

3. They require that the personages in a tale shall be alive, except in the case of corpses, and that always the reader shall be able to tell the corpses from the others.

4. They require that the personages in a tale, both dead and alive, shall exhibit a sufficient excuse for being there.

5. They require that when the personages of a tale deal in conversation, the talk shall sound like human talk, and be talk such as human being would be like to talk in the given circumstances, and have a discoverable meaning, also a discoverable purpose, and a show of relevancy, and remain in the neighborhood of the subject in hand, and be interesting to the reader, and help out the tale, and stop when the people cannot think of anything more to say. …

9. They require that the personages of a tale shall confine themselves to possibilities and let miracles alone; or, if they venture forth a miracle, the author must so plausibly set it forth as to make it look possible and reasonable. …

In addition to these large rules, there are some little ones. These require that the author shall

12. Say what he is proposing to say, not merely come near it.

13. Use the right word, not its first cousin.

> **CAUTION**
>
> **Danger, Will Robinson**
>
> Don't forget that clear writing always uses perfect grammar and usage. Ditto for spelling, punctuation, and capitalization.

14. Eschew surplus.

15. Not omit necessary details.

16. Avoid slovenliness of form.

17. Use good grammar.

18. Employ a simple and straightforward style.

I'll Have What's on His Plate

The grass is always greener over the septic tank, the dress always looks better in the window, and the food always looks better on someone else's plate, eh? I can't do anything about your lawn, loins, or lunch, but I *can* help you develop a better writing style. Start by analyzing different styles to figure out makes one writing style appeal to you more than another. Once you can isolate the elements that appeal to you—word choice, sentence length and variety, structure, and so on—you can start adapting these element of style to your own prose.

Read the following famous passages and analyze their style. Decide how the writer uses consistency, coherence, clarity to convey meaning. Then decide which passages you like the best and why.

1. It was the best of times, it was the worst of times, it was the age of wisdom, it was the age of foolishness, it was the epoch of belief, it was the epoch of incredulity, it was the season of Light, it was the season of Darkness, it was the spring of hope, it was the winter of despair, we had everything before us, we had nothing before us, we were all going direct to Heaven, we were all going direct the other way— in short, the period was so far like the present period, that some of the noisiest authorities insisted on its being received, for good or for evil, in the superlative degree of comparison only.

    There was a king with a large jaw and a queen with a plain face on the throne of England; there was a king with a large jaw and a queen with a fair face, on the throne of France. In both countries it was clearer than crystal to the lords of the State preserves of loaves and fishes, that things in general were settled for ever.

    —*A Tale of Two Cities* by Charles Dickens

Take My Word for It _____

Charles Dickens (1812–1870) vividly depicted the working class of British society in the Victorian era. He achieved immense popularity in his lifetime by providing a rich array of memorable, often humorous characters while showing the dark side of the Industrial Revolution as it affected the average person. He's also famous for producing more novels than children, but it was a close race: 14 novels to 10 children.

2. It is a truth universally acknowledged, that a single man in possession of a good fortune must be in want of a wife.

    However little known the feelings or views of such a man be on his first entering a neighborhood, this truth is so well fixed in the minds of the surrounding families that he is considered as the rightful property of some one or another of their daughters.

    "My dear Mr. Bennet," said his lady to him one day, "have you heard that Netherfield Park is let at last?"

    Mr. Bennet replied that he had not.

    "But it is," returned she; "for Mrs. Long has just been here, and she told me about it."

Mr. Bennet made no answer.

"Do you not want to know who has taken it?" cried his wife impatiently.

"*You* want to tell me, and I have no objections to hearing it."

This was invitation enough.

—*Pride and Prejudice* by Jane Austen

3. Four score and seven years ago our fathers brought forth on this continent, a new nation, conceived in Liberty, and dedicated to the proposition that all men are created equal.

Now we are engaged in a great civil war, testing whether that nation, or any nation so conceived and so dedicated, can long endure. We are met on a great battlefield of that war. We have come to dedicate a portion of that field, as a final resting place for those who here gave their lives that that nation might live. It is altogether fitting and proper that we should do this.

But in a larger sense, we cannot dedicate—we cannot consecrate—we cannot hallow—this ground. The brave men, living and dead, who struggled here, have consecrated it, far above our power to add or detract. The world will little note, nor long remember what we say here, but it can never forget what they did here. It is for us the living, rather, to be dedicated here to the unfinished work which they who fought so nobly advanced. It is rather for us to be here dedicated to the great task remaining before us—that from these honored dead we take increased devotion to that cause for which they gave the last full measure of devotion— that we here highly resolve that these dead shall not have died in vain—that this nation, under God, shall have a new birth of freedom—and that government of the people, by the people, for the people, shall not perish from the earth.

—"Gettysburg Address" by Abraham Lincoln

Take My Word for It

Abraham Lincoln built the "Gettysburg Address" on parallelism and repetition, drawn from his deep knowledge of biblical rhythms: "But in a larger sense, we cannot dedicate—we cannot consecrate—we cannot hallow—this ground." Notice the repetition of the parallel phrase "we cannot."

4. These are the times that try men's souls. The summer soldier and the sunshine patriot will in this crisis, shrink from the service of his country; but he that stands it now, deserves the love and thanks of man and woman. Tyranny, like hell, is not easily conquered; yet we have this consolation with us, that the harder the conflict, the more glorious the triumph. What we obtain too cheap, we esteem too lightly; 'tis dearness only that gives everything its value.

—*The Crisis, Number I* by Thomas Paine

Lie Like a Rug

You know the three big lies about reality: "The check is in the mail," "You don't look a day older," and "We'll keep your resumé on file." There are a lot of little lies, myths, and half-truths about effective writing styles, too. Take this snap quiz to see how much you know about good writing.

Write T if you think the statement is true or F if you think it's false.

_____ 1. You should write as you talk.

_____ 2. Never begin a sentence with a coordinating conjunction.

_____ 3. Never end a sentence with a preposition.

_____ 4. Never use *I* in your business writing.

_____ 5. Big words impress people.

Answers

Every item is false.

Let's take a look at some of these misunderstandings about writing style.

Lie #1: You should write as you talk.

Unless you've been granted the gift of an exceptionally fluent tongue, writing as you talk usually results in awkward and repetitive documents. Most of us hesitate as we speak to allow us time to gather our thoughts. We also backtrack to pick up points we might have missed on the first go-round. This works in speech, but not in writing. As a result, a document written "by ear" usually comes out badly organized.

Quoth the Maven

Although writing as you talk rarely works for most people, reading your draft out loud to see how it sounds is often a great way to catch stiff, overly formal word choice and sentence structure.

Writing as you speak may work well with a first draft to get your ideas flowing, but it's usually a waste with subsequent versions.

Lie #2: Never begin a sentence with a coordinating conjunction.

You remember your old friends the coordinating conjunctions: *for, and, nor, but, or,* and *yet.* For years, you've probably been told that starting a sentence with one of these babies, especially *but* and *and,* is verboten. Yes and no.

It is true that starting a sentence with a coordinating conjunction can make that sentence seem like an afterthought. It's usually better to use conjunctive adverbs such as *moreover, in addition*, and *furthermore* in the middle of a sentence to link ideas. Another effective way to connect related ideas is to link your clauses with *also*.

On the other hand, recall that the coordinating conjunctions function as important verbal signposts for your readers. These words alert readers that specific points are coming down the pike: *and* shows addition; *but* shows contrast. Therefore, beginning a sentence with a coordinating conjunction is fine if it makes your writing read more smoothly and makes your point more clearly.

Lie #3: Never end a sentence with a preposition.

Been there, done that, bought the T-shirt. You've already learned that it's okay to end a sentence with a preposition if doing otherwise will result in an awkward sentence. But it's not something to make a habit of.

Lie #4: Big words impress people.

In high school, you were probably taught that 25¢ words dazzle people. College continued the process, for academic writing is all too often verbose and didactic for the sake of mere pedantry. After you graduate and enter the business world, your task shifts from writing to impress to writing to communicate.

There will be times when you'll still have to use "big words," especially if they are technical terms or necessary jargon. Much of the time, however, big words just set up barriers between you and your audience. They create distance where none is required.

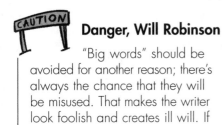

Danger, Will Robinson

"Big words" should be avoided for another reason; there's always the chance that they will be misused. That makes the writer look foolish and creates ill will. If you are going to use big words, be sure to use them correctly.

Lie #5: Never use *I* in your business writing.

It's true that using *I* too much in a document can make you seem self-centered and selfish. However, when you are describing events from your own viewpoint, *I* is both suitable and logical. It's much preferred to awkward phrases such as "This writer thinks …" and "One could say that …."

The Least You Need to Know

◆ Style is a person's distinctive way of writing.

◆ Every type of writing—both business and personal—needs the appropriate style.

◆ An effective writing style is characterized by consistency, coherence, and clarity.

◆ Don't write as you talk, you can begin a sentence with a coordinating conjunction, you can end a sentence with a preposition, you can use *I* in your business writing, and big words rarely impress people.

Chapter 20

In Style

In This Chapter

♦ Assess the importance of audience to writing style

♦ Use models to develop your own style

♦ Learn the four types of writing

What, in your opinion, is the most reasonable explanation for the fact that Moses led the Israelites all over the place for 40 years before they finally got to the Promised Land?

A. He was being tested.

B. He wanted them to really appreciate the Promised Land when they finally got there.

C. He refused to ask for directions.

In writing, as in travel, there are times when you've just *got* to ask for directions. In this chapter, I give you some easy directions for getting where you want to go on the road to good writing.

Audience: People Who Need People

To be an effective writer, you must understand how your *audience* is likely to react to what you say and how you say it. Knowing *who* you are

You Could Look It Up

A writer's **audience** are the people who read the document and influence its power to be implemented.

communicating with is fundamental to the success of any message. You need to tailor your writing style to suit the audience's needs, interests, and goals. It's vital to know where you stand—before you step somewhere you don't want to be.

There are several steps in the process of analyzing your audience. Let's take a look at them now.

Inquiring Minds Want to Know

Before you can analyze your audience, you have to identify them. Piece of cake, you say: I'm sending this memo to Joe over in accounting. Not so fast, partner. In a company, the person to whom your correspondence is addressed may not be your most important audience. In fact, like a pebble in a pond, your memo may reach a much wider audience than you realize. Here are the different audiences you must consider:

◆ *The primary audience:* The reader who decides to accept or reject your message. (That's Joe in accounting.)

◆ *The secondary audience:* People in the company who may be asked to comment on your message or implement it after it's been approved. (That could be the rest of Joe's staff.)

◆ *The gatekeeper:* The person who has the power to stop your message. The gatekeeper can be your immediate supervisor or someone higher up in the organization.

◆ *The watchdog audience:* People in the organization who don't have the power to stop your message but have political or economic power over its completion. Your future in the company may depend on what the watchdog audience decides. (That could be Joe's counterpart in production or manufacturing.)

I Share Your Pain

The most important weapon in your arsenal of audience analysis is your ability to put yourself in someone else's shoes. Fortunately, I'm talking figuratively rather than literally because some of those shoes can be really stinky.

To do an effective audience analysis, you need *empathy*, the ability to see things from someone else's point of view. You don't have to agree with the person at all; rather, you have to understand that the person's point of view is valid from his or her framework. This will color his or her perception of your message.

We tend to think that most people are like us. Flash—they're not. They may look the same, dress the same, and even talk the same, but they all think differently. Otherwise, how could we explain divorce, spandex, and salad in a bag?

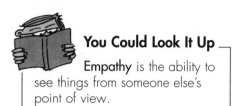

You Could Look It Up

Empathy is the ability to see things from someone else's point of view.

Before you write any important document, use the following form to analyze your audience.

Audience Survey

1. Who will be reading my document?

   _____

   _____

2. How much do my readers know about my topic at this point?

   _____

   _____

3. What else must they know about the subject for my message to be successful?

   _____

   _____

4. What is the basis of the information they have (for example: reading, personal experience)?

   _____

   _____

   _____

5. How does my audience feel about this topic? Are they neutral, hostile, enthusiastic—or somewhere in between?

   _____

   _____

6. Does my organization have a history of conflict or cooperation with this group?

   _____

   _____

7. Do *I* have a history of conflict or cooperation with this person or department?

_____

_____

8. What obstacles (if any) must I overcome for my message to be successful?

_____

_____

9. What style of writing does my audience anticipate and prefer?

_____

_____

10. How will my audience use my document (for example: general reference, detailed guidelines, the basis for a lawsuit)?

_____

_____

_____

Who's Who

Circle the audience for each of the following passages.

1. Humpty Dumpty sat on a wall,
   Humpty Dumpty had a great fall;
   All the King's horses and all the King's men
   Couldn't put Humpty back together again.

   Children

   Dieters who have fallen off the wagon

   Members of the mason's union

   Glue manufacturers

2. To get to the bowling alley, first drive south on I-95 for 3 miles. Next, take exit 13 (Enterprise/Island) to Island Avenue. At the end of Island Avenue, bear left onto the service road. The bowling alley is at the end of the service road.

   Mathematicians

   Trans-Am racers

Map makers

Directionally challenged bowlers

3. A new language can come into being as a pidgin. A pidgin is a makeshift jargon containing words of various languages and little in the way of grammar. Some of the best examples of the innate formation of a grammar system are linguist Derek Bickerton's studies of such pidgins. Bickerton noted that indentured workers on plantations in the South Pacific needed to communicate with each other in order to carry out practical tasks. However, the slave masters of the time were wary of their laborers being able to communicate with each other, so they formed mixed groups of laborers who spoke different languages. These laborers created their pidgin from rough mixtures of their own language and the language of the plantation owners. But this formation was not a sudden, conscious act. The formation of a pidgin is gradual shift from speaking a few words of the owner's tongue to speaking a new language.

Pigeons

A professor

Tourists in the South Pacific

Poor old Bickerton

4. To Whom It May Concern:

It is with enormous pleasure that we recommend Dr. Wilma Wacca as a recipient of this year's Service Award. As former recipient of this award, we fully understand the high standards it sets and the honor it confers. As a result, we can recommend Dr. Wacca as *the* most worthy recipient because she has contributed in all three areas we recognize: service, teaching, and scholarship. Let's start with service.

The IRS

An award committee

Dr. Wilma Wacca

Teachers

5. In Japan, gourmets relish aquatic fly larvae sautéed in sugar and soy sauce.

Venezuelans feast on fresh fire-roasted tarantulas. Many South Africans adore fried termites with cornmeal porridge. Merchants in Cambodia sell cooked cicadas by the bagful. Diners cut off the wings and legs before eating them.

People in Bali remove the wings from dragonflies and boil the bodies in coconut milk and garlic.

Insect cuisine may not be standard food in the United States, but Miguel Vilar notes in *Science World* that 80 percent of the world's population savors bugs, either as staples of their everyday diet or as rare delicacies. Entomophany (consuming insects intentionally) has yet to catch on in America and Europe in spite of the superior nutritional content of edible insects compared to other food sources. It's time that changed.

> Manufacturers of bug zappers
>
> Scientists
>
> A general audience
>
> Vegetarians

Answers

1. Children

2. Directionally challenged bowlers

3. A professor

4. An award committee

5. A general audience

Culture Vulture

No employee is an island, so tune into the culture of your particular company. An organization's *culture* consists of its values, beliefs, and attitudes. You can pick up hints about an organization's culture from the following sources:

♦ How employees dress

♦ The nature of parties and other social events

♦ Allocation of space

♦ Division of power

♦ Allocation of money

♦ Organizational heroes

♦ Channels of communication

♦ Behavior and language styles

You Could Look It Up

An organization's **culture** consists of its values, beliefs, and attitudes.

Model Behavior

Explaining how he learned to write, the famous nineteenth-century novelist and short story writer Robert Louis Stevenson said, "I have played the sedulous ape to Hazlitt, to Lamb, to Wordsworth, to Sir Thomas Browne, to Defoe, to Hawthorne, to Montaigne, to Baudelaire, and to Obermann. ... That, like it or not, is the way to learn to write."

"Sedulous," from the Latin word *sedulus*, meaning to be "careful," means diligent attention to detail, so the phrase "sedulous ape" describes someone who slavishly imitates somebody else. Stevenson claimed that he learned how to write by studying the best writing available. True or false?

True.

Think back, way back. Go a little more. How did you learn how to ride a bike, throw a ball, and cook a meal? How did you learn how to talk? To swim? To get that hole in one? You copied someone else, and then you practiced, practiced, and practiced some more. The same process works just as brilliantly when it comes to learning how to write well.

By studying the world's finest writers and then trying your hand at copying their style, you'll learn how to develop your own style. Here's what else this method can teach you:

- Which words work—and which ones don't
- How to make your sentences graceful
- The basic rules of grammar
- Where those itty-bitty punctuation marks go
- Spelling rules
- Various ways to organize your paragraphs
- Ways to achieve the correct tone
- How to arrange your material logically
- Methods for linking ideas
- Ways to use figures of speech
- The importance of details
- How to develop your own style

Quoth the Maven

Experts estimate that an astonishing 80 to 90 percent of the information we need comes from what we read. One sure way to become a better writer is to read more. Any type of reading will do: fiction, nonfiction, and drama. Try to read for at least one hour a night.

Danger, Will Robinson

Be careful about aping a specific writer's style too closely. Your aim is to use models to help you form your own style. More on this later.

Live and Learn

I always thought that if you want to be a writer, you've got literature … literature is all you need.

—Larry McMurtry, novelist

Each kind of writing has its own conventions and its distinctive features and content. Biographies, for example, tell a story, usually in chronological order. Business letters, in contrast, often present information in order of importance, from most to least important.

To learn the conventions of a specific genre, you need to read examples of that genre. At the same time, you should also practice writing in that genre.

Want to write boffo business letters, resumés, and memos? Read a lot of them. Use the good ones as models of what you should do and the bad ones as models of what you should not do. Part 6 of this book contains models of effective business communication. Study their form as well as content.

Good writers are avid readers. "Read, read, read … Just like a carpenter who works as an apprentice and studies the master. Read!" said Nobel laureate William Faulkner.

Make It Your Own

Reading is to the mind what exercise is to the body.

—Richard Steele, essayist

Reading is essential to writing. As you read examples of different kinds of writing, you begin to recognize the predictable patterns as well as possibilities for innovation. This is education, not imitation. However, working with a specific genre or type of writing doesn't mean that your writing will be a word version of "connect-the-dots" or "paint-by-numbers." Reading is essential to writing.

Each type of writing follows a broad set of reader expectations, but working within the framework will actually allow you to be more creative rather than less so. That's because once you know where the lines are, you'll be free to color inside them or outside them, depending on your audience, purpose, and tone.

Four Play

I know what you're thinking: *Okay, Doc, you've convinced me that if I analyze my audience and read widely, I can learn to write well, but haven't you forgotten something? What about all the different kinds of writing that I have to do? How can I possibly learn all of them?*

Hmm … good point, Gentle Reader.

How many different kinds of writing or modes of discourse are there? Circle the best answer:

(a) 75 to 100

(b) 50 to 75

(c) 25 to 50

(d) 4

And the answer is … 4. That's all there is— 1, 2, 3, 4. That's all! They are *exposition*, *narration*, *argumentation*, and *description*. Let's look at them now.

You Could Look It Up

The four types of writing—**exposition, narration, argumentation,** and **description**— are often called the "four modes of discourse."

Exposition: Writing That Explains

Exposition is writing that explains. The word *exposition* comes from the Latin word *exponere*, which means "to place out." When you write exposition, you try to place out or set forth specific information.

Exposition shows and tells by giving information about a specific topic. The topic can be anything—computers and the Internet, medicine, economics, social studies, history, math, science, or music. Different examples of expository writing that you may already be composing include the following:

◆ "How-to" essays, such as recipes and other instructions

◆ Business letters

◆ Personal letters

◆ News stories

◆ Press releases

◆ Reports

◆ Scientific reports

◆ Term papers

◆ Textbooks

◆ Wills

Quoth the Maven

You can remember that **exposition** is writing that explains by this memory trick: exposition = explain. Both words start with the same three letters, *exp.*

Most of the writing you do in school and in life will be expository.

Narration: Writing That Tells a Story

Scheherazade, the legendary queen of Samarkand, told her husband Schariar a story each night to keep him from killing her. By ending each story before the climax and thereby keeping his interest, Scheherazade won a delay of execution for 1,000 nights. On the 1,001st night, the king relented and granted her a pardon. Her stories include "Aladdin," "Sinbad the Sailor," and "Ali Baba and the Forty Thieves." And you thought storytelling didn't have a practical purpose! See? A good story might even save your life.

Narration is storytelling, writing that contains plot, characters, setting, and point of view. Here are some different forms that narration can take:

♦ Anecdotes

♦ Autobiography

♦ Biography

♦ Novels

♦ Oral histories

♦ Short stories

Take My Word for It _____

The Arabian Nights, also called *A Thousand and One Nights,* is a collection of stories, fairy tales, and fables gathered from Arabian and Indian folklore and passed down orally. Nearly 200 stories were compiled between 988 C.E. and 1011 C.E.; about 250 tales appear in standard collections today. Well-known stories include "Aladdin," "Sinbad the Sailor," and "Ali Baba and the Forty Thieves."

Argumentation: Writing That Persuades

Persuasion is writing that appeals to reason, emotion, or ethics (our sense of right and wrong). Writing that appeals specifically to reason is often called *argumentation.* When you argue a point in writing, you analyze a subject, topic, or issue in order to persuade your readers to think or act a certain way. *The Declaration of Independence* is a persuasive essay; so is the letter to the editor you read this morning in the daily newspaper. Here are some other forms that persuasion can take:

♦ Critical review

♦ Editorials

♦ Job evaluation

♦ Job application letter

- Letter of recommendation

- Letters to the editor

- Resumés

It's very likely that you've probably already written a great many persuasive essays, because they are common both on the job (recommendations, evaluations, resumés) and in daily life (letters to the editor).

Description: Writing That Describes

As you read the following passage, try to figure out how the writer helps you visualize the roller coasters.

> Busch Gardens in Williamsburg, Virginia, has two thrilling roller coasters, the *Big Bad Wolf* and the *Loch Ness Monster*. The four-passenger cars on *The Big Bad Wolf* hang from an overhead rail. *The Wolf* zooms at 48 miles per hour over rooftops, then plunges 80 feet to skim the river below. With its three steep drops and two 360-loops, the *Loch Ness Monster* is just as exciting. It flies along at more than 60 miles per hour along nearly 3,500 feet of track. The best part is the long, dark, twisting tunnel. Inside the tunnel, monsters shriek and strobe lights burst into the inky blackness. Water sprays from the walls.

The writer uses *description*—details drawn from the five senses: sight, taste, touch, sound, and smell. For example, the sentences "Inside the tunnel, monsters shriek and strobe lights burst into the inky blackness. Water sprays from the walls" appeal to sight, touch, and sound. See how many more descriptive details you can find in this passage.

Description is the only mode of discourse that's used in every type of writing. That's because you can't write a narration, persuasion, or exposition without description.

Take My Word for It

You want to write well, so let's tilt the scales in your favor. First, recognize that you can succeed. Many people who weren't very good at writing have learned more than enough to get where they want to be. Second, realize that you're not going to become an outstanding writer instantly. It will take you some time to master the information you need.

The Least You Need to Know

♦ Analyze your audience before you write.

♦ Tailor your writing to appeal to your audience.

♦ Study models of fine writing to help you develop your own style—so read, read, and read some more.

♦ The four types of writing are exposition, narration, argumentation, and description. The four types often overlap.

Chapter 21

Stylish Sentences

In This Chapter

- ◆ Learn how to write elegant sentences
- ◆ Try your hand at revising poor writing
- ◆ Explore the importance of punctuation to writing style

Joanne is having a relationship with a sentence. It is a beautiful sentence, and she loves it very much. They met in Haiti, a number of years ago, when Joanne was on vacation. The sentence was in French then, but Joanne didn't mind. Even through a language barrier, she knew what it was saying to her. She could see that the two of them were meant to be together.

The sentence was translated into English, and Joanne happily brought it back to America with her. She read it every day, mooning over every word, admiring her sentence's delicate phrasing. She knew she had the most perfect sentence in the whole world. And it was good to her, it made her life complete.

Joanne told her friends about her new lover. They were all shocked and confused and told her she was crazy. But she knew they were jealous because they didn't have a sentence like hers. No one else did. She was the only person in the world who felt this way. She never let them near her sentence, much less read it. It was too good for petty people like them.

The sentence spent almost a year translated into German for political reasons. Joanne worried about it every day. When it got back, would it still be the same sentence she had known before? She waited, and worried, and sure enough, it returned to her—a little different, perhaps, but what did semantics matter? It was still the sentence she knew and loved.

Years passed. Joanne and her sentence led very happy, fulfilled lives. They lived together, traveled together, and grew old together. Then, one day, Joanne read her sentence as she had in her youth. To her dismay, she discovered she no longer understood it. She had no idea what the sentence meant anymore.

Joanne is having a relationship with a sentence. But she no longer thinks it a beautiful sentence, and she no longer loves it. Now, all she has is a scrap of paper and a dependent clause.

Poor Joanne! I want you to stay in love with your sentences forever. In this chapter, I'll teach you how to write graceful sentences that express your exact meaning. To that end, you'll rewrite weak sentences to make them stronger. You'll also explore the impact that punctuation can have on sentence style and effectiveness.

Flexible Flyers

Clear writing uses sentences of different lengths and types to create variety and interest. Craft your sentences to express your ideas in the best possible way. Following are eight ways you can vary your sentences to create an effective, readable, and interesting style.

Vary Sentence Types

Mix *simple, compound, complex,* and *compound-complex* sentences for a more effective style. Review Chapter 13 for a complete discussion of the four sentence types.

But while you're here, label each sentence in the following passage. Write *simple, compound, complex,* or *compound-complex* for each sentence.

(1) The world's most costly meal began with a glass of vinegar. (2) When people are asked to think of the most expensive beverage, vinegar may not immediately come to mind, but it may take the prize for the most expensive drink in history!

(3) Cleopatra, queen of Egypt, made history when she made a bet that she could eat, at one meal, the value of a million sesterces, which was many years' wages for the average worker. (4) Everyone thought that her wager was impossible; after all, how could anyone eat so much at a single meal?

(5) Cleopatra was able to eat a meal worth so much by putting a million sesterces worth of pearls into a glass of vinegar. (6) She then set the goblet aside while the dinner was served and she waited for the vinegar to dissolve the pearls. (7) At the end of the meal, when it was time for her to fulfill her gamble, she simply drank the dissolved pearls! (8) Cleopatra won her bet because she knew that vinegar would dissolve pearls.

Answers

1. Simple

2. Compound-complex

3. Complex

4. Complex

5. Simple

6. Compound

7. Complex

8. Compound

Vary Sentence Lengths

Vary the length of your sentences, too. The unbroken rhythm of monotonous sentence length can lull a reader into unconsciousness.

◆ When your topic is complicated or full of numbers, use simple sentences to aid understanding. And keep them short!

◆ Use longer, more complex sentences to show how ideas are linked together and to avoid repetition.

The following passage has a boring mix of simple sentences. On a separate sheet of paper, rewrite the passage to vary the sentence types.

John Styth Pemberton was born in 1833. He was a pharmacist. He moved to Atlanta, Georgia, in 1869. He created so-called "patent medicines." These were homemade medicines that were sold without a prescription. He made these patent medicines to make a living. Pemberton registered a trademark for a medicine he called "French Wine Coca—Ideal Nerve and Tonic Stimulant." This happened fourteen years after he settled in Atlanta. In 1866, Pemberton came up with a headache medicine. He called it "Coca-Cola." He had taken the wine out of the

French Wine Coca and added some caffeine. The medicine tasted terrible. At the last minute he added some extract of kola nut and a few other oils. He sold it to soda fountains in used bottles. A few weeks later, a man with a terrible headache hauled himself into a drugstore. The man asked for a spoonful of Coca-Cola. Usually, druggists stirred such headache remedies into a glass of water. In this case, however, the person on duty was too lazy to walk over to the sink. Instead, he mixed the syrup in some seltzer water. He did this because it was closer to where he was standing. The customer liked the carbonated version better than the uncarbonated one. Other customers agreed. From then on, Coca-Cola was served as a carbonated drink.

Possible response:

Born in 1833, John Styth Pemberton was a pharmacist who moved to Atlanta, Georgia, in 1869. To make a living, he created so-called "patent medicines," homemade medicines that were sold without a prescription. Fourteen years after settling in Atlanta, Pemberton registered a trademark for a medicine he called "French Wine Coca—Ideal Nerve and Tonic Stimulant." In 1866, Pemberton came up with a headache medicine he called "Coca-Cola." He had taken the wine out of the French Wine Coca and added some caffeine. The medicine tasted so terrible that at the last minute he added some extract of kola nut and a few other oils. He sold it to soda fountains in used bottles. A few weeks later, a man with a terrible headache hauled himself into a drugstore and asked for a spoonful of Coca-Cola. Usually, druggists stirred such headache remedies into a glass of water. In this case, however, the person on duty was too lazy to walk over to the sink. Instead, he mixed the syrup in some seltzer water because it was closer to where he was standing. The customer liked the carbonated version better than the uncarbonated one. Other customers agreed. From then on, Coca-Cola was served as a carbonated drink.

However, we can't be so quick to throw out the baby with the bathwater! A passage with only simple sentences can create a very stately tone, as the following speech illustrates. Chief Joseph of the Nez Percé Indians delivered this speech in 1877 when he surrendered his family and people to the U.S. Army. As you read the speech, see how Chief Joseph uses only simple sentences to convey his sorrow.

Tell General Howard I know his heart. What he told me before I have in my heart. I am tired of fighting. Our chiefs are killed. Looking Glass is dead. The old men are all killed. It is the young men who say yes or no. He who led the young men is dead. It is cold and we have no blankets. The little children are freezing to death. My people, some of them, have run away to the hills and have no blankets, no food; no one knows where they are, perhaps freezing to death. I want time to look for my children and see how many of them I can find. Maybe I shall find them among the dead. Hear me, my chiefs, I am tired; my heart is sick and sad. From where the sun now stands, I will fight no more forever.

Add Questions and Commands

Break the pattern of your writing with an occasional mild command or question—if it is suitable for your topic and audience. Remember that you have only four basic types of sentences—*declarative, interrogative, exclamatory,* and *imperative*—to express your ideas. Nearly all your formal business and personal writing will be based on declarative sentences, but when you can, try for some variety.

Underline the question in the following paragraph.

There is a great deal of confusion over what the 40 different species that belong to the family *Delphinidae* are called. For example, is a small cetacean a "dolphin" or a "porpoise"? Some people distinguish a *dolphin* as a cetacean having a snout or beak, while a *porpoise* usually refers to one with a smoothly rounded forehead. The larger members of this porpoise and dolphin family are called "whales," but they nonetheless fit the same characteristics as their smaller relatives. The number of different names for these creatures reflects the confusion of long-ago sailors as they tried to classify them. Unfortunately, identifying them in their home in the sea is not easy, for the main differences between members of the species is in their skeleton structure.

Focus on the Subject

Select the subject of each sentence based on what you want to emphasize. Because readers focus on the subject of your sentence, make it the most important aspect of each thought.

The following sentences all contain the same information, but notice how the meaning changes in each one based on the choice of subject:

 Quoth the Maven

Keep the subject and verb close together in very long sentences to make the sentences easier to read and understand.

♦ Our research showed that 15 percent of employees' time is spent answering e-mail.

  (*Research* is the subject.)

Take My Word for It _____

The latest studies suggest that readers best remember a message delivered at the very beginning or the very end of a sentence. If the material you're presenting is especially important, position it at one of these key points.

◆ Employees spend 15 percent of their time answering e-mail.

(*Employees* is the subject.)

◆ Answering e-mail occupies 15 percent of employees' time.

(*Answering e-mail* is the subject.)

◆ Fifteen percent of employees' time is spent answering e-mail.

(*Fifteen percent*—the amount of time—is the subject.)

Add Details

A plain black suit has an undeniable elegance, but it's so much more interesting when brightened up with a classy tie or glittering diamond broach. It's the same with sentences. Add adjectives and adverbs to a sentence (when suitable) for emphasis and variety. Carefully selected details help your readers visualize the people, places, and scenes that you're describing.

◆ Base your decision to expand a sentence on its focus and how it works in the context of surrounding sentences.

◆ Expand sentences with phrases and clauses as well as words.

As you read the following essay, note how the writer (me!) added vivid details. Use the details to help you get a clear mental image of the scene.

By the 1800s, several hundred medicine shows traveled across America, giving a wide variety of shows. At one end of the scale were simple magic acts; at the other, complicated spectacles. From 1880 to 1910, one of the largest of these shows was "The King of the Road Shows," the Kickapoo Indian Medicine Company. Two experienced entertainers, Charles H. "Texas Charlie" Bigelow and John E. "Doc" Healy, had started the company more than two decades before. From their headquarters in New Haven, Connecticut, the partners sent as many as twenty-five shows at a time across America.

Texas Charlie managed the "medicine" end of the production, training the "Doctors" and "Professors" who gave the "Medical Lectures." Doc Healy was in charge of hiring the performers—from fiddlers to fire-eaters, including comedians, acrobats, singers, and jugglers. Both Indians and whites were hired. All the Indians, including Mohawks, Iroquois, Crees, Sioux, and Blackfeet, were billed as "pure-blooded Kickapoos," a completely fictional tribe.

All the entertainers wore outrageous costumes. The Native Americans were covered in feathers, colored beads, and crude weapons. The "Doctors" and "Professors" were equally glittery. Some wore fringed leather coats, silver-capped boots; others, fancy silk shirts, a type of tuxedo jacket called a "frock coat," and high silk hats. One of the most outlandish figures was the glib "Nevada Ned, the King of Gold." Born Ned T. Oliver, this entertainer wore a fancy suit studded with buttons made of gold. On his head he sported a huge sombrero dangling 100 gold coins.

During the summer, the Kickapoo shows were presented under enormous tents. When the weather turned chilly, the troupe moved into to town halls and opera houses. Most often, the show was free. Occasionally, adults were charged a dime to get in. Where did the profits come from? The sale of "medicine." According to the show's advertisements, these wonder-working Kickapoo brews were "compounded according to secret ancient Kickapoo Indian tribal formulas." Among the ingredients were "blood root, feverwort, spirit gum, wild poke berries, slippery elm, white oak bark, dock root, and other Natural Products." These "medicines" sold for fifty cents to a dollar a bottle, and were guaranteed to cure all the ills that afflict the human body.

Read the following two passages. They're both chintzy with adjectives, adverbs, and details. Add some juice in the spaces provided.

Model #1

Egypt, a _____ strip of land in _____, is the only place in the world where pyramids were built. Back then, all the water for the land and its people came from the _____ River. Natural barriers protected the land from invaders. There were _____ deserts to the east and west that cut off Egypt from the rest of the world. There were _____ rapids on the Nile to the south. Delta marshes lay to the _____. This circle of isolation allowed the Egyptians to work in _____. In addition, _____ materials were needed to build the pyramids. Ancient Egypt had an abundance of _____ . These rocks were quarried close to the banks of the Nile. But these rocks had to be brought from quarries to the building sites. Egypt's _____ resource— the great Nile River—provided the means for transportation.

Possible response:

Egypt, a long, narrow, fertile strip of land in northeastern Africa, is the only place in the world where pyramids were built. Back then, all the water for the land and its people came from the mighty Nile River. Natural barriers protected the land from invaders. There were vast deserts to the east and west that cut off Egypt from the rest of the world. There were dangerous rapids on the Nile to the south.

Delta marshes lay to the north. This circle of isolation allowed the Egyptians to work in peace and security. In addition, great supplies of raw materials were needed to build the pyramids. Ancient Egypt had an abundance of limestone, sandstone, and granite. These rocks were quarried close to the banks of the Nile. But these rocks had to be brought from quarries to the building sites. Egypt's most precious resource—the great Nile River—provided the means for transportation.

Model #2

We have airplanes because _____ built their biplane and took off from _____. We understand physics because Albert Einstein dared to think ahead of the curve. We made it into space because of the _____ at _____ who learned about space travel. Ford thought outside the box and created the _____; Banting and Best found out how to treat diabetes with insulin. These brave people—and so many more like them—found out how to solve problems that enabled them to do a job that needed doing.

Possible response:

We have airplanes because Orville and Wilbur Wright built their biplane and took off from Kitty Hawk. We understand physics because Albert Einstein dared to think ahead of the curve. We made it into space because of the scientists and astronauts at NASA who learned about space travel. Ford thought outside the box and created the Model T; Banting and Best found out how to treat diabetes with insulin. These brave people—and so many more like them—found out how to solve problems that enabled them to do a job that needed doing.

Danger, Will Robinson

Don't add detail merely to pad your writing, because that results in bloated, awkward sentences. And make sure that every word has meaning in the context of the passage. As George Orwell said in his famous essay "Politics and the English Language": "A scrupulous writer, in every sentence that he writes, will ask himself at least four questions, thus: What am I trying to say? What words will express it? What images or idiom will make it clearer? Is this image fresh enough to have an effect? And he will probably ask himself two more: Could I put it more shortly? Have I said anything that is unavoidably ugly?"

Use Vivid Verbs

Use verbs rather than nouns to communicate your ideas. This makes your writing more forceful and less wordy. For example, replace forms of *to be* with action verbs, as the following example shows:

- ◆ *Weak:* In 1850, 21-year-old Levi Strauss *went* from New York to San Francisco.

    Vivid: In 1850, 21-year-old Levi Strauss *traveled* from New York to San Francisco.

- ◆ *Weak:* The shrieking Arctic gales *sent* needles of ice into their faces.

    Vivid: The shrieking Arctic gales *shot* needles of ice into their faces.

Danger, Will Robinson

Place the adjectives, adverbs, phrases, and clauses according to the emphasis you want to achieve in each sentence. Remember that misplaced modifiers spell trouble, so be sure to place them as close as possible to the words they describe.

Invert Word Order

Most English sentences follow the subject-verb-direct object pattern, so varying this pattern automatically creates emphasis and interest. To create stylistic variety, occasionally place the verb before the subject, as these examples show:

Subject-verb order: The CEO walked in. The manager walked out.

Inverted order: In walked the CEO. Out walked the manager.

Play with Pronouns

Use the pronoun *you* to engage your readers. The second-person pronoun *you* (rather than the third-person *he, she, one*) gives your writing more impact because it directly addresses the reader, as this example shows:

Weak: Contributions to the employee's account will automatically be reinvested unless the employee has completed form 21-A.

Better: Contributions to your account will automatically be reinvested unless you have completed form 21-A.

Take My Word for It _____

Due to state laws, some companies require that documents such as consumer contracts and warranties meet a specific readability score that determines how easy or difficult they are to read. Such readability scores on the Frye, Gunning Fog Index, and Flesch Reading Ease Scale are calculated on the basis of word and sentence length. But using shorter words and sentences will not necessarily make a document easier to understand, especially if the words are technical in nature.

Between a Rock and a Hard Place

What happens if your supervisor likes an ornate, flowery style with big words and windy sentences? Or take a less extreme case: What if your company prefers writing in the passive voice to the active voice? If this is the case, you have several choices:

1. Write clearly and logically, based on what you learned in this chapter. Seeing effective writing may change your supervisor's mind.

Quoth the Maven _____

As you draft your message, use special care to avoid phrases that could seem hostile, rude, uncaring, or arrogant. Strike them from your style.

2. Confer with your supervisor about changing writing styles. People might be using weaker writing models because they don't have anything better to use.

3. Recognize that writing style serves to unify a company as well as communicate ideas. Even if the style isn't as strong and effective as clear writing, it may bring people together in a corporate culture.

Punctuation and Style: Little Things Matter a Lot

Your choice of punctuation also has a critical influence on your writing style because it determines the degree of linkage between sentences. Further, it suggests whether sentence elements are coordinating or subordinating. Here are some guidelines:

♦ Remember that a period shows a full separation between ideas.

♦ A comma and a coordinating conjunction show the following relationships: addition, choice, consequence, contrast, or cause.

♦ A semicolon shows that the second sentence completes the content of the first sentence. The semicolon suggests a link but leaves it to the reader to make the connection.

◆ A semicolon and a conjunctive adverb (a word such as *nevertheless, however,* etc.) shows the relationship between ideas: addition, consequence, contrast, cause and effect, time, emphasis, or addition.

◆ Using a period between sentences forces a pause and then stresses the conjunctive adverb.

Take My Word for It

So far, I've concentrated on the *content* of your writing, but the *form* also matters. To make your writing easier to read, break it into chunks of manageable length. That's the principle behind dividing telephone numbers into groups (212-555-2138 versus 2125552138). When you have a lot of facts, consider arranging them in a list, table, or chart. Use color to set off charts, graphs, or other visuals.

Try it yourself. Add punctuation to the following passage. First, make sure it's correct; then, make sure it's interesting—given your audience and purpose!

It stretches snaps and shatters when hit with a heavy object If you press a blob of it against a comic book or newspaper it picks up the image even the colors It can be used to build strength in a person's hands and remove lint from clothing It's out of this world literally because astronauts use it to hold tools to space capsule surfaces during the weightlessness of space travel What is it

That's the question James Wright asked himself in the early 1940s when he created the odd stuff As an engineer for General Electric Wright had been trying to develop a rubber substitute to do his part to help the Allies during World War I However instead of rubber he created a blob of sticky stuff that bounced when he dropped it It had no use but everyone liked to play with it

In 1949 Peter Hodgson named it "Silly Putty" and featured it in a toy store catalog Silly Putty was an instant hit

Possible response:

It stretches, snaps, and shatters when hit with a heavy object. If you press a blob of it against a comic book or newspaper, it picks up the image—even the colors. It can be used to build strength in a person's hands and remove lint from clothing. It's out of this world—literally—because astronauts use it to hold tools to space capsule surfaces during the weightlessness of space travel. What is it?

That's the question James Wright asked himself in the early 1940s when he created the odd stuff. As an engineer for General Electric, Wright had been trying to develop a rubber substitute to do his part to help the Allies during World War I. However, instead of rubber, he created a blob of sticky stuff that bounced when he dropped it. It had no use, but everyone liked to play with it.

In 1949, Peter Hodgson named it "Silly Putty" and featured it in a toy store catalog. Silly Putty was an instant hit.

The Least You Need to Know

- Mix simple, compound, complex, and compound-complex sentences for a more effective style. Also vary sentence lengths, add questions and commands, focus on the subject, use vivid verbs, and invert word order.

- In informal writing, use the pronoun *you* to engage readers.

- Your choice of punctuation also has a critical influence on your writing style.

- Always write clearly and logically.

22

Conciseness: The Department of Redundancy Department

In This Chapter

- ◆ Understand redundancy
- ◆ Simplify sentences
- ◆ Improve your writing style

In language, as in plane geometry, the shortest distance between two points is a straight line. As Thomas Jefferson once remarked, "The most valuable of all talents is that of never using two words when one will do." That's what this chapter is all about.

All good writing demands a polished style. Especially in business, writers impress their readers not with big words and convoluted prose, but rather with a straightforward, easy-to-read style. Learn how to accomplish this right now.

Slash and Burn

Redundant writing is cluttered with unnecessary words that fog your meaning. Wordy writing forces your readers to clear away unnecessary words and phrases before they can understand your message. *Redundancies* are the junk food of our language, filling us up on empty words.

You Could Look It Up

Redundancy is the unnecessary repetition of words and ideas.

Prove it to yourself. The following table is a series of redundant phrases I've culled from newspapers, magazines, friends, and foes. Rewrite each of the following phrases to eliminate the redundancy. Then give a reason for your revision. The first one is done for you.

Redundancy	Repair	Reason
1. honest truth	truth	truth *is* honest by definition
2. past experience	_____	_____
3. past history	_____	_____
4. fatally killed	_____	_____
5. revert back	_____	_____
6. foreign imports	_____	_____
7. partial stop	_____	_____
8. true facts	_____	_____
9. free gift	_____	_____
10. live and breathe	_____	_____
11. null and void	_____	_____
12. most unique	_____	_____
13. cease and desist	_____	_____
14. soup du jour of the day	_____	_____
15. at 8 A.M. in the morning	_____	_____
16. sum total and end results	_____	_____
17. living survivors	_____	_____
18. proceed ahead	_____	_____
19. successfully escaped	_____	_____

Redundancy	Repair	Reason
20. minus eight degrees below zero	_____	_____
21. forward progress	_____	_____
22. set a new record	_____	_____
23. kills bugs dead	_____	_____
24. at this point in time	_____	_____

Answers

Redundancy	Repair	Reason
1. honest truth	truth	truth *is* honest
2. past experience	experience	*all* experience is past
3. past history	history	all history is past
4. fatally killed	killed	fatal = dead
5. revert back	revert	revert = go back
6. foreign imports	imports	we have *domestic* imports?
7. partial stop	stop	stop = stop
8. true facts	facts	facts *are* true
9. free gift	gift	gifts *are* free
10. live and breathe	live	if you live, you breathe
11. null and void	null (or void)	null = void
12. most unique	unique	unique can't be modified; it is the most
13. cease and desist	cease (or desist)	cease = desist
14. soup du jour of the day	soup du jour	du jour = of the day
15. at 8 A.M. in the morning	at 8 A.M.	A.M. = morning
16. sum total and end results	total (or results)	sum total = end results
17. leaving no living survivors	leaving no survivors	survivors *are* alive
18. proceed ahead	proceed	you can't proceed *back*

continues

continued

Redundancy	Repair	Reason
19. successfully escaped	escaped	you can't escape *unsuccessfully*
20. minus eight degrees below zero	minus 8 degrees	minus = below zero
21. forward progress	progress	all progress is forward
22. set a new record	set a record	all records are new when they are set
23. kills bugs dead	kills bugs	kills = dead
24. at this point in time	now	wordy phrase

Thrift, Thrift, Thrift

When you sit down to write, you might get carried away by the sound of your own words. Even though you know you've packed in some unnecessary verbiage, each word is near and dear to your heart, like your cracked Little League catcher's mitt from '67 or the designer shoes you got on sale that never fit and never will.

Take My Word for It _____

Redundancy comes from the Latin word *undare* ("to overflow") and *re* ("back"). Because redundancy literally means "to overflow again and again," the word itself is redundant!

You want to save every one of your words; after all, they are *your* words. "Cut that phrase?" you howl. "I can't bear to part with such a beautiful (graceful, important, dazzling) phrase." Yes, you can; trust me. And your writing will be the better for it. An effective writing style shows an economy of language.

From now on, here's your mantra:

♦ Write simply and directly.

♦ Omit unnecessary details or ideas that you have already stated.

♦ Use a lot of important detail, but no unnecessary words. You want your writing to be concise.

Conciseness describes writing that is direct and to the point. This is not to say that you have to pare away all description, figures of speech, and images. No. Rather, it *is* to say that wordy writing annoys your readers because it forces them to slash their way through your sentences before they can understand what you're saying. Hard and lean sentences, like hard and lean bodies, require far more effort than flabby ones. And they are so much nicer.

Follow these five easy rules to create taut, effective sentences.

- ◆ Eliminate unneeded words and phrases.
- ◆ Revise sentences that begin with expletives.
- ◆ Combine sentences that repeat information.
- ◆ Don't say the same thing twice.
- ◆ Make passive sentences active.

Look at each of these rules in greater detail.

Eliminate Unneeded Words and Phrases

Unneeded words are like annoying little gnats that nip at your ankles during summer picnics. As a matter of fact, because these words and phrases are like so much empty noise, they are often called *buzzwords*.

Buzzwords come in different parts of speech, as the following table shows.

You Could Look It Up

Buzzwords are commonly used, extraneous phrases that aren't necessary to the meaning of the sentence and so should be cut.

Buzzwords

Part of Speech	Sample Buzzwords
Adjectives	nice, central, major, good, excellent
Adverbs	quite, very, basically, really, central, major
Nouns	field, case, situation, character, kind, scope, sort, type, thing, element, area, aspect, factor, nature, quality

Here's how they look in context:

Wordy: These types of administrative problems are really quite difficult to solve.

Better: Administrative problems are difficult to solve.

Redundant phrases are kissing cousins to buzzwords because they also repeat information that has already been stated. The following table lists 10 especially annoying examples. Add them to the ones you revised at the beginning of this chapter.

Ten Redundant Phrases Revised

Redundant	Better
repeat again	repeat
red in color	red
extra gratuity	gratuity
continue to remain	remain
small in size	small
few in number	few
new innovation	innovation
complete stop	stop
combine together	combine
final end	end

Then we have the big daddy of them all, really long-winded phrases. These are pre-fab phrases that seem to add instant sophistication to your sentences. They don't. Instead, they make your writing sound pretentious and gassy.

The following table lists some of these annoying redundancies and ways to revise them.

Twenty Redundant Phrases Revised

Wordy	Better
at this point in time	now
at the present time	now
for the purpose of	for
in the event that	if
until such time as	until
in view of the fact that	because
because of the fact that	because
due to the fact that	because
in order to utilize	to use
is an example of	is
free up some space	make room
my personal physician	my doctor
thunderstorm activity	thunderstorm

Wordy	Better
weather event	snow (rain, and so on)
it is believed by many that	many believe
experience some discomfort	hurt
in order to	to
making an effort to	trying to
completely surrounded on all sides	surrounded
reiterated over and over again	repeated

Following are 8 wordy phrases that should just be stricken from your writing, much as you destroy the pictures of your old flame when you find a new love. (You *did* destroy those photos, didn't you?)

Dead air:

1. the point I am trying to make

2. as a matter of fact

3. in a very real sense

4. in light of the fact that

5. in the case of

6. that is to say

7. to get to the point

8. what I mean to say

Wordy: In fact, the luncheonette that was situated in the local area was, in a very real sense, the heart of the neighborhood.

Better: The luncheonette was the heart of the neighborhood.

Take a second and slice the deadwood from the following sentences. Each refers to an actual law still on the books in some U.S. cities. (They prove why we need more lawyers.)

1. It is a true fact that in Tennessee, it's illegal to shoot any game (for the purpose of harming them) other than whales from a moving automobile.

2. What I mean to say is that in Boston, it is illegal to hold frog-jumping contests in nightclubs.

    _____

3. At this point in time, it is still illegal to drive more than 2,000 sheep down Hollywood Boulevard at one time.

    _____

4. It is a true fact that in Devon, Connecticut, it is unlawful to walk backward in a reverse direction after sunset when the sun has already set.

    _____

5. It is the honest truth that horses are forbidden to eat fire hydrants in a very real sense in Marshalltown, Iowa.

    _____

Answers

1. In Tennessee, it's illegal to shoot any game other than whales from a moving automobile.

2. In Boston, it is illegal to hold frog-jumping contests in nightclubs.

3. It is still illegal to drive more than 2,000 sheep down Hollywood Boulevard at one time.

4. In Devon, Connecticut, it is unlawful to walk backward after sunset.

5. Horses are forbidden to eat fire hydrants in Marshalltown, Iowa.

Revise Sentences That Begin with Expletives

Expletives are constructions that fill holes when writers invert subject-verb word order. Now, inverting subject-verb word order is a good way to achieve sentence variety, as you've already learned. But filling in the blanks with expletives just clutters your writing.

You Could Look It Up

Expletives are constructions that fill holes when writers invert subject-verb word order.

Here are the most common expletive constructions:

- It is
- There is
- There are
- There were

These constructions only delay the point of the sentence. For instance:

- *It is necessary for* all employees to select a health care plan.

- *There are* three health plans employees can choose.

Whenever possible, replace the expletive with an action verb, as these revised sentences show:

- All employees must select a health care plan.

- Employees can choose from three health plans.

  Or:

  Three health plans are offered.

Combine Sentences That Repeat Information

You can also combine sentences to achieve clarity. First, look for sentences that contain the same information or relate to the same ideas and so logically belong together. Then combine the related sentences. Finally, cut any words that just take up space like an unwanted house guest. Here are some examples:

Wordy: The Chamber was a best-seller. It was written by John Grisham. *The Chamber* was a courtroom thriller.

Better: The Chamber, by John Grisham, was a best-selling courtroom thriller.

Wordy: Sonnets, which are a beautiful poetic form, have 14 lines and a set rhythm and rhyme.

Better: Sonnets are a beautiful poetic form with 14 lines and a set rhythm and rhyme.

You can also eliminate unnecessary words by slicing and dicing extraneous relative pronouns and adjective clauses. For instance:

Wordy: Rosie O'Donnell, who was homecoming queen of her high school class, was raised in Commack, New York.

Better: Rosie O'Donnell, homecoming queen of her high school class, was raised in Commack, New York.

(The relative phrase "who was" jolts the rhythm of the writing; the sentence is much smoother without it.)

Danger, Will Robinson

Repetition is a good thing, redundancy is not. When you use repetition, you deliberately repeat words and phrases to create rhythm and emphasis. Redundancy, in contrast, is made up of unnecessary bits and pieces that need to be trimmed like fat from the federal budget.

Wordy: Many people are drawn to Goldie Hawn's vitality, which is delightful.

Better: Many people are drawn to Goldie Hawn's delightful vitality.

(Again, the relative phrase "which are" adds annoying clutter.)

Give it a shot. Rewrite the following paragraph to eliminate unnecessary words. Write your revision on the lines provided.

Wordy:

The high cost of multimedia presentations is due to the combined cost of studio shoots and expensive media compression. The costs of graphic design and technical support are also high.

Revised:

_____

_____

How does your revision compare to this version?

Studio shoots, media compression, graphic design, and technical support all contribute to the high cost of multimedia presentations.

Don't Say the Same Thing Twice

Phrases such as "cover over," "circle around," and "square in shape" are redundant—they say the same thing twice. This is the redundancy problem you corrected in the beginning of this chapter.

Wordy: We watched the big, massive, black cloud rising up from the level prairie and covering over the sun.

Better: We watched the massive, black cloud rise from the prairie and cover the sun.

Wordy: The package, rectangular in shape, was on the counter.

Better: The rectangular package was on the counter.

Danger, Will Robinson

As you learned, there are some legitimate reasons to use the passive voice. For example, passive is the voice of choice when you don't want to name the subject (as in "A mistake was made") or you want to focus on the object of the action (as in "A robbery occurred today").

Make Passive Sentences Active

In the *active voice*, the subject performs the action named by the verb. In the passive voice, the subject receives the action. The *passive voice* is often far wordier than the active voice. How many unnecessary words were cut by rewriting the following sentences from the passive voice to the active voice?

Passive: A turkey instead of an eagle was first wanted by Benjamin Franklin as our national symbol.

Active: Benjamin Franklin first wanted a turkey instead of an eagle as our national symbol.

Passive: From 1960 to 1981, a record $71 million was amassed by Muhammad Ali in his professional boxing career.

Active: From 1960 to 1981, Muhammad Ali amassed a record $71 million in his professional boxing career.

Rewrite each of these passive sentences into the active voice.

1. As the *Titanic* sank on April 15, 1912, "Nearer My God to Thee" was played by the band.

   _____

2. Four Pulitzer Prizes in poetry were won by Robert Frost.

   _____

3. In 1963, the presidency of her high school class was won by Bette Midler.

   _____

4. The first antislavery group in America was headed by Ben Franklin.

   _____

5. A job as a reporter for *The New York Tribune* was once held by Karl Marx.

   _____

Answers

1. As the *Titanic* sank on April 15, 1912, the band played "Nearer My God to Thee."

2. Robert Frost won four Pulitzer Prizes in poetry.

3. In 1963, Bette Midler won the presidency of her high school class.

4. Ben Franklin headed the first antislavery group in America.

5. Karl Marx was once a reporter for *The New York Tribune*.

The Least You Need to Know

◆ Redundancy is unnecessary repetition of words and ideas.

◆ Eliminate unnecessary words and phrases to make your writing clearer and more vigorous.

23

Diction: Find the Right Word, Not Its First Cousin

In This Chapter

◆ Define diction

◆ Learn the levels of diction

◆ Distinguish between confusing words

Few people use the same words every time they write any more than they wear the same clothes on every occasion. Successful writers adapt their language to the audience and circumstances because they know which words are appropriate in a specific situation. Just as people with style know how to select an outfit that will make the right impression, so do effective writers know how to select the words to fit their needs. That's what you learn in this chapter.

First, I define *diction* and explain the criteria for choosing words. You learn about the different levels of language, from very formal to very informal. Along the way, I explain the importance of *connotation* and *denotation*, too. This chapter concludes with a discussion of *homonyms* and other words that are often confused and misused.

Diction: Proper Words in Proper Places

The words you select as you write and speak make up your *diction*. There are words, and then there are words. The word you want in a specific instance depends on context: your audience, purpose, and *tone*.

You Could Look It Up

Diction is a writer's choice of words. The **tone** of a document is the writer's attitude toward his or her subject and audience.

Your diction affects the clarity and impact of your message. Diction is measured from *formal* to *informal* language usage. *Formal diction* is marked by 25¢ words, long sentences, and a formal tone; *informal diction* includes shorter words and sentences and a less formal tone. Neither level of diction (or any level in between) is intrinsically good or bad; rather, each is appropriate in different writing situations. The following chart shows the spectrum of diction and when each level is used.

Levels of Language	
Very formal	Legal documents
	Technical reports
	Job applications
	Letters/resumés
	Scientific magazine articles
	Political speeches
	Sermons
	Newspaper editorials
	Newspaper columns
	Letters of complaint
	Press releases
	Sales and marketing letters
	E-mail (depending on content)
	Popular magazine articles
Very informal	Notes to friends

Let's look at the different levels of diction in more detail, starting at most formal and working to the least formal.

Elevated Diction

The most elevated level of diction has abstract language, a serious tone, few personal references, few contractions, and considerable distance implied between reader and writer. It's used for the most formal documents such as a stock prospectus, deed, or last will and testament, as you learned from the preceding chart.

Here's some elevated diction from philosopher Ralph Waldo Emerson: "Whoso would be a man, must be a nonconformist. He who would gather immortal palms must not be hindered by the name of goodness, but must explore if it be goodness." Note the difficult words (*Whoso, nonconformist, hindered*), long sentences, formal tone, and complex ideas.

Edited American English

The set of language standards used in most academic and professional writing is called "Edited American English" or "Standard Written English." It's the writing you find in magazines such as *Newsweek, U.S. News & World Report*, and *The Atlantic*. Such language conforms to the widely established rules of grammar, sentence structure, usage, punctuation, and spelling that you've been learning in this book.

Danger, Will Robinson

The advertising industry often uses language that ignores conventional usage to appeal to a wider percentage of the population. Don't let these published ads influence you into believing that this level of diction is acceptable in a business setting. It's not.

Colloquial Language

Next comes *colloquial language*, the level of diction characteristic of casual conversation and informal writing. The following two sentences show the difference between standard diction and colloquial language:

Standard: I *failed* my driving test.

Colloquial: I *flunked* my driving test.

Slang

Less formal than colloquial language is *slang*, which is coined words and phrases or new meanings for established terms. Recent slang includes the words *yuppie, chill out, rad,*

You Could Look It Up

Slang is coined words and phrases or new meanings for established terms.

superheavy, or *phat*. Slang is fun, informal, and personal, and it's great for casual conversations with friends. Slang is never used in formal writing.

Vernacular

Vernacular is the ordinary language of a particular region, such as *hoagie, grinder,* or *sub* for a sandwich on a roll. *Dialect*, the language specific to a particular regional area, is a type of vernacular. It's different from slang because dialect reflects differences in regions and socio-economic status. Like colloquial language and slang, vernacular and dialect are not appropriate for formal writing, such as business letters, memos, and faxes.

Here's how the novelist and humorist Mark Twain used vernacular and dialect to describe the people and events in the American West in the 1880s. The following sentence describes a scam involving a frog stuffed with buckshot: "I do wonder what in the nation that frog throw'd off for—I wonder if there ain't something the matter with him—he 'pers to look mighty baggy, somehow."

Quoth the Maven

You may find it easier to use the appropriate tone if you put yourself in the reader's position for a moment. Ask yourself how you might feel or react if you received the letter you are sending.

The phrases *what in the nation* and *look mighty baggy* as well as the words *ain't* and *'pers* (for *appears*) capture the mood of the time and place. Notice the unusual spelling, especially the contractions.

Tone-on-Tone

When you write, you'll often find yourself shifting between levels of diction, as you look for the word, phrase, or expression that fits your writing situation and creates the tone you want. The tone of a document is the writer's attitude toward his or her subject and audience. For example, the tone may be formal or informal, friendly or distant, personal or pompous.

Danger, Will Robinson

Don't discount the importance of context and connotation. Words carry different connotations depending on how they are used, especially where gender is concerned. For example, an aggressive man and an aggressive woman are often perceived as two different animals: the former as an achiever; the latter as a word that rhymes with *witch* and *rich*.

Tone is not a constant, like death and taxes. The tone of a business letter, for example, varies as much as people and companies do. Letters that represent the opinions of companies and governments, for example, are often extremely formal. Letters between friends or longtime colleagues, in contrast, may have a casual tone—even though they are in the form of a business letter.

Ten Distinctions Worth Making (or at Least Worth Being Able to Make!)

1. *Affect and effect*

   Swear to get this one down and I promise to spare you *lie* and *lay*. (I lie, but no matter.) Most of the time, *affect* is the verb, implying influence. For example: "A nice big chunk of imported Swiss chocolate can affect your mood." *Effect* is the equivalent noun: "Chocolate has had an effect on my mood."

   But life in Grammarland is not *that* simple. Sometimes, *effect* can be a verb. Here's where the situation gets so ugly it can run a bulldog off a meat wagon. When used as a verb, *effect* means impact and purpose: "I must effect my plan to stop eating so much chocolate"; "By not eating so much chocolate, I have succeeded in effecting my plan." Of course, not eating chocolate may also have affected your plan (may have contributed to it), but here you're claiming that stopping eating chocolate was what really turned things around.

2. *Anxious and eager*

   Here's one of the famous language bulwarks: You're not *anxious* to spend an evening with old friends, you're *eager* to spend it. (Unless, of course, you've been sleeping with one of them for the past six months. Then you probably *are* anxious.)

    Danger, Will Robinson

   There's also the so-called *affect* (watch that noun) in psychology; all that emotional stuff about a particular state. But don't let it affect you too much.

3. *Assure, ensure, insure*

   Assure is a verb meaning "to reassure" or "to convince." It's generally followed by a direct object that names a person. For example: The doctor assured her patient that the rash looked worse than it was. *Ensure* and *insure* both mean "to make sure, certain, or safe." Insure is generally used to refer to a financial certainty. Check out this example: Luis hoped his college degree would ensure him a job, preferably one that would insure him in case of illness.

4. *Authentic and genuine*

   Something that's *genuine* is the real thing; something that's *authentic* tells the truth about its subject. So if you spent Monday morning thrilling your co-workers with the details of your weekend scuba diving in Barbuda when you'd really stayed home and watched reruns yet again, your account would be genuine but not authentic.

Now, if you were eavesdropping on the subway and overheard the story about scuba diving in Barbuda and repeated the story word for word to your co-workers, that account would be *authentic* (assuming the person in the subway was telling the truth) but not *genuine*, because you'd be passing off someone else's good time as your own.

5. *Compleat and complete*

This one's a snap; *compleat* is *archaic*. It's as classy as hot pants and hula hoops. If the world were a fair place, you'd never have to deal with this word again. Unfortunately, the world is not a just place.

You Could Look It Up

An **archaic** word is antiquated, and like Grammy's fine china, rarely used. People with names like "Sir Milton of Westchester" and "The Baroness Sydneyy of Lower Slobbovia" tend to trot out archaic words for company, but they always raise a few eyebrows with their pretension.

For the past few centuries, editors, publishers, and writers have used *compleat* to tart up book titles and boost sales. The first to cotton to this trick was Izaak Walton, back in 1653 with his *The Compleat Angler,* a rumination on fishing and morality. Now we have such noble imitators as *The Compleat Stripper, The Compleat Wyoming Traveler,* and *The Compleat Backpacker (on Ten Cents a Month!).*

No matter how you spell it, the word means "perfectly skilled or equipped."

6. *Farther and further*

This one has kept Greta the Grammarian as busy as a mosquito in a nudist colony. Here's the deal: *farther* means "far"; *further,* "more forth, more to the fore." So it's *farther* from Long Island to Boca Raton than it is from Long Island to New Jersey. And if you hate malls, you might want to go *farther* away still, Bora Bora, maybe. Once you've pitched your tent in Bora Bora, no *further* moves should be necessary.

Of course, real estate and grammar being what they are, nothing's that simple. *Farther* can be applied to time as well as space; you may have packed up and left Long Island *farther* back than you can recall.

7. *Flaunt and flout*

Flaunt means to "parade oneself ostentatiously." If you *flaunt* it, you show it off. Think Pamela Anderson, Cher, and Howard Stern. Now, *flout* means "to be scornful of, to show contempt for" as in "The government cannot flout the will of the people." Although both words describe over-the-top behavior, they are virtual opposites.

8. *Imply and infer*

   This pair's a matter of perspective, whether you're receiving or sending. You *imply* something in a remark to a buddy, who then *infers* something from your words. Therefore, anyone who goes around muttering, "What are you inferring?" is a dolt.

9. *Oral and aural*

   Oral is spoken, rather than written. And don't confuse *oral* (from the Latin word for "mouth") with *aural* (from the Latin word for "ear"). Of course they're pronounced alike, just to make your life a little more stressful.

Take My Word for It

A movie mogul once said, "A verbal contract ain't worth the paper it's written on." And it wasn't.

10. *Sensuous and sensual*

   Sensuous applies to the delight you get from things that appeal to the senses, such as art, flowers, music, and high-fat ice cream. *Sensual* is linked to erotic pleasures, lust, gluttony, and other yummy self-indulgent pastimes.

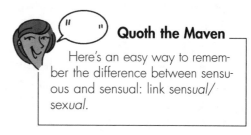

Quoth the Maven

Here's an easy way to remember the difference between sensuous and sensual: link sensual/sexual.

Twenty-Five Headaches

You've been so good; why am I doing this to you? Because you know you love it, you bad boy. But more about that later.

Here are 25 word pairs or ménage à trois often mixed up with each other. Sometimes it's because the words sound alike; other times it's because they're spelled alike.

Twenty-Five Often Confused Words

Word	Definition	Example
accept	take	Accept my thanks.
except	leave out	Everyone except him.
already	before	Elvis already left the room.
all ready	prepared	He was all ready to go.
all together	everyone at once	They yell all together.

continues

Twenty-Five Often Confused Words   (continued)

Word	Definition	Example
altogether	completely	It was altogether wrong.
altar	table of worship	Put the Bible on the altar.
alter	to change	Alter the skirt to fit.
ascent	rising	The rocket's ascent took an hour.
assent	agreement	Nod to show assent.
bare	uncovered	The window was bare.
bear (n.)	animal	The bear growled.
bear (v.)	endure	Can you bear the noise?
brake	stop	Use the car's brake.
break	destroy	Don't break the dish!
capital	government seat	Visit the capital.
capitol	where the U.S. legislature meets	Congress meets in the Capitol.
conscience	morally right	Listen to your conscience.
conscious	awake	She was conscious during the surgery.
desert (v.)	leave behind	Never desert a sinking ship!
desert (n.)	arid region	Camels travel in the desert.
dessert	sweet	I love a rich dessert.
emigrate	leave a country	She emigrated from France.
immigrate	enter a country	Immigrate to a new homeland.
lead	writing material	That's a lead pencil.
led	conducted	We were led to safety.
learn	receive facts	You learn grammar.
teach	give facts	I teach grammar.
loose	not fastened	The clasp is loose.
lose	misplace	I might lose the necklace.
passed	went by	The tortoise ultimately passed the hare.
past	gone by	They helped in the past.
principal (adj.)	main	The principal road is 5th Avenue.
principal (n.)	head of a school	Mr. Cantor is the principal.
principle	rule	The principles of grammar.

Word	Definition	Example
rise	get up	The cost of living will rise.
raise	lift	Raise your arms.
respectfully	with respect	The audience clapped respectfully.
respectively	in the stated order	The red, blue, and green books belong to John, Billie, and Lee, respectively.
simple	not complicated	It's a simple game.
simplistic	watered down	The explanation was simplistic.
stationary	staying in place	The car was stationary.
stationery	writing paper	Hotels have nice stationery.
than	comparison	Kansas is bigger than Rhode Island.
then	at that time	The state was then very dry.
their	belonging to them	It is their book.
there	place	Put it there.
they're	they are	They're good friends.
to (prep.)	distance	Go to the corner.
too (adv.)	also	He can come, too.
two	the number 2	I have two books.
weather	atmospheric conditions	The weather is rainy.
whether	if	Whether or not you agree.
your	belonging to you	Is that your jacket?
you're	you are	You're late again.

~~Your~~ You're On

Choose the correct word in each set of parenthesis.

1. Bigamy: One wife (to/two/too) many. Monogamy: same idea.

2. Police in Wichita, Kansas, arrested a 22-year-old man at an airport hotel after he tried to pass (to/too/two) counterfeit $16 bills.

3. The feud between East Coast and West Coast rappers continues. It all started over the usual: who controls what, who insulted whom, (weather/whether) the theories of Kierkegaard still have relevance.

4. There is never enough time—unless (your/you're) serving it.

5. Smokey the (Bare/Bear) warns us not to start forest fires.

6. Living with a (conscience/conscious) is like driving a car with the brakes on.

7. Being (conscious/conscience): that annoying time between naps.

8. Egotist: a person more interested in himself (than/then) in me.

9. In America (there/their) are two classes of travel—first class and with children.

10. Just remember (you're/your) unique, just like everyone else.

Answers

1. too
2. two
3. whether
4. you're
5. Bear

6. conscience
7. conscious
8. than
9. there
10. you're

Homophones: Give Piece a Chance

More, more, more! Distinguishing between words can be fun and games. Have some fun; try the following game:

What do the following 20 words have in common?

1. aisle
2. hour
3. knap
4. knave
5. kneed
6. knew
7. knickers
8. knight
9. knit
10. knot

11. llama
12. psalter
13. scent
14. whole
15. wrap
16. wrest
17. wretch
18. wright
19. write
20. wrote

In each case, if you remove the first letter of each word, what remains is a homonym of the original word. For example, *aisle* becomes *isle*.

Now take a gander at another list of 20 words. How do they form homonyms?

1.	add	4.	block
2.	bee	5.	borne
3.	belle	6.	butt
7.	bye	14.	lamb
8.	canvass	15.	lapse
9.	caste	16.	ore
10.	damn	17.	please
11.	flue	18.	sow
12.	fore	19.	too
13.	inn	20.	wee

Give up yet? (Naw, you broke the code by the second word.) The answer lies in the last letter. Remove it, and you get a homophone of the original word: *Add* becomes *ad* and so on.

Grin and ~~Bare~~ Bear It

Virtually none of the following words is covered in this chapter; putting them here is my sneaky way of getting in more confusing words. Use a dictionary if necessary.

1. A (waste/waist) is a terrible thing to mind.

2. I have a rock garden. Last (weak/week) three of the rocks (dyed/died).

3. Two farmers each claimed to own a certain cow. While (won/one) pulled on its head and the other pulled on its (tale/tail), the cow was milked (buy/by) a lawyer.

4. Archaeologist: A person (who's/whose) career lies in ruins.

5. Mae West said, "Brains (are/our) an asset, if you hide them."

6. (Buy/By) old masters. They bring better prices than young mistresses. —Lord Beaverbrook

7. You live in Alaska … when you have more (than/then) (won/one) recipe for (mousse/moose).

8. You live in Colorado … when the top of (you're/your) head is bald but you still have a pony (tail/tale).

9. You live in California when … you make more than $250,000 a year and you still can't afford (to/too/two) (buy/by) a house.

10. You live (in/inn) Alaska … when you have only (four/for) spices: salt, pepper, ketchup, and Tabasco.

11. Bumper sticker: "Very funny, Scotty. Now beam up my (cloths/clothes)."

12. Ben Franklin said, "Let thy maid servant be faithful, strong, and (plane/plain)."

13. You live in Alaska when … sexy lingerie is anything flannel with less than (ate/eight) buttons.

14. Oscar Wilde said, "I never travel without my diary. One should always have something sensational to (reed/read)."

15. You live in New York City when … you think that (I/eye) contact is an act of aggression.

Answers

1. waist
2. week, died
3. one, tail, by
4. whose
5. are
6. Buy
7. than, one, moose
8. your, tail

9. to, buy
10. in, four
11. clothes
12. plain
13. eight
14. read
15. eye

The Least You Need to Know

◆ Diction is word choice.

◆ Select words that suit your topic, purpose, and audience.

◆ Learn the difference between homonyms and other confusing words.

Chapter 24

Don't Go There: Words and Expressions to Avoid

In This Chapter

- ◆ Don't be sexist
- ◆ Ditch doublespeak
- ◆ End euphemisms
- ◆ Can clichés

Here are three rules to live by:

- ◆ No one is paying attention until you make a mistake in speech or writing.
- ◆ Experience is something you don't get until just after you need it, especially when it comes to grammar and style.
- ◆ People who think before they write are probably right.

No one wants to make a mistake choosing words. In this chapter, I help you gain the experience you need to say and write what you want with confidence. So don't even think of unpacking. Just wash out yesterday's socks, grab a snack, and prepare to discover what words and expressions to avoid.

Sexist Language: Political Roadkill

Exhibit A:

> A man was waiting in the doctor's office. The doctor came in and said, "Well, I've got some good news and some bad news. The bad news is that you need a brain transplant. The good news is our hospital has two available brains. The man's brain is $100,000 and the woman's brain is $30,000."
>
> The patient couldn't help but ask, "Why such a large difference between the male and the female brain?"
>
> The doctor replied, "The female brain is used."

Exhibit B:

> Why did the blonde scale the chain-link fence? To see what was on the other side.
>
> How do you get a blonde out of a tree? Wave.
>
> Why are dumb blonde jokes so short? So brunettes can remember them.
>
> Why can't blondes put in lightbulbs? They keep breaking them with the hammers.

We all know that such blatant sexist attitudes aren't acceptable today. But *sexist language* can be much less obvious—and every bit as offensive.

Sexist language assigns qualities to people on the basis of their gender. It reflects prejudiced attitudes and stereotypical thinking about the roles of the two sexes and traits of both men and women. As a result, sexist language discriminates against people by limiting what they can do. And if that's not bad enough, sexist language also …

- Lies.
- Annoys and alienates readers.
- Can cause legal problems.
- Perpetuates sexist attitudes.

You Could Look It Up

Sexist language assigns qualities to people on the basis of their gender. It reflects prejudiced attitudes and stereotypical thinking about the sex roles and traits of both men and women.

On Thin Ice

Let's look at each of these problems in detail.

Sexist Language Lies

More than half of all Americans are of the female persuasion. If you write *he* and *him*, you're ignoring half the people in the country. If you talk about a doctor as *he*, you're giving the cold shoulder to female medical doctors—more than one-third of all physicians graduating today. In a similar way, don't refer to an unknown nurse as *she*, because there are some excellent nurses of the male persuasion. So what do we say to sexist language? Liar, liar, pants on fire.

Sexist Language Annoys and Alienates Readers

According to the latest edition of the *World Almanac*, we've come a long way, baby. Here's proof:

◆ Of the 103 million women age 16 and over in America, 61 million are working.

◆ Women accounted for 59 percent of labor-force growth between 1985 and 1995.

◆ Women have made substantial progress in obtaining jobs in virtually all managerial and professional specialty occupations.

◆ Of the approximately 69 million families in the United States, 12 million (18 percent) are maintained by women. In black families, it's 46 percent; in Hispanic families, 24 percent.

Because more than half the women in the United States are in the workforce, women are an economic and political power that can't be ignored. Modern women get angry at writers and speakers who stereotype and patronize them with sexist language. Ditto for stay-at-home fathers and men in nontraditional jobs.

Sexist Language Causes Legal Problems

The law is increasingly intolerant of biased documents and hostile work environments. Because federal law forbids discrimination on the basis of gender, people writing policy statements, grant proposals, or any other official documents must be very careful not to use any language that could be considered discriminatory. Otherwise, they're just looking for a lawsuit.

Sexist Language Perpetuates Sexist Attitudes

A steady diet of sexist language encourages women to have low aspirations, to seek jobs rather than careers, and to think the so-called "glass ceiling" can't be shattered. Sexist language makes it more difficult for people who have been pushed to the margins to enter the mainstream.

Sexist language is so pervasive that it sometimes seems natural. Nonetheless, sexist language sends a message that the only people with power are white middle-class males. When a single woman gets a letter address to *Mrs.* instead of *Ms.*, she realizes that the writer neither knows her nor cares about her. Job descriptions with male pronouns automatically disregard more than half the population.

Nonsexist Language: Level the Playing Field

Nonsexist language treats both sexes neutrally. It does not make assumptions about the proper gender for a job, nor does it assume that men take precedence over women. Here are some guidelines to help you use nonsexist language when you write and speak:

1. Avoid using *he* to refer to both men and women.

   Sexist: He is a good writer so he knows how to select suitable words.

   Nonsexist: Good writers know how to select suitable words.

2. Avoid using *man* to refer to men and women.

   Sexist: Man is a social creature.

   Nonsexist: People are social creatures.

3. Avoid expressions that exclude one sex. Here are some of the most offensive examples and acceptable alternatives.

Out	In
mankind	humanity
the common man	the average person

4. Avoid language that denigrates people.

   Sexist: stewardess, male nurse, old wives' tale

   Nonsexist: flight attendant, nurse, superstition

   The following chart shows the preferred terms for many common occupations.

Out	In
waitress	server
woman lawyer	lawyer
workman	worker, employee (or a specific work title)
salesman	salesperson
foreman	supervisor
chairman	chair, moderator
businessman	the person's specific title

5. Use the correct courtesy title.

   Use *Mr.* for men and *Ms.* for women, with these two exceptions:

   ♦ In a business setting, professional titles take precedence over *Mr.* and *Ms.*

   For example, when I'm teaching in the university, I'm referred to as *Dr.* Rozakis rather than *Ms.* Rozakis.

   ♦ Always use the title the person prefers. Some women prefer *Miss* to *Ms.*

   If you are not sure what courtesy title to use, check in a company directory and on previous correspondence to see how the person prefers to be addressed. Also pay attention to the way people introduce themselves.

6. Use plural pronouns and nouns whenever possible.

   Sexist: **He** must check all **his** employees' timecards.

   Nonsexist: **Supervisors** must check all employees' timecards.

Danger, Will Robinson

Watch for phrases that suggest women and men behave in stereotypical ways, such as *talkative women, rugged men, giggling girls, rowdy boys.* Expunge such phrases from your writing and speech.

Quoth the Maven

If you do not know the person's gender, you can call the company and ask the receptionist, use the reader's full name in the salutation (*Dear J. Rickels*), or use the person's position or job title (*Dear Bursar*).

Quoth the Maven

Remember to use nonsexist language on *visuals* (such as slide captions, posters, and videos) as well as in speech and writing.

Top of Your Game

You're not out of the woods yet, bunky. Language can trap you by being *racist* and *ageist* as well as sexist. You wouldn't discriminate against people based on their race, age, or disability—and neither should your words. So what you want to use is *bias-free language*. This type of language uses words and phrases that don't discriminate on the basis of gender, physical condition, age, race, or anything else. Here are three ways to play fair when you write and speak:

1. Refer to a group by the term it prefers.

   Language changes, so stay on the cutting edge. For example, a hundred years ago, black people were called *colored*. Fifty years later, the term *Negro* was used. Today, the preferred terms are *African American* and *black*. Here are some other changes to put in your Rolodex:

You Could Look It Up

Bias-free language uses words and phrases that don't discriminate on the basis of gender, physical condition, age, race, or anything else.

   ◆ *Asian* is preferred over *Oriental.*

   ◆ *Inuit* is preferred over *Eskimo.*

   ◆ *Latino* is the preferred designation for Mexican Americans, Puerto Ricans, Dominicans, and other people with Central and Latin American backgrounds.

   ◆ *Senior citizen* is preferred over *old person.*

2. Focus on people, not their conditions.

   Biased: mentally retarded people

   Nonbiased: people with mental retardation

   Biased: the blind

   Nonbiased: people with vision impairments

   Biased: cancer patients

   Nonbiased: people being treated for cancer

   Biased: abnormal, afflicted, struck down

   Nonbiased: atypical

Take My Word for It

One in every six Americans has a disability, defined as a physical, emotional, or mental impairment. Expect the ratio to increase as the population ages.

3. Identify someone's race only if it is relevant to your story. And if you do mention one person's race, be sure to mention everyone else's.

Spin Doctors

When's the last time someone tried to sell you an "underground condominium"? It's the newest term for a *grave*. (Would I lie to *you?*) See any "personal manual databases" being hawked on the home shopping network? They're what we used to call *calendars*.

If you're like me, you're probably having some trouble understanding some of the latest phrases you read in the newspaper, hear on the radio, or see on television. Let's see how bad things really are. Try to decode the following phrases:

1. Vertically challenged

   _____

2. Nonpositively terminated

   _____

3. Revenue enhancement

   _____

4. Unauthorized withdrawal

   _____

5. Outplaced

   _____

6. Mechanically separated meat

   _____

7. Cheese analogs

   _____

8. Involuntarily leisured

   _____

Answers

Did you get these answers?

1. a short person	5. fired
2. fired	6. salvaged meat
3. tax increase	7. fake cheese
4. robbery	8. fired

Score Yourself

All 8 correct	You *must* be working for the government.
5 to 7 correct	You applied for a job with the government.
3 to 4 correct	There's hope for you yet.
1 to 2 correct	You call it as you see it; I like you.

What can we expect in a world where "a personal time control center" is a watch, "writing fluid" is ink, and "social expression products" are greeting cards? Teachers are now "learning facilitators," a sick person is "a compromised susceptible host," and a deadly missile is a "peacekeeper." Save yourself.

Each of the these phrases is an example of *doublespeak*—artificial, evasive language. Doublespeak pretends to communicate but really doesn't. It is language that makes the bad seem good, the negative appear positive, the unpleasant become pleasant. It shifts responsibility and deliberately aims to distort and deceive. With doublespeak, words and facts don't agree. At the heart of any doublespeak is an incongruity between what is said and what is meant.

When writers use doublespeak, they hide the truth. Always avoid doublespeak; use language truthfully.

You Could Look It Up

Doublespeak is artificial, evasive language.

Doublespeak includes the following subcategories:

- ◆ Jargon
- ◆ Bureaucratic language
- ◆ Inflated language
- ◆ Euphemisms

Let's look at each of these subcategories now.

Jargon: "Phasers on Stun, Cap'n"

What's *love?* To teenagers, it's a sweet stolen kiss by the lockers; to tennis players, it's zero, zip, nada. In the context of tennis, the word *love* is an example of *jargon*, the specialized vocabulary of a particular group. Jargon features words that an outsider unfamiliar with the field might not understand. There's medical, legal, educational, and technological jargon. All sports, hobbies, and games have their own jargon, as do the arts.

You Could Look It Up

Jargon is the specialized vocabulary of a particular group.

There's even nonsense jargon, such as the *dilithium crystals*, *warp field*, *warp drive*, and *phasers* of the *Star Trek* crew.

As you write, consider your purpose and audience to decide whether a word is jargon in the context of your material. For example, a baseball fan would easily understand the terms *shutout* and *homer*, but these terms would be jargon to a nonfan. Using jargon with the appropriate audience communicates your meaning—but using jargon can unnecessarily confuse readers. Here's the rule to live by: If a technical term has an equivalent in plain English, use the simpler term.

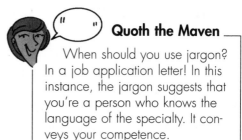

Quoth the Maven

When should you use jargon? In a job application letter! In this instance, the jargon suggests that you're a person who knows the language of the specialty. It conveys your competence.

Bureaucratic Language: Piled Higher and Deeper

Bureaucratic language is stuffy, overblown language. It has two main characteristics:

◆ Wordiness

◆ Unnecessary complexity

You Could Look It Up

Bureaucratic language is stuffy, overblown language.

Bureaucratic language becomes meaningless because it is evasive and wordy. Call my bluff. Take a minute to simplify the following example:

> The internal memorandum previously circulated should be ignored and disregarded and instead replaced by the internal memorandum sent before the previous one was sent. The memorandum presently at the current time being held by the appropriate personnel should be combined with the previous one to call attention to the fact that the previous one should be ignored by the reader.

How about this simplification:

> Replace the previous memorandum with the one sent before the previous memorandum. (Use the older version.)

You Could Look It Up

Inflated language makes the ordinary seem extraordinary.

Quoth the Maven

Instead of using whoopee words when you write an over-the-top letter of recommendation, include specific details and examples that highlight the person's accomplishments.

Inflated Language: Full of Hot Air

Inflated language makes the ordinary seem extraordinary. Here are some examples:

- *Automotive internists* for car mechanics
- *Vertical transportation corps* for elevator operators

So-called "whoopee" words are a type of inflated language. These are words that are so overused that they've become practically meaningless. Here are some of the most annoying examples: *fantastic, excellent, terrific, wonderful, fabulous,* and *marvelous.*

As you learned in the previous chapter, use words that are appropriate to your audience and purpose. In nearly all cases, the best choices are those most easily understood by your readers.

Euphemisms: Sleeping with the Fishes

What do all the following expressions have in common?

- Cashed in his/her chips
- Bit the big one
- Kicked the bucket
- Pushing up daisies

- Visiting the W.C.
- Potty trained
- Powdering my nose
- Seeing a man about a horse

They're are all *euphemisms*, inoffensive or positive words or phrases used to avoid a harsh reality. The phrases on the left refer to death; those on the right refer to bathroom activities. Euphemisms are a type of doublespeak because they cloud the truth. You find them used with all potentially embarrassing topics, such as death, nudity, body parts, sex, aging, and bathroom activities.

Euphemisms are not doublespeak when they are used to spare someone's feelings or out of concern for a recognized social custom, as when you say, "I am sorry your sister passed away," rather than "I am sorry your sister died." But most of the time, euphemisms drain meaning from truthful writing. Avoid euphemisms if they obscure your meaning. Use them to spare someone's feelings, especially in delicate situations.

Take My Word for It _____

Perhaps no one has made better use of the sexual nuances that connect bathrooms and parts of the body than American humorist Dorothy Parker. Distressed that she was not meeting any men at her office, she hung a simple sign over her office door. It said, "Gentlemen." Parker's office was soon inundated with a stream of male visitors. A triumph for the power of the euphemism!

Search and Destroy

Use the following checklist to identify doublespeak in all its guises. As you reread your own work to eliminate doublespeak, ask yourself these five questions:

- ❏ What am I saying?
- ❏ To whom is the remark addressed?
- ❏ Under what conditions is the remark being made?
- ❏ What is my intent?
- ❏ What is the result of the remarks?

The Cliché Expert

As you read this section, be sure to keep your eyes peeled, your fingers crossed, and your head above water, and you may be able to keep up with the Joneses. But that's only if you're on the ball, beam, go, level, and up-and-up, rather than on the fly, fence, ropes, rocks, or lam. Or you can just go fry an egg.

The previous paragraph is chock full of *clichés*, descriptive phrases that have lost their effectiveness through overuse. If you have heard the same words and phrases over and over, so has your reader. Replace clichés with fresh, new descriptions. If you can't think of a way to rewrite the phrase to make it new, delete it completely.

You Could Look It Up _____

Clichés are descriptive phrases that have lost their effectiveness through overuse.

Give it a shot now. Complete this list by defining each cliché and then rewriting it to convey a more precise and descriptive meaning.

Cliché	Meaning
1. on the carpet	_____
2. on the fritz	_____
3. on the lam	_____
4. on the make	_____
5. on the spot	_____
6. on the spur of the moment	_____
7. on the wagon	_____
8. sweet as sugar	_____
9. raining cats and dogs	_____
10. straight as an arrow	_____

Answers

Did you get these answers?

Cliché	Meaning
1. on the carpet	reprimanded
2. on the fritz	broken
3. on the lam	fleeing
4. on the make	eager for financial or sexual gain
5. on the spot	great difficulty
6. on the spur of the moment	spontaneously
7. on the wagon	not drinking
8. sweet as sugar	sweet
9. raining cats and dogs	raining heavily
10. straight as an arrow	honest

Remember, if you have a tough row to hoe, be a tough nut to crack and tough it out. Truth will win out and you can turn over a new leaf, turn the tables, other cheek, or the corner. Under a cloud? Not up to par, scratch, or snuff? Use your head; it's all water over the dam. After all: The world is your oyster—you can bet your bottom dollar!

Gorgeous George

George Orwell was the pen name of Eric Blair, one of the most brilliant English stylists ever. In his landmark essay "Politics and the English Language," Orwell wrote, "Modern English prose consists less and less of *words* chosen for the sake of their meaning, and more and more of *phrases* tacked together like the sections of a prefabricated henhouse." He concluded: "The great enemy of clear language is insincerity. When there is a gap between one's real and one's declared aims, one turns as it were instinctively to long words and exhausted idioms, like a cuttlefish squirting out ink." You've read about Orwell before in this book. He deserves more ink, because he nailed style in writing.

But Orwell didn't just complain. Fortunately, he suggests a number of remedies. I've yet to come across six guidelines that make more sense than Orwell's. And here they are:

1. Never use a metaphor, simile, or other figure of speech that you are used to seeing in print. (In other words, cut all those clichés!)

2. Never use a long word where a short one will do. (Remember what you learned in Chapter 23 on word choice, or *diction*.)

3. If it is possible to cut a word out, always cut it out. (Look back to Chapter 22.)

4. Never use the passive voice when you can use the active. (This was covered in Chapter 22.)

5. Never use a foreign phrase, a scientific word, or a jargon word if you can think of an everyday English equivalent.

6. Break any of these rules sooner than say anything outright barbarous.

Danger, Will Robinson

Proverbs are often confused with clichés, but then again, I'm often confused with Cindy Crawford. Such is the way of the world. Unfortunately, I'm not Cindy, and proverbs aren't clichés. Proverbs are economical phrases that pack a great deal of meaning in a brief wallop; a cliché, on the other hand, is bloated and meaningless.

Take My Word for It

Steer clear of *slanted language*, too. These are emotionally loaded words and phrases designed to inflame readers. Describing a lab experiment as "viciously maiming helpless rats" is an example of slanted language. At its most offensive, slanted language descends into propaganda; at its best, slanted language *merely* offends readers.

A Note on Words and Expressions to Avoid for Non-Native Speakers

If you are a non-native speaker of English, this chapter is especially important to you for several reasons:

◆ Many other countries are not as concerned with "politically correct" language as America has become recently. Thus, the issue of sexist and biased language is not as significant or likely to cause offense in your native language.

◆ Ornate and flowery language may be considered more polite than direct discourse in your native language. This is true in Japanese, for example. In general, direct, blunt speech is judged as very rude in Japanese culture.

◆ Certain bodily functions may not be referred to with euphemisms in your culture. However, these functions are cloaked indirect expressions in English. Thus, knowing when to use euphemisms and when not to use euphemisms may present special problems for you.

To deal with these issues, study the documents in your workplace and read well-respected newspapers such as *The New York Times*. Listen to the language used by public speakers and leaders who are held in high esteem. Do *not* rely on television, entertainers, or sports figures to help you master correct usage.

The Least You Need to Know

◆ Use bias-free language.

◆ Avoid doublespeak, including jargon, bureaucratic language, inflated language, and euphemisms.

◆ Nix on clichés, too.

◆ Write simply and directly.

Part **6**

In Your Write Mind

Brenda Starr and Lois Lane can whip out a story in a flash, with nary a chipped nail. According to the movies and television, even L.A. lawyers, New York City cops, and lowly office workers sit at computer terminals and bang out perfectly crafted memos, letters, or reports at breakneck speed. Hollywood would have us think that effective writing is a cakewalk—without the cake, of course.

On the other hand, we have Hollywood's picture of the starving writer, toiling away in anonymity in a garret, painfully facing that blank sheet of paper while waiting for the muse. The floor is littered with a mountain of crumpled pages; towers of empty coffee cups teeter against the stained walls.

Of course, both are equally unrealistic views of the writing process, yet each contains a germ of truth. In this part, you explore the process of writing and learn how to produce powerful resumés, cover letters, business communications, and personal writing.

Chapter 25

Business Writing: Write Angles

In This Chapter

◆ Design effective business letters

◆ Create winning resumés and cover letters

◆ Send business thank you letters

◆ Deliver good news and bad news in writing

Today, there's stiff competition for positions, and people who can communicate often win out over those who can't. Many companies don't advertise at all, preferring to do their recruiting through formal and informal networking. The stock market is a wild roller coaster—and people are edgy. Knowing how to write a powerful resumé and cover letter can help you get the job you want. If you've already got a job, these tools—along with the ability to write effective business letters and memos—can help you get where you want to be. Those are the skills you learn in this chapter.

Letter Perfect

Successful business writers know that an effective document reads well and looks good. Here are my top 10 ways to make your documents look as professional as they read:

1. Use *white space* (the empty space on a page) to separate and emphasize key points within a letter. Provide sufficient white space around paragraphs, too. Figure 1 inch to 1½ inches on all sides.

2. To help readers locate key elements, use indented lists, bullets, or numbers—just like this book does!

3. Use *headers* (words or phrases that group points) to lead the reader through the document.

4. To get maximum impact, put key elements such as return addresses and company contact information in the top-left and lower-right quadrants of the page.

 " " Quoth the Maven

Templates (available on standard software) can make formatting business letters, resumés, and memos a breeze.

5. Go easy on the bells and whistles such as highlighting, decorative devices, fonts, and color.

6. Decide whether to justify the right margin (line up the type), based on the situation and audience. Justified margins let you add about 20 percent more text on the page. However, use them only with proportional type to avoid distracting, wide spaces between words.

7. For all important business writing, such as letters of application and resumés, use good quality, heavy, white bond paper and matching envelopes. Traditionally, local printers typeset letterhead, but a good-quality laser printer and software package can create fine letterhead as well.

8. When possible, limit your letters and resumés to one page.

9. Consider your audience's needs and expectations. Show that you understand the purpose for the business communication and the context in which it is read.

10. Use conventional formats, explained in the following section and shown in Appendix A.

Form and Function

Business letters are single-spaced on 8½ by 11-inch letterhead. There are three different formats you can use: the block style, the modified block style, and the semiblock style. The differences among the three styles relate to paragraph indentations and the placement of headings and closings.

♦ The *block style* has all parts of the letter placed flush left.

♦ The *modified block style* places the heading in the upper-right corner and the closing and signature in the lower-right corner, parallel to the heading. The paragraphs are *not* indented.

♦ The *semiblock style* places the heading in the upper-right corner and the close and signature in the lower-right corner, parallel to the heading. The paragraphs *are* indented.

> **Danger, Will Robinson**
>
> Pick one letter style—the block style, the modified block style, or the semiblock style—and stick with it. You're less likely to make mistakes if you're consistent.

The following list contains the guidelines for the block style. Vary it as explained earlier if you want to use the modified block or semiblock style instead.

Date	Month (spelled out), day (followed by a comma), year.
Inside address	The recipient's address; place two lines after the date.
Salutation	Recipient's title, last name, colon (Dear Ms. Streisand:).
Body	Short, single-spaced paragraphs stating the information.
Close	Capitalize the first word, conclude with a comma (Yours truly,). Place two lines after the last line of the letter.
Signature	Sign your name in ink. Leave three lines of space after the close for your signature.
Initials	If the letter is typed by someone other than the writer, insert the typist's initials below the typed name of the signatory. Capitalize the writer's initials; use lowercase for the typist's (LR:st or LR/st).
Enclosures	"Enclosures" or "Enc." indicates that additional material is included with the letter.
Copies	List other recipients alphabetically or by rank (cc: Samantha Harris, Tracey Jefferson).

Kissing Cousins

Although no two kinds of business letters are identical, they *do* share certain features besides their format.

- They are brief but clear.

- The relationship between the writer and reader is established at the beginning of the letter.

- Any necessary background information is provided.

- If action is required on the part of the reader, the action is stated outright.

- If the letter is a response, it mentions the date of the previous contact.

- The *tone* matches the occasion. A letter to a colleague is appropriately friendly, but general business correspondence is formal.

- The overall tone is always polite.

Danger, Will Robinson

Using e-mail addresses like sonofsatan, hotlips69, and imababy will get you kicked out of the pile so fast you'll get whiplash. Your e-mail should read: Firstname_Lastname@carrier, as in Laurie_Rozakis@Farmingdale.edu.

Business communication falls into the following general categories: letters of application, informational letters, and memos. Let's check out these categories.

Resumés and Cover Letters: Get on the Fast Track

You don't have to rescue a child from under a flaming Chevy or donate a kidney to get the job you want (although it probably wouldn't hurt). You *do* have to write effective *resumés* and cover letters—and writing is a lot less painful than heroics.

A resumé is a persuasive summary of your qualifications for employment. It is always accompanied by a *cover letter.* Employers use resumés and cover letters to decide whom to interview. An effective cover letter and resumé are not like sweat pants: One size doesn't fit all. To get you some face time, a winning cover letter and resumé must be tailored to suit the employer's needs and your qualifications as closely as possible. For that reason, many people have several different versions of their resumé. Here's how to make your resumé work for you.

You Could Look It Up

A **resumé** is a persuasive summary of your qualifications for employment.

Resumés

As you write your resumé, emphasize the things you've done that are most relevant to the position for which you are applying and show how you are superior to other candidates. Emphasize what *you* can do for the company, not what the company can do for you. Be realistic, use the layout to emphasize key points, and relate your experience to the job you want.

Here are the facts you *must* include:

◆ Name, address, phone number, e-mail address

◆ Education

◆ Relevant experience

Here are the facts you *can* include:

◆ Career objective

◆ Previous and current employment

◆ Promotions

◆ Foreign language and computer language proficiency

◆ Volunteer positions

◆ Education and course work

◆ Honors and achievements

◆ References

Here are the facts you *never* include:

◆ Age

◆ Health (It's assumed that every candidate's health is excellent.)

◆ Religious affiliation, political affiliation

◆ Race or ethnicity

◆ Gender or sexual orientation

◆ Marital status (as in married, widowed, divorced, or single)

◆ Information about children or pets

You're expected to put your accomplishments in the best possible light, but *always* tell the truth. Background checks are a hot topic in personnel circles today. Experts say a decade of litigation has nervous employers turning more and more to professional background checkers, who report that caseloads are growing at 30 percent a year. Investigators find discrepancies or outright lies in about one-third of the resumés they check. *Gloryoski!*

Shooting Yourself in the Foot

Here are the top resumé turnoffs.

Resumé No-No's

Turnoff	Example
Poor formatting and exotic fonts	John J. JobSeeker, *Ann Applicant*
Unnecessary personal information	I'm a single white male. I'm a Libra.
Buzzwords that obscure meaning	As the Director of Integral Operations, my mission involves convergences in delivering synergized solutions to my strategic customers.
Vague descriptions of achievements	"I increased widget sales." Instead, say "I increased widget sales by 25 percent or $2 million."
Incomplete contact information	Some people actually forget to give their own names and telephone numbers!
Spelling and grammar mistakes	The worst is misspelling the name of the company or contact person.

Chronological Resumé

There are two kinds of resumés: *chronological* and *skills*. Although each type of resumé lists basically the same information, the information is arranged very differently.

A *chronological resumé* summarizes your accomplishments in reverse chronological order (starting with the most recent and working backward). It stresses degrees, job titles, and dates. Consider using a chronological resumé when …

◆ Your education and experience are logical preparation for the job you want.

◆ You have an impressive education or job history.

The following chronological resumé shows a candidate steadily moving up the job ladder.

Name
Street Address
City, Town, ZIP Code
Telephone number

OBJECTIVE	To secure a promotional or editorial position in the publishing industry.	
EDUCATION	*Boston College*, Boston, MA Candidate for Masters in business and public relations GPA 3.72	May, 2003
	Boston College, Boston, MA Bachelors of business in marketing	May, 2001
PUBLISHED	Articles on comic books published in *Comics Weekly*, *The Comics Scene*, and *Boston Tab*	2000–
WORK RELEVANT EXPERIENCE	*Comics International*, Boston, MA	2001–

Promotions assistant

◆ Wrote press releases

◆ Conducted research to introduce comics to student population through symposia and articles

Comics Close-Up, Boston, MA   2002–2003

◆ Developed and produced an innovative weekly radio program on WQBC

◆ Examined the comics field and literature

◆ Arranged and conducted interviews with noted comic book artists and writers

ACTIVITIES	Student Senate, elected representative English and writing tutor Student Activities Council	2002–2003 2001–2003 2001–2003
HONORS	Boston College Award of Excellence	2002
AWARDS	Phi Beta Kappa	2002

Skills Resumé

A *skills resumé* emphasizes your skills. Consider using a skills resumé when …

◆ You are no longer a spring chicken and wish to hide your age because of the common bias against more mature and experienced workers.

◆ Your education and experience are not the usual preparation for the job you want.

Take My Word for It

A curriculum vitae (CV to those in the know) is the Goodyear Blimp of resumés: It contains every relevant thing you've ever done. Scientists and academics use CVs instead of resumés to include all their publications, conferences, and professional affiliations. My CV is more than 20 pages long.

♦ You lack an impressive education or job history.

♦ Arranging your recent work history in reverse chronological order would create the wrong impression (perhaps because you have been demoted, fired, or hopped from job to job).

A middle-aged candidate with a great deal of experience prepared the following skills resume. The format allows her to place the emphasis on her most recent jobs and place far less emphasis on her age.

Danger, Will Robinson

Claire includes her job as Assistant Manager, which she held from 1973–1980. The original resumé had that section omitted, a very good idea. I put it back in to show you the full range of Claire's employment—and to tell you to leave this entry out. If you are middle-aged, I *strongly recommend* that you list only 10 years' of experience. Never lie, but don't parade your age. Once you get your foot in the door at the interview, you can share as much of your job history as necessary, or as you wish.

Claire De Lune

315 Elmo Avenue, Riverdale, CA 81711
681-732-9373 (H); 681-865-7166 (W)
Claire_DeLune@yahoo.com

EDITORIAL   **Supervising Editor**

CURRENT POSITION   Big Books (a division of Bigger Books), Oakland, CA

- Oversee publishing process from inception to bound book, producing elementary through high school materials on time and under budget
- Manage editorial development, creative process, and content of test-preparation materials for 30–50 titles per year
- Supervise project teams and senior editors
- Hire authors and evaluate manuscripts
- Prepare and maintain editorial schedules and budgets
- Strategic planning and product development of test-preparation materials

Senior Editor   1998–2001   Big Books (a division of Bigger Books), Oakland, CA
- Research and lay out books
- Supervise editors, junior staff, freelance editors, and proofreaders
- Approve art, photos, page layouts and designs, page proofs, and bluelines

Editor   1996–1997   Big Books (a division of Bigger Books), Oakland, CA
- Edit, copyedit, proofread
- Write test questions and introductory copy addressing teachers

Freelance Editor   1993–1996
- Varied projects, including PR brochures, advertisements, and a cookbook

Assistant Manager   1973–1980   Dewey Cheatem and Howe Law Offices, Cincinnati, OH

- Accountable for accuracy of legal briefs
- Copywrite, copyedit, and proofread
- Oversee print production and schedules
- Train junior staff

WRITING   **Freelance Author**
- Two study guides for series *What's the Big Idea?* (First Steps, Inc.), Winter, 2001
- Essays, LI Parenting News and Newsday

TEACHING   **Teacher, First and Fifth Grades;** Drama Club Director, Family Math Presenter, 1990–1993
Washington Elementary School, Oakland, CA

Corrective Math Teacher, Grades 3–6; 1990   Washington Elementary School, Oakland, CA

CERTIFICATION   **New York State Permanent Certification: Elementary Education, N-6/English, 7–9**

EDUCATION   **Master of Arts, English Literature**   New York University, New York, NY

Bachelor of Arts, Cum Laude, English and Creative Writing
Brooklyn College, Brooklyn, NY

SKILLS   Theatre Arts: Acting, Directing, Playwriting
PLATFORMS: Windows/Mac; Software: MS Word, Excel, QuarkXPress

Cover Letters

Like a resumé, the purpose of a cover letter (or a "job application letter") is to get an interview. Although a resumé and a cover letter do overlap in certain areas, there are three crucial differences:

◆ A *cover letter* is adapted to the needs of a particular organization; a *resumé* is usually adapted to a position.

◆ A *cover letter* shows how your qualifications can help the organization meet its needs; a *resumé* summarizes all your relevant qualifications.

◆ A *cover letter* uses complete sentences and paragraphs; a *resumé* uses short phrases.

Tailor each cover letter to the specific company or organization. If you can substitute another inside address and salutation and send out the letter without any further changes, it isn't specific enough. Here's what to include:

◆ The major requirements for the job.

◆ Facts and examples that show how you can do the job.

◆ Details that show your knowledge of the company.

◆ Qualities that employers seek: the ability to read and write well, think critically, speak effectively, and get along with others.

Danger, Will Robinson

If you decide to do some name dropping in your cover letter, only drop the names of those people who will speak well of you. Be sure to get prior permission from the person to mention his or her name.

Some people find it difficult to write effective cover letters because they don't want to toot their own horns. My advice? Toot away. Good work rarely speaks for itself—it usually needs a microphone to be heard. Studies have shown that successful executives spend about half their time on their job and the other half on self-promotion and office politics.

Five final points:

1. Take the time to know the company or organization you are contacting.

2. Know what you have to offer. Analyze your strengths and weaknesses.

3. Be prepared to show the employer that you can do the job—and do it well.

4. Target your letter to an individual rather than a position.

5. Spend the time to get it right. You have a snowball's chance in Hades of getting an interview if your letter contains errors.

Here's the cover letter that accompanied the first resumé:

May 5, 2003

Mr. Big Executive, Vice President
Major American Comic Book Company
1325 Important Street
New York, NY 10019

Dear Mr. Big Executive:

If you are interested in someone to join your editorial or promotions team who has a passion for comic books, formal training in comic book production, an understanding of the industry, and a variety of related experiences, then please take a moment to review the enclosed resumé and writing samples.

As my resumé indicates, I received my undergraduate degree in marketing from Boston College, and will be completing my graduate studies in business and public relations next month. My emphasis is on public relations writing, marketing, promotional strategies, and research methods. My current grade-point average is 3.72.

The pleasure that comics brought me when I was a child has never left. It has, however, matured from simply an affection for the product to a respect for the process. This evolution has been cultivated in both my undergraduate and graduate studies, extracurricular activities, and work experience. I would like to point out some of my accomplishments that help illustrate this point.

As an undergraduate, I developed and produced *Comics Close-Up*, an innovative weekly radio program that aired on WQBC in the greater Boston area. The program examined the comics field and literature and featured interviews with noted comic book artists and writers. Also, I have had several articles published in *Comics Weekly*, *The Comics Scene*, and *Boston Tab*. Recently, I received the Boston College Award of Excellence from the Communications Department for a research prospectus on the development of computerized comic book production. Furthermore, as part of my graduate internship, I worked for several months at Comics International as a promotions assistant.

In short, my education, coupled with other vital experiences, has prepared me for a role in the promotions field, particularly in the field of comics. I would welcome an opportunity to discuss helping Major American Comic Book Company meet its promotional or editorial objectives. I will contact you soon to answer any questions you may have, and perhaps arrange an appointment. Thank you in advance for your time and attention.

Sincerely,

J. P. JobSeeker

J. P. JobSeeker

Remember to use correct forms of address on your letter (*Mr., Ms., Dr.,* and so on) and nonsexist language.

Bread-and-Butter Notes

Remember how your Mom used to force you to write thank you letters to Aunt Shirley and Uncle Irving for those ugly, itchy sweaters? "Aw, Ma," you whined, "Aunt Shirley and Uncle Irving won't care. I bet they don't even read those stupid letters." Think again. It's not only your relatives who are impressed by your good manners; it's prospective employers as well. You should always write a business thank you letter when you've:

- Had a phone conversation with someone at the company about an actual job opening or any matter relating to employment

- Been granted an informational interview

- Had an actual job interview

- Been offered a job and declined it

In today's tight job market, many employers expect applicants to be more aggressive. Following up after an interview can give you the winning edge. In this situation, a thank you letter really functions as a follow-up. The letter should remind the interviewer:

- Who you are

- What position you want

- Your outstanding qualifications

- What he or she liked in you

- What new information you learned about the company during the interview

Also use the letter as a chance to counter any negative impressions that might have come up during the interview. Be very sure that the letter is well-written and completely free of errors.

Here's a model thank you note:

Inside address

Date

Dear Mr. Harris:

I am writing this letter to thank you again for the opportunity to work at Acme as an intern. The description of the internship that you gave me leads me to believe that I will enjoy working there immensely. I hope to do so during the months of June and July of this year.

I'd like to specifically thank you for the advice and counsel that you gave me concerning my job search. I found your advice very helpful and I wanted you to know how much I appreciate it.

I look forward to working with you.

Sincerely,

J. P. JobSeeker

J. P. JobSeeker

Good News, Bad News

Myth #1: Good news messages are easy to write.

Myth #2: Bad news messages are hard to write.

Stop! Both are wrong—both are right. How easy a message is to write (and deliver) depends on how well you know the situation as well as the message you have to deliver. It's also crucial to know what information each type of message must contain. Even good news can be hard to deliver when you have a lot of facts to include. Let's do some special deliveries now.

Danger, Will Robinson

A true pitfall of delivering good news is the potential for going overboard. Congratulating someone on a job well done shouldn't mislead the person into thinking he or she has practically clinched that promotion, which might not be the case.

Good News

Compared to some of the situations we face every day at work, delivering good news seems to be the least of our worries. But even such a seemingly pleasant task as giving welcome news has its sand traps. To avoid getting bogged down, try these guidelines.

First, recognize that good news letters provide information, downplay the downside, and build a good image of the writer. They cement a good relationship between the writer and reader and reduce the need to send any further correspondence so you can finally get to the bottom of the pile of paper on your desk. They do this by following these five steps:

1. Start with the good news.

2. Summarize the main points.

3. Provide details and any needed background information.

4. Present any negative elements—as positively as you can.

5. End on a positive note.

The next page shows a model letter.

Bad News

You should live and be well, but into each life a little trouble always comes. And when it does, you'll probably have to be the one to write the letter about it.

Bad news letters deliver the lousy news and help readers accept it. They also build a good image of the writer and his or her organization. To be effective, bad news letters leave readers feeling that the decision was reasonable and that even if they were in the writer's position, they would make the same decision. Bad news letters accomplish this by using the following pattern:

1. Give reasons for the action.

2. Don't overly stress the negative.

3. End with a positive statement.

Rte. 453 and Cowplop Road
Gassy Point, Idaho 67819

WHATSAMATTER U

May 1, 2003

Solid Community College
Kneejerk, Nevada 98761

Dear Professor Schmendrick:

We are pleased to offer you a term appointment as an Assistant Professor of Self-Actualization, effective August 31, 2003. You will be teaching two classes in Barefoot Aluminum Foil Dancing, one class in Underwater Fire Prevention, and one class in Advanced Quantum Physics. In addition, you will mentor six undergraduate students in the "I'm Okay, You're Okay" department.

Whatsamatter U is a select liberal arts college on the cutting edge of the 21st century. We pride ourselves on our wide and eclectic course offerings, focus on self-awareness, and high tuition costs. This year we are especially excited about our new major, "Fen Shu and You," which already has three enrollees.

Your salary will be $20,000, and you will be considered for a tenure-track position at the end of your five-year probationary period. This is the standard procedure at our University.

Please send your written acceptance as soon as possible and let me know if you need any software or supplies. On August 31, please report to the personnel office, located on the second floor of Cheez Whiz Hall. Please stop by my office at noon, and I'll take you out to lunch at the Dew Drop Inn.

Welcome to Whatsamatter U!

Sincerely,

Seymour Glass, Dean

Danger, Will Robinson

If you have to present some negative news, give the facts a positive spin, but don't be dishonest. You'll lose credibility and may even expose yourself and the company to litigation.

Remember that the person you reject for a job or promotion today might be someone you want to keep on friendly terms with for the future; letting people down graciously not only keeps the door open for future relations, it wins your company a good reputation as a people company. If it's a client you're delivering bad news to, the reasons for kindness are even greater. Study the following model letter:

April 4, 2003

Dear Fellow Resident:

Over the past four years, Faulty Towers has enjoyed excellent service at a cost lower than the prevailing rates in this part of Icy Falls. Through careful planning, the condominium board has been able to maintain services in spite of changing economic conditions.

We are happy to report that we can continue to provide excellent service but we are no longer able to avoid a fee increase. Accordingly, at the January meeting your directors authorized a 5 percent increase in condominium fees for the 2003–2004 fiscal year.

The directors know that any increase in fees is unwelcome. The fee increase was mandated by the following conditions:

1. a 6 percent increase in county taxes;

2. a 7 percent increase in utility costs; and

3. a new labor contract with the maintenance staff that calls for a 9 percent wage increase over 2 years.

You will note that the 5 percent increase is below the average of increases in comparable condominiums in the Icy Falls area. Faulty Towers still costs less per month than comparable buildings.

We will continue to work hard to provide outstanding service at a competitive price.

Sincerely,

Rick Taylor

Rick Taylor
President, Condominium Board of Directors

The Least You Need to Know

♦ A resumé is a persuasive summary of your qualifications for employment; it is always accompanied by a cover letter.

♦ Tailor your resumé and cover letter to the specific job you want.

♦ Follow up every job contact with a thank you note.

♦ How easy a message is to write (and deliver) depends on how well you know the situation and the message you have to deliver.

Chapter 26

Personal Writing: In Your Write Mind

In This Chapter

- ◆ Write friendly letters
- ◆ Send social notes
- ◆ Learn how to write effective letters of opinion
- ◆ Tune into writing technology

As often as we use the telephone to reach out and touch someone, there are times when only a letter will do. *Friendly letters* share personal feelings and information among friends and family, while *social notes* relay or refuse an invitation. They also express our gratitude, congratulations, or condolences. There are also *letters of opinion*, sent to newspapers, businesses, and the media.

In this chapter, you learn how to write other important and useful types of letters. Sometimes these concern your personal life; at other times, they are more business-centered.

Friendly Letters: My Baby, She Wrote Me a Letter

Letters are a testimony to the enduring attempts of human beings to bridge the communication gap between themselves and others. Letters pack an astonishingly big wallop for their size. In some cases, they even become the stuff of history.

Quoth the Maven

We could make a case that some e-mail correspondence is a contemporary form of the friendly letter. It follows a different format, however, as described in detail later in this chapter.

Although a friendly letter is an informal type of correspondence, it still matches the letter format you learned in Chapter 25.

Because friendly letters express your own ideas, you generally have a far wider choice of content with them than you do with a business letter. Nonetheless, an effective friendly letter must still be clearly organized and carefully thought out.

Signed, Sealed, Delivered: I'm Yours

An astonishing number of people would rather get a root canal, pay their tax bill, or jump from a moving train than write a friendly letter. If you're one of these, the following 10 tips should make your task easier:

1. Don't apologize for not having written or for running out of ideas. You're not on trial here.

2. Reread any recent letters you received from the person to whom you are writing. This helps you answer the person's questions and include items of interest to the reader.

3. To make your ideas come alive, use vivid sensory impressions, descriptions that appeal to sight, hearing, smell, and so on.

4. Include figures of speech, such as similes and metaphors. Tap into what you learned in Part 5 of this book.

5. Add dialogue to make your writing more specific and interesting, too.

6. Identify all unfamiliar people and places you mention. Never assume that your reader knows the complete cast of characters in your life, especially newcomers like your daughter's boyfriend (the one with the ring in his navel and hole in his head).

7. Check your grammar and usage carefully.

8. Reread for errors in spelling, punctuation, capitalization, and logic.

9. Make your letter easy to read. Write legibly or type.

10. Try to end your letter on a positive note. Avoid lame endings like, "Well, that's all I have to say" or "It's late so I'll end this letter." A strong ending leaves your readers thinking good thoughts—and thinking well of you.

Model Letter

Personal letters are written for several important and intriguing reasons. These include an urge to record an experience, the desire to respond to a situation, the craving to maintain contact, a wish to offer congratulations or comfort, and the longing to be creative. Elinore Rupert Stewart, a pioneer trekking west at the turn of the century, wrote for all these reasons. Today, letters such as hers offer us a fascinating record of the westward expansion.

Quoth the Maven

What happens when you get a gift you detest (I mean it's a real *stinker*)? It still deserves a thank you note. Don't lie and gush about the gift. Instead, be polite and more general in your thanks. After all, a gift is just that—a gift rather than an obligation.

September 28, 1909

Dear Mrs. Coney,

Your second card just reached me and I am plumb glad because, although I answered your other, I was wishing I could write to you, for I have had the most charming adventure.

I was awakened by a pebble striking my cheek. Something prowling on the bluff above us had dislodged it and it struck me. It was four o'clock, so I arose and spitted my rabbit. The logs had left such a big bed of coals, but some ends were still burning in such a manner that the heat would go both under and over my rabbit. So I put plenty of bacon grease over him and hung him up to roast. Then I went back to bed. I didn't want to start early because the air is too keen for comfort early in the morning ….

—Elinore Rupert Stewart

B & B Revisited

In the previous chapter, you learned the importance of thanking interviewers for their time. Thank you notes are equally important in a nonbusiness setting. In addition to acknowledging someone's thoughtfulness and generosity, a thank you note can prevent misunderstandings, such as a misrouted gift, that can set off a family feud.

Quoth the Maven

Letters of condolence are *always* handwritten.

When you write a thank you note, try to ...

♦ Mention the specific gift or act of kindness.

♦ Explain why the gift or action was appreciated.

♦ Write promptly.

Here's a model:

Dear Aunt Mabel:

Thank you for the lovely afghan. The colors exactly match the decor of my den: lime green, bright purple, and day-glow orange. It was very thoughtful of you to make me a gift that is functional as well as beautiful: You know how I always get cold at night watching "Wheel of Fortune" reruns. Now I can snuggle up in my afghan and dream of being Vanna White and turning those big letters myself. You know I will treasure the afghan for years and think of you with great affection.

Fondly,

Dilly

I Feel Your Pain: Letters of Condolence

No, you don't, and don't even try. But a letter of condolence is much more appreciated than a phone call because it's tangible proof that the person cared enough to write. Many people keep meaningful letters of condolence and reread them in times of pain.

Letters of condolence must be written with tact and sincerity. Although it's always best to write promptly after the person's loss, a letter of condolence is the rare situation where "better late than never" holds true. If you put off writing the note because you couldn't think of appropriate words of comfort, it's not too late to do it now. Here are some ideas to get you started:

1. Keep the letter sincere. Write from the heart.

2. Don't rehash the tragedy and the gory details.

3. Show your reader that you care and you have been affected by the loss, but never try to show that your loss is greater than the other person's loss. It isn't.

4. Offer friendship or love, whatever the relationship.

5. If you're offering help, offer help: "May I come over next month and take down your storm windows?" not "I'm here for you."

6. If you knew the person well, try to include specific details about the deceased person's admirable traits. Tell a brief story about the time the person picked you up from the airport at midnight, for example.

Abraham Lincoln wrote the following letter of condolence:

Executive Mansion, Washington

November 21, 1864
Mrs. Bixby
Boston, Massachusetts

Dear Madam:

I have been shown in the files of the War Department a statement of the Adjutant-General of Massachusetts that you are the mother of five sons who have died gloriously on the field of battle. I feel how weak and fruitless must be any words of mine which should attempt to beguile you from the grief of a loss so overwhelming. But I cannot refrain from tendering to you the consolation that may be found in the thanks of the Republic they died to save. I pray that our Heavenly Father may assuage the anguish of your bereavement and leave you only the cherished memory of the loved and lost, and the solemn pride that must be yours to have laid so costly a sacrifice upon the altar of freedom.

Yours very sincerely and respectfully,

Abraham Lincoln

Letters of Opinion

How about those Mets? Everybody's got an opinion, and few of us are shy about expressing it. That's where letters of opinion come in. By stating your point of view in writing, letters of opinion give legitimacy to your feelings.

Letters of opinion are like telephone books: They have a wide variety of uses. Here are some of the most common ones:

- Praise or criticize a company
- Register your viewpoint on a social issue
- Comment on public policy
- Respond to an editorial or article
- Evaluate a project

All letters of opinion state your opinions clearly and provide reasons to support them. Here's how it works with a letter of complaint.

Complain, Complain, Complain

The toaster incinerated your lovely sesame-seed bagel; the hair dryer has more hot air than your local senator. You're mad as hell and you're not going to take it anymore. What to do? Why not write a letter of complaint? "Ah, they never work," you scoff. Here's how to lodge a consumer complaint and accomplish more than just venting your spleen.

Quoth the Maven

If you don't have the company's phone number or address because aliens stole your paperwork, check out your library's reference desk. They should be able to help you locate toll-free customer service numbers or the address of the company's corporate offices.

1. Gather up all the paperwork related to the product or service in question—which you saved, like the careful consumer you are, rather than throwing it away with the box. Here's the proof you need to make your case:

   - Sales receipt
   - Work order
   - Canceled check or charge slip
   - Warranty booklet

2. Contact the company by letter. The letter approach allows you time to frame your complaint more carefully and completely.

3. Follow these guidelines as you write:

   ◆ Address the letter to the company president or the consumer complaint department.

   ◆ Explain your problem with the product or service.

   ◆ Include the model number, serial number, and any receipts.

   ◆ State what you want. Be specific but reasonable. If the toaster broke after a month, a reasonable replacement is another toaster or a refund, not a side-by-side refrigerator/freezer or a week in Barbados.

   ◆ Be sure to include your return address and a daytime telephone number.

   ◆ Keep the letter brief.

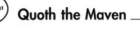

Quoth the Maven

Many consumer agencies are now on the Net. For example, you can reach the New York office of the Better Business Bureau at www.newyork.bbb.org. You may have to pay a small fee when you contact the Better Business Bureau by phone, but the service is free through e-mail.

4. Give the company sufficient time to respond to your complaint.

5. If you haven't received satisfaction after what you judge to be a reasonable length of time, you can take the following steps:

   ◆ Assume the letter was misplaced and write again.

   ◆ Contact your local consumer affairs office or regulatory agencies.

The next page shows a model letter of complaint.

Days of Wine and Roses
1221 GrapeLeaf Terrace
The Valley, California, 17226

Dear Product Manager:

On May 17, 2003, I purchased a Whine and Cheese corkscrew, model number 4157Z, from Wal-Mart, for $29.99. When I inserted the corkscrew into the cork of a Merlot that evening, the handle broke off. I have enclosed the receipt and all parts of the corkscrew in this package.

Because the Whine and Cheese corkscrew is highly recommended as a Best Buy in *Bottom's Up* magazine, I can only conclude that the corkscrew I purchased is defective. Please replace my corkscrew with the same model or another of comparable value that you recommend.

Thank you for your attention to this matter.

Sincerely,

Charlotte Chardonney

Charlotte Chardonney

My 2¢ Worth

A letter of opinion can state a positive viewpoint as well as a negative one. For example, you might write to a park to praise its rangers or a school district to applaud its teachers. Or your letter of opinion might state a dissenting viewpoint—a different way of looking at the same issue. You might write to a newspaper, magazine, or television station about its editorial viewpoint. Whatever your purpose or audience, here are some suggestions to consider as you write.

1. For letters of praise …

   ◆ State exactly who or what you are praising.

   ◆ Give the dates of the exemplary service.

   ◆ Identify outstanding employees by name and title.

   ◆ Include your name, address, and telephone number.

2. For letters of dissent …

  ◆ State what editorial, article, or other item prompted your response.

  ◆ Keep your cool; name-calling works against you.

  ◆ Stay on the issue; avoid pointless digressions.

  ◆ Include your name, address, and telephone number.

Here's a model letter of praise:

Dear Manager:

I must acknowledge the beautiful cake your staff baker Jodi Saviuk made for us on February 9, 2003, for our niece's Sweet Sixteen birthday party. The top of the cake had a delicate pattern of pink and yellow flowers joined by a pale green ribbon. The same motif was repeated around the base. The cake was as delicious as it was pretty, as shown the by the fact that our guests kept returning for seconds!

In addition, you should know that we put in our order at the last minute. Nonetheless, Ms. Saviuk found the time to bake and decorate our cake. Considering how busy your bakery is, we know that this entailed a great deal of extra work on her part. She made it seem easy, but we know that she worked very hard for us.

Erica Bakery is fortunate indeed to have such a talented and pleasant baker as Ms. Saviuk. You can be sure that we will come to Erika Bakery for all our cakes, cookies, and breads— especially our special occasion cakes!

Sincerely,

Sammi Weinstein

Sammi Weinstein

E-Mail: Instant Gratification

The Internet is a vast computer network of computer networks. It's composed of people, hardware, and software. With the proper equipment, you can sit at your computer and communicate with someone any place in the world as long as that person also has the proper equipment. You communicate through *e-mail*, short for *electronic mail*. For electronic newbies out there, e-mail is so easy, cupcake. It's also a lot less expensive than telephoning!

You Could Look It Up

Electronic mail (e-mail) is the transmission of messages over a communications network.

Internet mail uses a hierarchical system of names to make sense of the millions of computers served. The name of each computer (or "domain") contains from two to five words or abbreviations, separated by periods, with the top of the hierarchy at the right. The following figure shows the hypothetical Internet address of Bob Smith, managing director of Acme Incorporated:

The Internet address, up close and personal.

user ID; identifies the user's personal mailbox

bsmith@admin.acme.com

indicates type of organization; ".com" is commercial; some other domains include ".edu" (education) and ".gov" (government)

specifies the company name and appropriate division

Take My Word for It

Want to e-mail the world's movers and shakers? You can look up their electronic mail-boxes in the e-mail phone book *E-Mail Addresses of the Rich and Famous* (Addison-Wesley, 1997). President George W. Bush is at president@whitehouse.gov, for instance.

Boot Up

First of all, don't be seduced by the seeming informality of the medium: Write all e-mail as you would any important written communication. Follow these steps as you write e-mail:

1. **Draft the e-mail.** Working offline, write one or more rough drafts. Resist the temptation to toss off a quick note. Once you push that "send" button, you've lost the chance to revise.

   As with all types of writing, your audience's expectations determine your tone and diction. For example, when using e-mail or real-time communication ("instant messages"), you may be tempted to write informally, overlooking some of the accepted conventions of grammar, usage, spelling, and punctuation. Resist the temptation. If I had a dime for every e-mail that contained a crucial typo, I'd be sitting on a tropical isle right now, enjoying one of those drinks that comes with a little umbrella.

2. **Write a subject line.** The *subject line* is a brief description of the message. An effective subject line grabs your reader's attention and summarizes the content of the e-mail. As an added courtesy, if your message doesn't require a reply, type FYI (For Your Information) at the beginning of the subject line.

   And while we're here, if necessary, change the subject line when you reply. Any change in topic requires a change in the subject line. This helps your reader identify your purpose and topic at a glance.

3. **Use order of importance.** Place the most important facts first. These might include results or recommendations, for example. Busy readers will appreciate your consideration—and you'll get better results.

4. **Be brief.** Write concise messages and make your point fast. In general, make your sentences and paragraphs shorter than you would in a letter, memo, or other offline communication.

   In addition, skip lines between paragraphs rather than indenting to make your e-mail easier to read.

5. **Make your purpose clear.** Be very clear why you're sending the e-mail. Are you just saying hello to an old friend? Do you want the reader to make a decision? Do you expect a telephone call? Don't make the reader hunt for the message.

6. **Edit and proofread.** As with any written communication, e-mail can become a legal document. Therefore, before you send your message, review it carefully to make sure it conveys your precise meaning and is free of errors in grammar, spelling, punctuation, and usage.

7. **Always sign your e-mail.** Never assume that your recipient knows your identity from your screen name.

Think Before You Flame

If you use e-mail (and you will soon if you don't already), consider these implications:

1. Because writers using e-mail feel as if they're speaking, they tend to be less concerned with spelling, grammar, usage, and punctuation. But readers judge e-mail as they would any written document. Errors reflect badly on the writer.

2. E-mail can be sent to others online or printed and passed around the office, house, or community. This magnifies the potential exposure of any errors in the document.

You Could Look It Up

Flaming is the term for sending rude e-mail messages.

3. In addition to style, the informal nature of e-mail leads some people to write things that are better left undocumented. This can cause embarrassment—and worse.

4. Intra-office e-mail is a permanent record. It can be used in legal proceedings.

5. One wrong keystroke, and your e-mail can be sent someplace you don't want it to go.

Take My Word for It

Sometimes I think e-mail is like the Hotel California: You can check out any time you like, but you can never leave. The folks who have spent too much time online invented the following smiley faces (called emoticons) to convey a light tone for informal communications. Read these sideways:

:-) basic happy smiley face	;-) winking smiley face
:-(sad face	:-D laughing face
:-X lips-are-sealed face	:-C really bummed
:-/ skeptical	%-) bleary-eyed

These cutsie-pie symbols are *not* appropriate for business communication.

The Least You Need to Know

◆ Friendly letters share personal feelings and information among friends and family.

◆ Social notes relay an invitation or refuse one and express gratitude, congratulations, or condolences.

◆ Letters of opinion express viewpoints.

◆ Get wired; anybody who's anybody is on the Net.

Appendix A

Glossary

adjectives   Words that modify—describe or limit—nouns and pronouns.

adjective clause   A clause that describes nouns and pronouns.

adverb clause   A dependent clause that describes a verb, adjective, or other adverb.

adverbial phrase   A prepositional phrase that modifies a verb, adjective, or adverb.

agreement   Means that sentence parts match. Subjects must agree with verbs, and pronouns must agree with antecedents.

antecedent   The noun the pronoun stands for.

appositive   A noun or a pronoun that renames another noun or pronoun.

appositive phrases   Nouns or pronouns with modifiers.

bias-free language   Uses words and phrases that don't discriminate on the basis of gender, physical condition, age, race, or anything else.

case   The form of a noun or pronoun that shows how it is used in a sentence. Case is the grammatical role a noun or pronoun plays in a sentence. English has three cases: *nominative*, *objective*, and *possessive*.

clause   A group of words with its own subject and verb.

collective nouns   Nouns that name a group of people, places, or things. Examples of collective nouns include *class*, *committee*, *flock*, *herd*, *team*, *audience*, *assembly*, and *club*.

complex sentences   Sentences that have one independent clause and at least one dependent clause.

compound sentences   Sentences that have two or more independent clauses.

compound-complex sentences   Sentences that have at least two independent clauses and at least one dependent clause.

conjugate   To list the singular and plural forms of the verb in a specific tense.

conjunctions   Words that connect words or groups of words.

conjunctive adverbs   Adverbs used to connect other words. Conjunctive adverbs are also called transitions because they link ideas.

connotation   A word's emotional overtones.

dangling modifiers   Words or phrases that describe something that has been left out of the sentence.

denotation   A word's dictionary meaning.

dependent (subordinate) clause   Part of a sentence; it cannot stand alone.

diction   A writer's choice of words.

doublespeak   Artificial, evasive language.

elliptical clauses   Clauses that intentionally omit words for conciseness.

form letter   A prewritten, fill-in-the-blank letter designed to fit standard situations.

gerund   A form of a verb used as a noun.

grammar   A branch of linguistics that deals with the form and structure of words.

indefinite pronouns   Pronouns that refer to people, places, objects, or things without pointing to a specific one.

independent clause   A complete sentence; it can stand alone.

indirect objects   Tells *to whom* or *for whom* something is done.

infinitive   A verb form that comes after the word *to* and functions as a noun, adjective, or adverb.

interjections   Words that show strong emotion. Often, interjections are set off with an exclamation mark.

jargon   The specialized vocabulary of a particular group.

linking verbs   Words that indicate a state of being (*am, is, are,* and so on), relate to the senses (*look, smell, taste,* and so on), or indicate a condition (*appear, seem, become,* and so on).

mechanics   Involves aspects of correct writing format, such as spelling; punctuation; use of abbreviations, numbers, capitalization, and italics.

metaphors   Figures of speech that compare two unlike things. The more familiar thing helps describe the less familiar one.

misplaced modifier   A phrase, clause, or word placed too far from the word or words it modifies.

mixed metaphors   A combination of images that do not work well together. They occur when writers string together clichés.

mood   Shows the attitude expressed toward the action. It refers to the ability of verbs to convey a writer's attitude toward a subject.

noun clause   A dependent clause that functions as a noun.

nouns   Words that name a person, place, or thing.

number   Refers to the two forms of a word: *singular* (one) or *plural* (more than one).

parallel structure   Means putting ideas of the same rank in the same grammatical structure.

participle   A form of a verb that functions as an adjective. There are two kinds of participles: *present participles* and *past participles.*

phrase   A group of words, without a subject or a verb, that functions in a sentence as a single part of speech.

predicate adjectives   Adjectives separated from the noun or pronoun by a linking verb. Predicate adjectives describe the subject of the sentence.

predicate nominative   A noun or pronoun that follows a linking verb. A predicate nominative renames or identifies the subject.

prepositional phrases   Groups of words that begin with a preposition and end with a noun or a pronoun.

prepositions   Words that link a noun or a pronoun to another word in the sentence.

pronouns   Words used in place of a noun or another pronoun.

redundancy   Unnecessary repetition of words and ideas.

relative clause   An adjective clause that begins with one of the relative pronouns.

run-on sentences   Two incorrectly joined independent clauses. A comma splice is a run-on with a comma where the two sentences run together.

sentence   A group of words that expresses a complete thought.

sentence coordination   Links ideas of equal importance.

sentence fragment   A group of words that does not express a complete thought.

sexist language   Language that assigns qualities to people on the basis of their gender. It reflects prejudiced attitudes and stereotypical thinking about the sex roles and traits of both men and women.

simple sentence   A sentence made of one independent clause.

slang   Coined words and phrases or new meanings for established terms.

split infinitive   Occurs when an adverb or adverbial phrase is placed between *to* and the verb.

style   A writer's distinctive way of writing.

subordination   Connecting two unequal but related ideas with a subordinating conjunction to form a complex sentence.

tense   Shows the time of a verb.

tone   The writer's attitude toward his or her subject and audience.

usage   The customary way we use language in speech and writing. The correct level of usage is the one that is appropriate for the occasion.

verbal   A verb form used as another part of speech.

verbs   Words that name an action or describe a state of being.

voice   The form of the verb that shows whether the subject performed the action or received the action.

writing   A way of communicating a message to a reader for a purpose.

Model Documents

Use these models to help you create winning business communications.

Resumés

Model resumé for an entry-level financial services position.

Charles Rozakis

Street Address
Anytown, City Zip Code
Home: (516) 555-5555, School: (609) 555-5555
crozakis@princeton.edu

Education

Princeton University, Princeton, NJ
AB Economics, June 2003

September 1999–Current

- ◆ Senior Independent Work in Internet Business Models

- ◆ Finance, Financial Accounting

- ◆ Advanced Macro- and Microeconomics, Econometrics and Statistics

- ◆ Public Finance and Tax-Related Economics, Law and Economics: Introduction to Property, Tort, and Criminal Law

- ◆ Computer Science: Algorithms and Data Structures, Programming Systems

Job Experience

Morgan Stanley, New York, NY
Summer Analyst, Prime Income Trust Group

June 2002–September 2002 and June 2001–September 2001

- ◆ Built financial models using Microsoft Excel, created presentations for prospective clients, researched the growth of the loan market, reconciled accounts and closed trades.

- ◆ Learned a great deal about leveraged loans and portfolio management. Gained a broad-view understanding of how the market works overall, and a close-up, hands-on experience managing accounts on a day-to-day basis.

AirClic, Inc., West Conshohocken, PA
Intern, Wireless Engineering Division

August 2000–September 2000

- ◆ AirClic builds bar code scanners into wireless devices such as cell phones and Palm Pilots, linking print media with an interactive, online databases.

- ◆ Created working demos of scanable advertisements, performed internet research, and assisted in creating presentations for client corporations.

Johns Hopkins University, Center for Talented Youth
Teaching Assistant: Mathematics

June 2000–August 2000 and June 1999–August 1999

- ◆ CTY Instructors and TAs teach highly intelligent young people fast-paced, high school-level courses. In one three-week session, a student usually covers a year's worth of material.

- ◆ As a TA for the Math Sequence course, helped students work at their own pace and explained topics they found difficult.

Leadership Experiences

- ◆ Director/Producer *See How They Run* play, Wilson Blackbox Theater (9/00–12/00)

  Directed 9 actors and 12 crew members; oversaw all aspects of the production; managed a budget of $2,000.

- ◆ President (2001–2002), Treasurer (2000–2001), *FireHazards* a cappella group

- ◆ Business Manager (2000–2001) and member, *Koleinu* a cappella group

- ◆ Treasurer (2000–2002) and contributor, Princeton University *Distractions* puzzle magazine

- ◆ Disk Jockey, 103.3 WPRB, weekly radio show (Princeton area)

- ◆ Achieved the rank of Eagle Scout, after eight years in the Boy Scouts of America

Computer Programs

In-depth knowledge of Microsoft Excel, Access, Powerpoint, Outlook and Word. Also worked with Portfolio Management Database, Wall Street Office, PCDOCS, Netscape, and numerous online services including Intralinks, LoanX and LPC's LoanConnector.

Model resumé for a purchasing director with experience.

T'AYSHA EMERSON

OBJECTIVE

To gain full-time employment as a purchasing director

EXPERIENCE

| 1999–present | Sbarro, Inc. | Southridge, SC |

Purchasing Agent

- ◆ Negotiate with vendors vigorously to save $3 million yearly as a result of corporate rebate programs, maximum discounts, and rapid payment discounts.
- ◆ Maintain and upgrade all equipment as necessary, saving $100,000 in leasing costs.
- ◆ Train and supervise staff on procedure and daily assignments.
- ◆ Estimate preconstruction costs for equipment based on design drawings.

| 1997–1999 | Sbarro, Inc. | Commack, NY |

Office Services Manager

- ◆ Negotiated and ordered all office supplies and business machines.
- ◆ Implemented training course for new recruits—speeding profitability.
- ◆ Distributed bi-weekly payroll packages to 650 company restaurants.

| 1990–1997 | Sonoma Grill | Brookhaven, NY |

Purchasing Assistant

- ◆ Negotiated bids with trucking services and scheduled deliveries.
- ◆ Secured warehouse space for equipment storage, saving $150,000 yearly.
- ◆ Tracked orders to insure timely delivery, resulting in 35% greater on-time rate.

EDUCATION

| 2000–2004 | SUNY Empire College | Hauppaugh, NY |

- ◆ B.A., Business Administration.
- ◆ Graduated Summa Cum Laude.

SKILLS

Excellent oral and written communication skills. Proficient in AS400 computer system regarding purchasing, payroll, and accounting. Knowledge of various computer programs, including Microsoft Word and Excel for Windows.

FAX (123) 098-7654 • E-MAIL ME@MYCOMPANY.COM

12345 MAIN STREET • ANY CITY, STATE OR PROVINCE 12345-6789 • PHONE (123) 456-7890

Model chronological resumé for a technical writer/engineer with extensive experience.

JOHN ENNIS

192 Plitt Avenue   Pensacola, FL 81901

(555)555-5555   JohnEnnis@compuserve.com

EXPERIENCE

Extensive experience in technical writing on both technical and business subjects, in a variety of formats including proposal preparation, technical reports, software manuals, management directives and position papers, technical briefing slides, ISO 9000 certification procedures, procurement specifications, and business analysis.

1987–present   NORTHROP GRUMMAN CORPORATION   Pensacola, FL 81901

Engineering Specialist, A-10 Program

- ◆ Write technical analysis reports and proposals: define system requirements, evaluate software and hardware platforms and technical approaches, perform trade studies, develop design concepts, and plan and manage work efforts. Analyze, manage, and implement systems analysis solutions under contract to the USAF. Edit engineering inputs and produce deliverable documents.

- ◆ Lead author for the A-10 Prime proposal Executive Summary, Past Performance, and Management volumes. Principal interface to the proposal center production staff (layout, graphics, presentation style). Website content author. Designed marketing brochure for real-time simulation laboratory. Authored ISO 9000 certification procedures.

- ◆ Present technical and management briefings to employees, management, and customers. Ghostwrite executive presentations and position papers.

- ◆ Train employees and customers in the use of various computer systems.

Spring 2001   Florida State University   Pensacola, FL 81901

Adjunct Professor

- ◆ Taught EGL 209 Technical Communications: business and technical writing/presentations for a targeted audience including technical research reports, technical manuals, proposal preparation, ISO 9000 certification procedures, procurement specifications, etc.; use of appropriate commercial, industry, and government specs for technical writing (such as IEEE, ANSI, ISO, and DOD); preparation and use of electronic media.

1977–1987   FAIRCHILD REPUBLIC COMPANY   Pensacola, FL 81901

Supervisor of Engineering Personnel

- ◆ Succession plan author.

- ◆ Trained supervisors in the writing of Management By Objectives performance appraisals and job evaluations.

- ◆ Author of five-year facilities capital plan, AAP reports, engineering policies and procedures. Executive ghostwriter for all manner of business documents.

- ◆ Designed and presented college recruiting briefings at engineering colleges.

- ◆ Resumé ghostwriter for outplacement center.

Associate Administrator

- ◆ Wrote and edited A-10 Aircraft Structural Integrity Plans for both the A-10 and T-46 Aircraft (annual technical analysis report approximately 600 pages).

- ◆ Wrote Corrosion Prevention and Control Plan contractual documents for the T-46.

- ◆ Wrote portions of the NGT proposal Technical and Cost Analysis volumes.

- ◆ Wrote portions of the annual Tri-Services Research and Development report.

- ◆ Conducted training classes in several computer systems (CMS, ADRS).

EDUCATION

MBA Management Information Systems with distinction May 1988 New York Institute of Technology

BS Computer Science/Business/English May 1982 New York Institute of Technology

Advanced Computer Engineering Certificate Client Server Computing April 1997

University of California Irvine (Extension program at Northrop Grumman, NY)

Flight and Ground Simulation Certificate Jan 1996 State University of New York Binghamton

Cover Letter

Model cover letter to accompany the resumé for an entry-level financial services position.

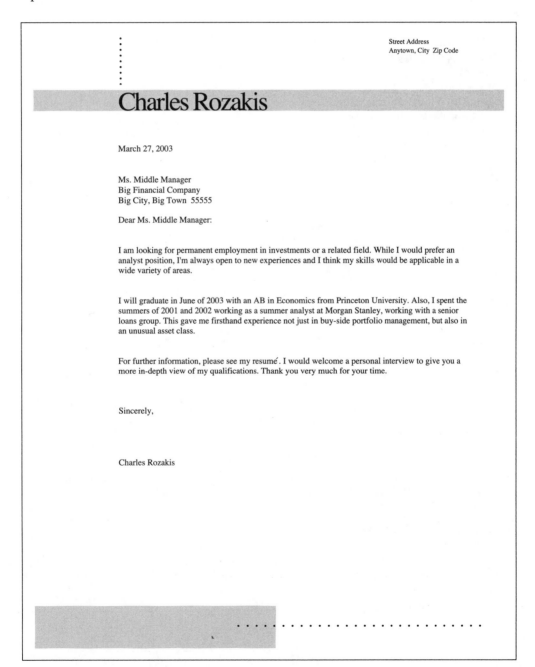

Street Address
Anytown, City Zip Code

Charles Rozakis

March 27, 2003

Ms. Middle Manager
Big Financial Company
Big City, Big Town 55555

Dear Ms. Middle Manager:

I am looking for permanent employment in investments or a related field. While I would prefer an analyst position, I'm always open to new experiences and I think my skills would be applicable in a wide variety of areas.

I will graduate in June of 2003 with an AB in Economics from Princeton University. Also, I spent the summers of 2001 and 2002 working as a summer analyst at Morgan Stanley, working with a senior loans group. This gave me firsthand experience not just in buy-side portfolio management, but also in an unusual asset class.

For further information, please see my resumé. I would welcome a personal interview to give you a more in-depth view of my qualifications. Thank you very much for your time.

Sincerely,

Charles Rozakis

Thank You Letters

Model business thank you letter:

Dear Mr. Harris:

Than you for the interview today. I enjoyed the tour of the facility as well as getting a chance to meet the staff. I appreciate the warmth and friendliness your staff showed me. I remain highly interested in your company.

I was also pleased to learn a little more about the operations and the way your company is run. It is refreshing to see the level of care that goes into running such a complicated business while maintaining the highest level of customer care and quality control.

I look forward to hearing from you and would greatly appreciate the chance to become part of your company. Thank you again.

Sincerely,

J. P. Jobseeker

J. P. Jobseeker

Model business thank you letter:

Inside Address

Date

Dear Mr. Harris:

I spoke to my cousin Alan and he told me that the marketing position at Big Publishing Company is open again and that you had told him that I might have another shot at it. Unfortunately, I won't be able to pursue the job this time. As you can see from the stationery, my job search was successful. I started at Hearst Publications in January as a Product Manager. I am involved in marketing such titles as *Redbook*, *Country Living*, and *Esquire* at the newsstand level. It is similar to what I did at Time and maybe to some extent what I would have been doing at Big Publishing Company.

In any event, I wanted to thank you for your help and for thinking of me again. The job at Big Publishing Company sounds exciting and I would have enjoyed being involved in the marketing of such great products. I plan on building a long career at Hearst, but please stay in touch in the future about any possible opportunities at Big Publishing Company. You never know.

Again, thank you very much for your help.

Sincerely,

J. P. Jobseeker

J. P. Jobseeker

Guide to Grammar and Usage

A

Adjectives

Adjectives are words that describe nouns and pronouns. Adjectives answer the questions "What kind?" "How much?" "Which one?" or "How many?"

Examples: pretty, blue, weak, many

There are four kinds of adjectives:

- ◆ Common adjectives
- ◆ Proper adjectives
- ◆ Compound adjectives
- ◆ Articles

Let's look at each.

- ◆ Common adjectives describe nouns or pronouns.

  Examples: strong, green, handsome, rich

- ◆ Proper adjectives are formed from proper nouns.

  Examples: California oranges, Chinese silk

- ◆ Compound adjectives are made up of more than one word.

  Examples: far-off country, teenage person

Articles are a special type of adjective. There are three articles: *a, an, the. The* is called a "definite article" because it refers to a specific thing. *A* and *an* are called indefinite articles because they refer to general things.

Follow these rules to use adjectives correctly:

◆ Use an adjective to describe a noun or a pronoun.

◆ Use an adjective after a linking verb. A linking verb connects a subject with a descriptive word. Here are the most common linking verbs: *be (is, am, are, was, were,* and so on), *seem, appear, look, feel, smell, sound, taste, become, grow, remain, stay,* and *turn.*

Example: Chicken made this way *tastes* more *delicious* (not deliciously).

Adverbs

Adverbs are words that describe verbs, adjectives, or other adverbs. Adverbs answer the questions "When?" "Where?" "How?" or "To what extent?"

Examples: always, often, quietly, slowly

Most adverbs are formed by adding *-ly* to an adjective. Here is a list of the most common adverbs that do not end in *-ly:*

afterward	here	now	there
almost	how	often	today
already	late	quick	tomorrow
also	long	rather	too
back	low	slow	when
even	more	so	where
far	near	soon	yesterday
fast	never	still	
hard	next	then	

Use an adverb to describe a verb, an adjective, or another adverb.

Examples:

Describe a verb: Experiments using dynamite must be done *carefully*.

Describe an adjective: Sam had an *unbelievably huge* appetite for pizza.

Describe an adverb: They sang *so clearly*.

Agreement of Pronoun and Antecedent

Pronouns and antecedents (the words to which they refer) must agree or match. Follow these rules:

- ♦ A pronoun replaces a noun. To make sure that your writing is clear, always use the noun first before using the pronoun.

- ♦ Be sure that the pronoun refers directly to the noun.

- ♦ A pronoun agrees (or matches) with its antecedent. Use a singular personal pronoun with a singular indefinite pronoun.

  Example: If *anyone* questions the amount, refer *him* or *her* to payroll. The singular pronouns *him* or *her* refer to the singular pronoun *anyone*.

Here is a list of the common singular indefinite pronouns:

anyone	every (person, etc.)	no one	someone
each	everyone	one	
either	neither	somebody	

Agreement of Subject and Verb

Agreement means that sentence parts match.

Follow these rules to match sentence parts:

- ♦ A singular subject takes a singular verb.

  Example: I <u>am</u> going to the movies.

- ♦ A plural subject takes a plural verb.

  Example: Lou and Shai <u>are</u> going to the movies.

- ♦ Some verbs have irregular forms. The following table lists the most common ones.

	Be	**Do**	**Have**
Singular:	is, am, was	does, did	has, had
Plural:	are, were	do, did	have, had

- ♦ Ignore words or phrases that come between the subject and the verb.

  Example: Too many *onions* in a stew often cause an upset stomach.

  The plural subject *onions* requires the plural verb *cause*. Ignore the intervening prepositional phrase "in a stew."

♦ Subjects that are singular in meaning but plural in form require a singular verb. Examples include *measles, news, economics,* and *mathematics.*

Example: The *news* <u>was</u> good.

♦ Singular subjects connected by either ... *or, neither ... nor, and not only ... but also* require a singular verb.

Example: Either the witness or the defendant *was* lying.

♦ If the subject is made up of two or more nouns or pronouns connected by *or, nor, not only, but also,* the verb agrees with the noun closer to the pronoun.

Example: Neither the contract nor the page *proofs are* arriving in time to meet the deadline.

Example: Neither the page proofs nor the *contract is* arriving in time to meet the deadline.

Antecedent

The noun the pronoun stands for.

Apostrophes

See Possession.

C

Capitalization

♦ Capitalize the first word of ...

A sentence: It rains on the Spanish plain.

A line of poetry: I think that I shall never see
A poem as lovely as a tree

The greeting of a letter: Dear Ms. Ramirez:

A complimentary close: Yours very truly,

Each item in an outline:

    I. Introduction

        A. Topic sentence

        B. First major point

        C. Second major point

- Capitalize the titles of books, plays, newspapers, and magazines.

  Examples:

  A book title: *The Big Book of Dates*

  A play: *Dance of the Vampires*

  A newspaper: *The Daily News*

  A magazine: *The Atlantic Monthly*

- Capitalize titles before a person's name.

  Examples: Dr. Frankenstein, Ms. Schmendrick, Rev. Smith, Mr. Myles

- Capitalize abbreviations that appear after a person's name.

  Examples: Martin Luther King Jr., Laurie Rozakis, Ph.D.

- Capitalize titles of parents and relatives not preceded by a possessive word.

  Examples: We saw Mother kissing Santa Claus. I saw my father with my mother.

- Capitalize geographical places and sections of the country.

  Examples: Europe, Asia, United States of America, Lake Erie, the South, Yellowstone National Park

- Capitalize the names of historical events, era, and documents.

  Examples: the Civil War, the Renaissance, the Magna Carta

- Capitalize the names of languages, nationalities, and races.

  Examples:

  Language: French, German, Russian

  Nationalities: American, Japanese, Indian

  Races: African American

- Capitalize religions and references to the Supreme Being.

  Examples:

  Religions: Judaism, Catholicism

  References: the Creator, Him, His name, He, Heaven

- Capitalize proper nouns and proper adjectives.

  Examples:

  Proper nouns: Shakespeare, Mexico

  Proper adjectives: Shakespearean, Mexican

- Capitalize brand names.

  Examples: Jell-O pudding, Kleenex tissues

- Capitalize the names of organizations, institutions, courses, and famous buildings.

  Examples:

  Organizations: The Girl Scouts of America

  Institutions: The United Nations

  Courses: French 101, Mathematics 203 (but not mathematics)

  Buildings: The Empire State Building

- Capitalize days, months, and holidays.

  Examples:

  Days: Monday, Tuesday, Wednesday

  Months: February, March, April

  Holidays: Thanksgiving, Fourth of July, Kwanzaa

- Capitalize abbreviations for time.

  Examples: 6 A.M., 6 P.M.

- Capitalize the words I and Oh.

  Examples: Quickly, I turned around.

  Oh! Did you see that?

Case

Case is the form of a noun or pronoun that shows how it is used in a sentence. English has three cases: *nominative, objective,* and *possessive.*

- Use the nominative case to show the subject of a verb.

  Example: We spoke to the agent about the deal.

- Use the objective case to show the noun or pronoun receives the action.

  Example: The agent was willing to speak to *us.*

- Use the possessive case to show ownership.

  Example: The agent gave us *his* advice.

  The following chart shows the three cases.

Nominative (Pronoun as Subject)	Objective (Pronoun as Objective)	Possessive (Ownership)
I	me	my, mine
you	you	your, yours
He	him	his
she	her	her, hers

Nominative (Pronoun as Subject)	Objective (Pronoun as Objective)	Possessive (Ownership)
it	it	its
we	us	our, ours
they	them	their, theirs
who	whom	whose
whoever	whomever	whoever

Clauses

Clauses are groups of words that have a subject and a verb.

- *Independent clauses* are complete sentences.
- *Dependent clauses* are fragments. They cannot stand alone; they can only be part of a sentence.

Clichés

Clichés are descriptive phrases that have lost their effectiveness through overuse.

Examples: sweet as sugar, tried and true, raining cats and dogs slow but sure

Replace clichés with fresh, new descriptions.

Colons

See Punctuation.

Commas

See Punctuation.

Comparative Adjectives and Adverbs

Follow these rules to make correct comparisons with adjectives and adverbs.

- Use the comparative degree (*-er* or *more* form) to compare two things.
- Use the superlative form (*-est* or *most* form) to compare more than two things.
- Never use *-er* and *more* or *-est* and *most* together.

Review the following chart.

Part of Speech	Positive	Comparative	Superlative
adjective	wide	wider	widest
adverb	widely	more widely	most widely
adjective	faithful	more faithful	most faithful
adverb	faithfully	more faithfully	most faithfully

Good and *bad* do not follow these guidelines. They have irregular forms.

Part of Speech	Positive	Comparative	Superlative
adjective	good	better	best
adverb	well	better	best
adjective	bad	worse	worst
adverb	badly	worse	worst

Conjunctions

Conjunctions connect words or groups of words.

Examples: and, but, or for, because, although

Contractions

Contractions are two words combined. When you contract words, add an apostrophe in the space where the letters have been taken out.

Examples:

◆ does + not = doesn't

◆ we + re = we're

◆ I + will = I'll

Don't confuse contractions with possessive pronouns. Study this chart.

Contraction	Possessive Pronoun
it's (it is)	its
you're (you are)	your
they're (they are)	their
who's (who is)	whose

D

Dangling Modifiers

A dangling modifier is a word or phrase that describes something that has been left out of the sentence.

- ◆ *Dangling:* Making startling new discoveries in science, the Renaissance was a time or rebirth.
- ◆ *Correct:* The Renaissance was a time of rebirth when people made startling new discoveries in science.

Diction

Diction is a writer's choice of words. Be sure you select words that are suitable for your audience, purpose, and tone. Depending on your audience, you can use words that are formal or words that are informal. Informal language includes slang. This level of diction is not suitable for formal discourse.

Be sure to avoid sexist language. This is language that assigns qualities to people on the basis of their gender. This language discriminates against people by limiting what they can do. Here are some guidelines:

- ◆ Avoid using *he* to refer to both men and women.

  Sexist: He is a good writer so he knows how to select suitable words.

  Okay: Good writers know how to select suitable words.

- ◆ Avoid using *man* to refer to men and women.

  Sexist: Man is a social creature.

  Okay: People are social creatures.

- ◆ Avoid language that denigrates people.

  Sexist: lady lawyer, male nurse

  Okay: lawyer, nurse

Double Negatives

Use only one negative word to express a negative idea. Here are the most frequently used negative words:

-n't	no	not	only
neither	no one	nothing	scarcely
never	nobody	nowhere	

E

Exclamation Marks

See Punctuation.

F

Fragments

A sentence fragment is a group of words that does not express a complete thought. Most times, a fragment is missing a subject, a verb, or both. Other times, a fragment may have a subject and a verb but still not express a complete thought.

Example: The writer *gone* to the office.

The verb is not complete. The sentence should read:

> The writer *has gone* to the office.

You can correct a fragment two ways:

- ◆ Add the missing part to the sentence
  Fragment: In the cabinet over the bookshelf.
  Complete: I keep the aspirin in the cabinet over the bookshelf.
- ◆ Omit the subordinating conjunction or connect it to another sentence.
  Fragment: When you go to the convention.
  Complete: When you go to the convention, be sure to wear comfortable shoes.

I

Interjections

Interjections show strong emotion. Often, interjections are set off with an exclamation mark.

Examples: Oh!, Wow!, Look out!

M

Misplaced Modifiers

A misplaced modifier is a describing word that is placed too far away from the noun or the pronoun that it is describing. As a result, the sentence does not convey its meaning. It may also produce confusion or amusement. To convey the error, move the modifier as close as possible to the word or phrase it is describing.

Example: The writer read from his new book wearing glasses.

The modifier *wearing glasses* is in the wrong place. The sentence states that the book, not the writer, was wearing glasses. Move the modifier so that the sentence reads:

> The writer *wearing glasses* read from his new book.

N

Nonstandard English

Nonstandard English are words and phrases that are not considered correct usage. Here is a list of words and phrases to avoid in writing and speech.

Nonstandard English	Standard Written English
irregardless	regardless
kind of a	kind of
off of	off
being that	because
had ought	ought
this here	this

continues

continued

Nonstandard English	Standard Written English
hisself	himself
the reason is because	the reason is that
like I told you	as I told you
that there	that

Nouns

A noun is a word that names a person, place, or thing. Nouns come in different varieties.

- ◆ Common nouns name a type of person, place, or thing.

  Examples: boy, city, food

- ◆ Proper nouns name a specific person, place, or thing.

  Examples: Harris, Pensacola, Rice-a-Roni

- ◆ Compound nouns are two or more nouns that function as a single unit. A compound noun can be two individual words, words joined by a hyphen, or two words combined.

  Examples:

  Individual words: time capsule

  Hyphenated words: step-brother

  Combined words: sunshine

P

Parts of Speech

English words are divided into eight different parts of speech according to their function in a sentence. *See* Adjectives, Adverbs, Conjunctions, Interjections, Nouns, Prepositions, Pronouns, and Verbs for a description of each kind.

Periods

See Punctuation.

Phrases

Phrases are groups of words that function in a sentence as one part of speech. Phrases do not have subjects or verbs.

Examples: by the lake, near the closet, with them, a large publishing house

Plural Nouns

Plural nouns name more than one person, place, or thing. Follow these guidelines to form the plural of nouns:

◆ Add *s* to form the plural of most nouns.

Singular	Plural
bird	birds
hat	hats

◆ Add *es* if the noun ends in *s*, *sh*, *ch*, or *x*.

Singular	Plural
class	classes
inch	inches
box	boxes

◆ If the noun ends in *y* preceded by a *consonant*, change the *y* to *i* and add *es*.

Singular	Plural
city	cities
lady	ladies

◆ If the noun ends in *y* preceded by a *vowel*, add *s*.

Singular	Plural
essay	essays
monkey	monkeys

◆ If the noun ends on *o* preceded by a *vowel*, add *s*.

Singular	Plural
radio	radios
ratio	ratios

◆ If the noun ends in *o* preceded by a *consonant*, the noun can takes *es*, *s*, or either *s* or *es*.

Singular	Plural
Takes es	
potato	potatoes
hero	heroes
Takes s	
silo	silos
solo	solos
Either	
zero	zeros, zeroes
tornado	tornados, tornadoes

◆ Add *s* to most nouns ending in *f*.

Singular	Plural
brief	briefs
chief	chiefs

Exceptions: Change the *f* or *fe* to *v* and add *es*.

Singular	Plural
self	selves
wolf	wolves
leaf	leaves
knife	knives
life	lives
wife	wives
half	halves
thief	thieves

◆ In compound words, make the main word plural.

Singular	Plural
sister-in-law	sisters-in-law
mother-in-law	mothers-in-law

◆ Some nouns change their spelling when they become plural.

Singular	Plural
child	children
man	men
foot	feet
tooth	teeth
louse	lice
mouse	mice

◆ Some nouns have the same form whether they are singular or plural.

Singular	Plural
swine	swine
series	series
deer	deer
sheep	sheep
moose	moose
species	species

Possession

Possession shows ownership. Follow these rules to create possessive nouns.

◆ With singular nouns, add an apostrophe and *s*.

Examples: girl, girl's manuscript; student, student's ideas

◆ With plural nouns ending in *s*, add an apostrophe after the *s*.

Examples: girls, girls' manuscript; students, students' ideas

◆ With plural nouns not ending in *s*, add an apostrophe and *s*.

Examples: women, women's books; mice, mice's tails

Prepositions

Prepositions are words that link a noun or a pronoun follow it to another word in the sentence.

Here are some of the most common prepositions:

about	below	from	outside
above	beneath	in	over
across	beside	inside	past
after	between	into	since
against	beyond	like	through
along	but	near	toward
amid	by	of	under
around	despite	off	underneath
as	down	on	until
at	during	onto	upon
before	except	opposite	with
behind	for	out	within

A prepositional phrase is a preposition and its object.

Examples: on the wing, in the door

Pronoun and Antecedent Agreement

See Agreement of Pronoun and Antecedent.

Pronouns

Pronouns are words used in place of a noun or another pronoun.

◆ Personal pronouns refer to a specific person, place, object, or thing.

	Singular	Plural
First person	I, me, mine, my	we, us, our, ours
Second person	you, your, yours	you, your, yours

	Singular	Plural
Third person	he, him, his she, her, hers, it	they, them, their theirs, its

◆ Possessive pronouns show ownership.

Examples: yours, his, hers, its, ours, theirs, whose

◆ Interrogative pronouns begin a question.

Examples: who, what, which, whom, whose

◆ Indefinite pronouns refer to people, places, objects, or things without pointing to a specific one. Here are the most common indefinite pronouns.

Singular	Plural	Singular or Plural
another	both	all
anyone	few	any
each	many	more
everyone	others	most
everybody	several	none
everything		some
much		
nobody		
nothing		
other		
someone		
anybody		
anything		
either		
little		
neither		
no one		
one		
somebody		
something		

Punctuation

Using the correct punctuation is more than following the grammar rules—it enables your audience understand your ideas more clearly.

◆ Periods

Use a period after a complete sentence.

Example: My dog is named Spot.

Use a period after a command.

Example: Fasten your seatbelt.

Use a period after most abbreviations.

Examples: Dr., Ms., Jr.

Use a period after an initial.

Example: John F. Kennedy

Use a period after each Roman numeral, letter, or number in an outline.

Example: I.

    A.

    B.

       1.

       2.

◆ Question marks

Use a question mark after a question. Place the question mark inside closing quotation marks if it is part of the quotation. If not, place it outside the quotation marks.

Examples:

"Where are you going?" Chris asked.

Do you know who wrote "The Raven"?

◆ Exclamation marks

Use an exclamation mark after an exclamatory sentence.

Example: What a terrible day!

◆ Commas

Use a comma to separate items in a series.

Example: Shoppers need comfortable shoes, patience, and money.

Use a comma to set off interrupting words and expressions.

Examples:

Oh, my back aches from lifting weights.

My baby, a light sleeper, awakens easily.

Use a comma after introductory words and expressions.

Examples:

Along the route from the stadium, the crowd cheered loudly.

When I graduated college, I started paying back my loans.

Use a comma to separate parts of a compound sentence. Use the comma before the coordinating conjunction.

Example: Henry didn't pay for dinner, but he promises that he will pay next time we go out.

Use a comma to set off a direct quotation.

Examples:

"Tomorrow I will start my diet," she said.

"Tomorrow," she said, "I will start my diet."

Use a comma after the greeting of an informal letter and the close of any letter.

Examples: Dear Sammi, Dear Mudface, Yours truly, Sincerely,

Use a comma between the day of the month and the year.

Examples: December 7, 1941, July 20, 1969

Use a comma to separate the parts of an address. Do not use a comma before the ZIP Code.

Example: She lives at 763 Main Street, Farmingdale, New York 11735.

◆ Semicolons

Use a semicolon to separate items in a series when the items contain commas.

Examples: We elected Courtney Kassinger, president; Shelby Kravitz, vice president; Elisabeth Fink, secretary; and Joe Schulman, treasurer.

Use a semicolon between main clauses when the conjunction (and, but, yet, so, for, or) has been left out.

Example: We have made many suggestions for your landscaping; you haven't accepted a single one.

◆ Colons

Use a colon before a list.

Example: The grader will be looking for the following elements: a topic sentence, specific details, and a strong conclusion.

◆ Parenthesis

Use parentheses to enclose additional information.

Example: The decline in literacy has been astonishing (see the following chart).

Use parentheses to enclose numbers or letters.

Example: A book owned by a public library is usually catalogued by (1) title card, (2) author card, (3) subject card.

- Hyphen

  Use a hyphen to show a word break at the end of a line.

  Example: By the time he finishes this book, your grandfather will be an octo-grammarian.

  Use a hyphen in certain compound nouns.

  Examples: pint-size, great-grandmother

  Use hyphens in fractions and in compound numbers from twenty-one to ninety-nine.

  Examples: one-half, sixty-six

- Quotation marks

  Use quotation marks to set off a speaker's exact words.

  Example: "Is that poem a sonnet?" we asked.

  Use quotation marks to set off the titles of short works such as poems, essays, songs, short stories, and magazine articles.

  Examples:

  "The Rime of the Ancient Mariner"

  "The Poet"

  "We've Only Just Begun"

- Apostrophes

  Use an apostrophe to show ownership.

  Examples: Lisa's book, Jillian's manuscript, women's room, men's room

  Use an apostrophe to show that letters have been left out of contractions.

  Examples: can't, won't, I'll

Q

Question Marks

See Punctuation.

Quotation Marks

See Punctuation.

R

Run-On Sentences

A run-on sentence is two incorrectly joined sentences.

Example: The teacher walked into the room there was a mouse in her desk.

You can correct a run-on sentence four ways:

- ◆ Separate the run-on into two sentences.

  Example: The teacher walked into the room. There was a mouse in her desk.

- ◆ Add a coordinating conjunction. The coordinating conjunctions are *and, but, or, for, yet,* and *so.*

  Example: The teacher walked into the room, and there was a mouse in her desk.

- ◆ Add a subordinating conjunction.

  Example: When the teacher walked into the room, there was a mouse in her desk.

- ◆ Use a semicolon.

  Example: The teacher walked into the room; there was a mouse in her desk.

S

Semicolons

See Punctuation.

Sentence Types

There are four types of sentences in English: declarative, exclamatory, interrogative, and imperative.

- ◆ Declarative sentences state an idea. They end with a period.

  Example: Students are made, not born.

- ◆ Exclamatory sentences show strong emotions. They end with an exclamation mark.

  Example: What a good essay this is!

- ◆ Interrogative sentences ask a question. They end with a question mark.

  Example: Which parts of the book do you have to study the most?

- Imperative sentences give orders or directions. They end with a period or an exclamation mark.

    Example: Sit down and write!

Sentence Variety

Unless you are writing certain kinds of dialogue, all your sentences should be grammatically correct. In addition, craft your sentences to express your ideas in the best possible way. Strive for rhythm, pattern, and variety as well. Here are some ideas to try:

- Expand short sentences by adding detail.

    Short: The plane took off.

    Expanded: The plane took off, a shrieking golden ribbon in the morning sky.

- Combine short sentences.

    Short: O. Henry wrote a short story called "The Gift of the Magi." A husband sells his watch to buy his wife combs. They are for her beautiful hair.

    Combined: In O. Henry's short story "The Gift of the Magi," a husband sells his watch to buy his wife combs for her beautiful hair.

- Change sentence openings.

    Sentence: I unlocked the attic door with great difficulty.

    Revised: With great difficulty, I unlocked the attic door.

Sentences

A sentence is a group of words that express a complete thought. A sentence has two parts: a subject and a predicate. The subject includes the noun or pronoun that tells what the subject is about. The predicate includes the verb that describes what the subject is doing.

Subject	Predicate
New York City	is called the "Big Apple."

Subject and Verb Agreement

See Agreement of Subject and Verb.

T

Tense

Avoid shifting tenses in the middle of a sentence of a paragraph.

Wrong: I *was walking* to class when a huge dog *jumps up* and *attacks* me.

Right: I was *walking* to class when a huge dog *jumped up* and *attacked* me.

Transitions

Transitions are words that connect ideas and show how they are linked. The following chart shows some of these transitions and the relationships they create.

Relationship	Transition Words
Addition	also, and, besides, too, in addition to, further
Example	for example, for instance, thus, namely
Time	next, then, finally, first, second, third, fourth, afterward, before, during, soon, later, meanwhile, subsequently
Contrast	but, nevertheless, yet, in contrast, however, still
Comparison	likewise, in comparison, similarly
Result	therefore, consequently, as a result, thus, due to this, accordingly
Summary	as a result, in brief, in conclusion, hence, in short, finally
Place	in the front, in the back, here, there, nearby

Use transitions to show how ideas are linked.

Without transition: Lisa completed her research. She started her outline.

With transition: After Lisa completed her research, she started her outline.

V

Verb Tense

The *tense* of a verb shows its time. Every verb has three parts.

Verb Part	Example
Present tense	break
Past tense	broke
Past participle	broken

♦ Some verbs are regular. This means they form the past tense by adding *-d* or *-ed* to the present form.

♦ Other verbs are irregular. This means their form changes in the past tense. The following chart shows the most common irregular verbs.

Present Tense	Past Tense	Past Participle
arise	arose	arisen
bear	bore	born or borne
beat	beat	beaten
become	became	become
begin	began	begun
bend	bent	bent
bite	bit	bitten
blow	blew	blown
break	broke	broken
bring	brought	brought
burst	burst	burst
catch	caught	caught
choose	chose	chosen
come	came	come
creep	crept	crept
dig	dug	dug
dive	dived or dove	dived
do	did	done
draw	drew	drawn
drink	drank	drunk
drive	drove	driven
eat	ate	eaten
fall	fell	fallen
fight	fought	fought
fly	flew	flown
forget	forgot	forgotten
forgive	forgave	forgiven
freeze	froze	frozen
get	got	gotten or got
give	gave	given

Present Tense	Past Tense	Past Participle
go	went	gone
grow	grew	grown
hang	hung	hung
hang (execute)	hanged	hanged
hide	hid	hidden
hold	held	held
hurt	hurt	hurt
kneel	knelt	knelt
know	knew	known
lay	laid	laid
lead	led	led
lie (horizontal)	lay	lain
lie (falsehood)	lied	lied
lose	lost	lost
prove	proved	proved or proven
ride	rode	ridden
ring	rang	rung
rise	rose	risen
run	ran	run
say	said	said
see	saw	seen
shake	shook	shaken
show	showed	showed or shown
sing	sang	sung
speak	spoke	spoken
steal	stole	stolen
swim	swam	swum
take	took	taken
teach	taught	taught
throw	threw	thrown
wake	woke or waked	woken or waked
write	wrote	written

Verbs

Verbs are words that name an action or describe a state of being. There are four basic types of verbs: action verbs, linking verbs, helping verbs, and verb phrases.

- Action verbs tell what the subject does.

  Examples: jump, kiss, laugh

- Linking verbs join the subject and the predicate and name and describe the subject.

  Examples: be, feel, grow, seem, smell, remain, appear, sound, stay, look, taste, turn, become

- Helping verbs are added to another verb to make the meaning clearer.

  Examples: am, does, had, shall, can, did, may, should, could, have, might, will, do, has, must, would

- Verb phrases are made of one main verb and one or more helping verbs.

  Examples: will arrive, could be looking

W

Word Choice

See Diction.

Wordiness

Write simply and directly. Omit unnecessary details or ideas that you have already stated. Use a lot of important detail, but no unnecessary words.

- Omit unnecessary words.

  Wordy: We watched the big, massive, black cloud rising up from the level prairie and covering over the sun.

  Better: We watched the massive, black cloud rising from the prairie and covering the sun.

- Rewrite the sentence to eliminate unnecessary words.

  Wordy: Sonnets, which are a beautiful poetic form, have 14 lines and a set rhythm and rhyme.

  Better: Sonnets are a beautiful poetic form with 14 lines and a set rhythm and rhyme.

Words Often Confused

Some pairs of words are mixed up with each other. Sometimes it is because the words sound alike; at other times it is because they are spelled alike. The following words are often confused, misused, and abused.

Word	Definition	Example
accept	take	Accept my thanks.
except	leave out	Everyone except him.
affect	influence	This affects your ear.
effect	result	The effect of the law.
already	before	Elvis already left.
all ready	prepared	He was all ready to go.
all together	everyone at once	They yell all together.
altogether	completely	It was altogether wrong.
altar	table of worship	Put the Bible on the altar.
alter	to change	Alter the skirt.
ascent	rising	The rocket's ascent took an hour.
assent	agreement	Nod to show assent.
bare	uncovered	The window was bare.
bear	animal	The bear growled.
	endure	Can you bear the noise?
brake	stop	Use the car's brake.
break	destroy	Don't break the dish!
capital	government seat	Visit the capital.
Capitol	where the U.S. legislature meets	Congress meets in the Capitol.
conscience	one's sense of right and wrong	Listen to your conscience.
conscious	awake	She was conscious during surgery.
desert	leave behind	Desert a sinking ship.
	arid region	Camels travel in the desert.
dessert	sweet served at the end of a meal	I love a rich dessert.
emigrate	leave a country	She emigrated from France.

continues

continued

Word	Definition	Example
immigrate	enter a country	To immigrate means to enter a new homeland.
lay	put down	present: Lay your cards down.
		past: He laid the cards down.
		future: He will lay his cards down.
		perfect: She has laid her cards down.
lie	be flat	present: The cat lies down.
		past: The cat lay down.
		future: The cat will lie down.
		perfect: The cat has lain down.
lead	writing material	That's a lead pencil.
led	conducted	We were led to safety.
learn	receive facts	You learn grammar.
teach	give facts	I teach grammar.
loose	not fastened	The clasp is loose.
lose	misplace	I might lose the necklace.
passed	went by	We passed the new library.
past	gone by	They helped in the past.
principal	main	The principal road is Main Street.
	head of a school	C. J. Jarvis is the principal.
principle	rule	You know the principles of grammar.
rise	get up	The cost of living will rise.
raise	lift	Raise your arms.
respectfully	with respect	The audience clapped respectfully.
respectively	in the stated order	The red, blue, and green books belong to John, Billie, and Lee, respectively.
stationary	staying in place	The car was stationary.
stationery	writing paper	Kings have nice stationery.
than	comparison	Kansas is bigger than Rhode Island.
then	at that time	The state was then very dry.
their	belonging to them	It is their book.
there	place	Put it there.
they're	they are	They're good friends.
weather	atmospheric conditions	The weather is rainy.
whether	if	Whether or not you agree.

Index

Q-R

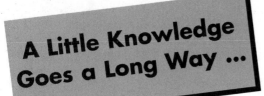
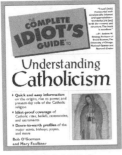

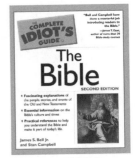

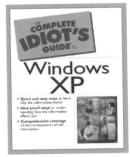